In a world that promises false liberty and incites inappropriate anger regarding sexuality and gender, Branson Parler is a winsome, loving voice of truth. With the wisdom of a theologian and the heart of a pastor, father, and friend, Parler expertly guides his readers through sex and gender myths toward a flourishing, embodied life.

—**LAURIE KRIEG**, author of *An Impossible Marriage*, host of the *Hole in My Heart Podcast*

This book is not a shot fired in a culture war, and it's not a set of simplistic rules. Rather, it is a call to faithfully enact a beautiful story with our bodies. As Branson Parler demonstrates, Christians have failed as often as anybody to practice and perform love in the daily work of our lives. But Parler turns to the gospel to find the redemptive script our bodies have been given to follow. In clear and delightful prose, this book offers the good news that our confused culture desperately needs.

—**JEFFREY BILBRO**, associate professor of English at Grove City College, editor in chief at Front Porch Republic

Every Body's Story is a readable, scholarly engagement of sexual discipleship for our times. Brilliantly deconstructing the sexual mythologies that control our lives, Branson Parler opens the door to the new worlds of covenantal faithfulness with God and his long story of saving the world. It's been a long time since I've been this encouraged after reading a book about sex!

—**DAVID FITCH**, Lindner Chair of Evangelical Theology, Northern Seminary, Chicago

Parler is such a careful thinker and has such deep biblical knowledge that even when the reader feels challenged, they will come away from this book with fresh insight; they will think more carefully and, indeed, more broadly on these issues. They will, in fact, find themselves wrestling with new questions, and this might be a significant part of what the church needs to reframe its conversation about human sexuality.

—**REW ZWART**, director of interdisciplinary studies, Kuyper College

T0043532

It is hard to imagine a more timely and articulate theology of bodies, sex, and marriage. Branson Parler has masterfully diagnosed what ails both our culture and our churches' sexual thinking and practice. *Every Body's Story* is biblically adept, historically aware, culturally astute, and philosophically sophisticated. At the same time, it is imminently practical and hauntingly convicting. I truly wish someone would have given me this book decades ago!

–JOHN NUGENT, professor of Bible and theology,
Great Lakes Christian College

With in-depth theological and cultural analysis and pastoral sensitivity, *Every Body's Story* enters the all too often polarized discourse on sexuality, bodies, marriage, and singleness. In it, Parler offers a rousing, timely critique of pervasive stories about our bodies, countering them with a compelling, beautiful corrective. By asking, "What are our bodies for?" Parler uncovers the way that Christians in the West have, intentionally or unintentionally, twisted the biblical story of bodies, marriage, sex, and singleness. With a keen eye toward not only the problems "out there" but the unhelpful and harmful teachings within the church, he contrasts the biblical story with both the story of the secular age and the distorted stories Christians have told about sex and bodies. We have failed, and we must do better. Parler offers us a gospel-centered way, inviting us to explore and embody not only God's "no" to sin but also the wide and beautiful "yes" to God's good gifts that we find in the story of Jesus. This is a needed book for our day.

–JESSICA JOUSTRA, assistant professor of religion and
theology, director of Albert M. Wolters Centre for
Christian Scholarship, Redeemer University

In this accessible book, Branson Parler shows that is not enough to object to secular stories about sex; we must inhabit and commend a more capacious one. These are complicated issues, and readers may not agree with all his conclusions. But the underlying vision is both countercultural and compelling, inviting readers to ask: What stories have we unwittingly imbibed? What stories are we embodying? And what could it look like for us to tell the story of God's suffering, faithful love in a ruptured world?

—JUSTIN ARIEL BAILEY, associate professor of theology at Dordt University, author of *Interpreting Your World*

The church needs the fresh hope Branson is offering in *Every Body's Story*. It's biblical, relevant, mind-stretching, Christ-centered. A must-read for our times.

—BOB BOUWER, senior pastor of Faith Church, author, and church coach

EVERY BODY'S STORY

*6 Myths about Sex
and the Gospel Truth
about Marriage
and Singleness*

BRANSON PARLER

ZONDERVAN
REFLECTIVE

ZONDERVAN REFLECTIVE

Every Body's Story
Copyright © 2022 by Branson Parler

Requests for information should be addressed to:
Zondervan, *3900 Sparks Dr. SE, Grand Rapids, Michigan 49546*

Zondervan titles may be purchased in bulk for educational, business, fundraising, or sales promotional use. For information, please email SpecialMarkets@Zondervan.com.

ISBN 978-0-310-12461-0 (audio)

Library of Congress Cataloging-in-Publication Data
Names: Parler, Branson L., 1980- author.
Title: Every body's story : 6 myths about sex and the gospel truth about marriage and singleness / Branson Parler.
Description: Grand Rapids : Zondervan, 2022.
Identifiers: LCCN 2022014476 (print) | LCCN 2022014477 (ebook) | ISBN 9780310124597 (paperback) | ISBN 9780310124603 (ebook)
Subjects: LCSH: Sex—Religious aspects—Christianity. | Sex—Biblical teaching. | BISAC: RELIGION / Christian Theology / Anthropology | RELIGION / Sexuality & Gender Studies
Classification: LCC BT708 .P365 2022 (print) | LCC BT708 (ebook) | DDC 241/.664—dc23/eng/20220627
LC record available at https://lccn.loc.gov/2022014476
LC ebook record available at https://lccn.loc.gov/2022014477

Cover design: Darren Welch Design
Cover photos: © Duncan1890; ThePalmer; NSA Digital Archive / Getty Images
Interior design: Sara Colley

Printed in the United States of America

22 23 24 25 26 27 28 29 30 /TRM/ 12 11 10 9 8 7 6 5 4 3 2 1

To my wife, Sarah, who embodies
the gospel every day

CONTENTS

PART 3

PART 4

FOREWORD

Preston Sprinkle

I first heard of Branson from a mutual friend of ours who listened to me give a talk about sexuality. He came up afterward and said, "You must know Branson Parlor?" With a name like that, I assumed he was referring to some movie star, so I told him I wasn't in the film industry and wasn't good at remembering actors' names at any rate. "No, he's a theologian like you," he said. "And you sound *exactly* like Branson in everything you've said tonight about sexuality." I was immediately both shocked and encouraged. When it comes to the sexuality and gender conversation, I have two main passions: theological faithfulness and courageous love. The former comes natural to me. I'm a biblical scholar who loves to read books all day. The love part, though, has taken a bit more work. Like most scholars, loving people courageously has not come easily. But over the years, I've worked hard at centralizing love in my theology of sex, sexuality, and gender, especially a love for those who have been marginalized because of their sexual orientation or gender identity. And preaching this sort of radical love for sexual and gender minorities hasn't always landed well with Christians, especially those of a more conservative persuasion.

So when our mutual friend said I sounded exactly like Branson, I was intrigued. I think it was a year later when I was finally able to grab a meal with Branson and talk theological shop. It was one of those rare movements where you barely meet somebody and yet end up finishing each other's sentences. We immediately became friends and like-minded colleagues in the sexuality conversation. Several years later, Branson told me he was writing a book—the book you now hold in your hands. From everything I knew about Branson, I was confident that it was going to be a good book. And after reading through the manuscript, I was not disappointed.

Every Body's Story gets to the heart of one of the most urgent and complex set of ethical questions facing the church today. What are our bodies *for*? What is sex *for*? Why did God create marriage? And what is marriage *for*? Conversations around sex, sexuality, and gender typically race to prohibition passages where God tells us to do this or not to do that. These rules and regulations certainly have their place in a Christian worldview, but they must be understood within a larger story of God's covenant with Abraham. This is what I love about Branson's book. He considers questions about the body, sex, sexuality, and marriage through the thick theological lens of covenant. Sex isn't just a pleasurable act that two humans do with each other. Rather, it's a sign of a marriage covenant, which itself points to a greater covenant that the Creator has made with his people. We cannot adequately understand the Creator's design for sex, marriage, and gender, nor can we fully appreciate the various "dos and don'ts" in Scripture, without first bathing ourselves in the beautiful story of God's red-hot desire to repair his creation. Sex—and marriage and embodiment and gender—cannot be understood apart from creation, covenant, and resurrection.

If all Branson did in this book was to connect marriage and sex to the greater story of God, it would be a much needed and worthwhile read. But there's more. One of my favorite aspects of this book is Branson's ability to put a robust theology of marriage and sex in conversation with other philosophical views, like naturalism and individualism, so that the distinctiveness of the Christian way can be considered against the backdrop of our other options. Branson is also able to salt this intellectual journey with references to pop culture—something not many theologians are able to do, and often if they try, you kind of wish they wouldn't.

What I appreciate most about this book, though, is what I appreciated about Branson when I first met him: his love for people. Branson is a theologian. He's also a biblical scholar. I'm sure he, like me, could spend hours in the books. But Branson writes this book as a pastor, father, and husband. This comes out most movingly when he talks about the death of his first child in the context of discussing the very difficult topic of procreation and contraceptives. Branson also discusses sexual ethics while revealing the difficulty of being kicked out of his church after his father (the pastor of the church) had an affair. If Branson had simply written a theologically robust book about marriage, sex, and gender, it still would have been a worth your time. But the book you're about to read is a slice of both the mind *and the heart* of a pastor-theologian who loves Jesus more than theology—which makes him a truly *Christian* theologian.

INTRODUCTION

WHAT ARE BODIES FOR?

M ainstream American culture is saturated with sex. *The Bachelor*, a reality TV show that turns romance into a competition, gives one man (or woman, in the case of *The Bachelorette*) a pool of potential romantic partners they eventually narrow down to "the one." Tinder, a dating app that allows people to date and hook up with other users, has 7.8 million active monthly users in the US and 75 million users globally.[1] Pornography is a $97 billion global industry, and a recent study shows that 43 percent of American men and 9 percent of women report watching pornography in the previous week.[2] Even many films released theatrically contain explicit material—as does much popular music—and for many people, sexting has become normal, with 1 in 4 teens ages 12 to 17 receiving explicit texts or emails, and 1 in 7 teens sending them.[3]

On college campuses, hook-up culture and sexual assault run rampant. In their study of sexuality and sexual assault on campuses, sociologists Jennifer Hirsch and Shamus Khan gathered student responses to the crucial question, "What is sex for?"[4] Some students made reference to "making babies," but most gave blank looks. Eventually, the sociologists gave up asking that question because too few could give an answer.

Mainstream American culture is saturated with sex, but many people cannot articulate why they do what they do. Although it might be tempting to look down on those students, would the responses be dramatically different if we posed the same question in our churches?

What is sex for? What are bodies for? What are marriage and singleness for? And what do these questions have to do with Jesus and the gospel? Many churches are fracturing over debates about marriage and sexuality. Denominations such as the Reformed Church in America and the United Methodist Church are in the process of dividing in large part over these matters, and every denomination and church is going to have to clarify its stance on these matters in the coming years.

We get caught up in discussions and debates about same-sex marriage, purity culture and shame, transgender rights, masturbation, porn and sex in a digital age, monogamy, and polyamory. Yet rarely do we stop, step back, and return to the most foundational questions about bodies, marriage, singleness, and sex. What are bodies *for*? Having clarity about these foundational questions is crucial, because every single one of us and every single one of our churches will walk through real-life situations that will reveal whether we've answered these questions in a biblical, thoughtful way.

I got the call from my brother early on Sunday morning while I was still in bed. This was a couple of months into the pandemic lockdown, and my brother lived out of state. "You need to go to Cheyenne's house," he said. "Andrew is leaving her." Shock ran through me. My sister and brother-in-law were both active in their church. He was the worship pastor. They have three young girls, and I didn't have a clue that things weren't going well.

As I raced to her house that morning, I could hardly think straight. But I was worried about how their church family would respond. My parents' marriage broke apart when I was 19, and our church did not respond well (a story I'll share later). As I embraced my sister that morning and cried and prayed with her, in the back of my mind I couldn't help but wonder, *How is the church going to respond to this separation (and their eventual divorce)?* Would people react out of anger and frustration, or were there solid sisters and brothers around her who had processed the foundational questions about sex, marriage, and the gospel?

On another occasion, I sat with some friends as they processed what they had heard from their elementary school–aged daughter. One of her young friends, a girl, had confided in her that she had a crush on her, a revelation that raised questions about romantic relationships and gender. Our friends have always been open with their kids, willing to engage in an age-appropriate way on matters of relationships and sex, but this was accelerating the conversation. As they walked with their daughter through her experience, she also raised questions of gender identity, expressing some level of struggle and questioning as she tried to sort this all out in her young mind. "We want to be prepared, but we can't share any of this with our parents or broader family," our friends said. "They would have no idea how to respond well. So we're trying to find all the resources we can to help us walk alongside our daughter as she continues to grow and ask hard questions of herself and us."

I was thankful for the wisdom of these parents. But their journey can be isolating. Even as they try to protect their daughter, they often don't have friends and resources to come alongside them as they seek to support her on her journey.[5] How do they help her ask and answer the foundational questions she needs to answer? As parents, how do they answer foundational questions about gender, sex, bodies, and the gospel so they can walk lovingly and faithfully with their daughter?

Just as individuals wrestle with these questions, churches and church leaders face them as well. I remember vividly the weekend in July 2020 when everything blew up in our church and neighborhood, in part because of the stance our church takes on marriage and sexuality. Before serving as our pastor, my friend Eric had founded a nonprofit in partnership with our church that was dedicated to holistic youth ministry in our neighborhood, pioneering a number of great programs that combined discipleship with learning core life skills. Under his leadership, this nonprofit started several programs, including a summer day camp; after-school tutoring during the school year; a weekly evening with a meal, games, and Bible study; a bakery for middle schoolers; and an urban farm. This nonprofit shared our church building and property and was largely sustained by church members as volunteers and donors. Unfortunately, after he stepped down as director of this organization, it went through several difficulties, leading to a shutdown of its discipleship programs, leaving only the farm.

When the nonprofit decided to hire a new director, it chose someone who was gay and in a same-sex relationship heading toward marriage. The organization promised to redevelop some of the discipleship programs that had been shut down, but for our church, this raised a foundational question: What kind of discipleship? What does Jesus have to say about sex, marriage, and singleness? Our church stands within the historic stream of orthodox Christianity, affirming that marriage is between a man and woman. This organization did not. Church leaders engaged in numerous conversations and intense times of prayer about the way forward and, in the end, asked this organization to relocate from church property because of this different understanding of discipleship and what it means to follow Jesus with our bodies.

When a local news station got wind of this and ran a story on it, many people in the community responded with vitriol and outrage. Of course, the storyline portrayed by the media was of a homophobic church booting out a great organization. The complexity of the backstory and the church's long relationship with the organization were completely overlooked. Our church and pastor, both with great reputations in the community, were hammered on social media because they stood firm on the connection they saw between sex, bodies, and the gospel. As we follow Jesus together in a life of discipleship and answer foundational questions about bodies, sex, and marriage, we should expect some level of conflict and clash with our broader culture's narrative around these questions.

Each of the three experiences I've described above reveals a critical need for us to provide a definitive and biblical answer to one fundamental question: What are bodies *for*? Three big cultural stories answer this question very differently: the secular story of liberty, the church story of authority, and the gospel story of fidelity. The first is the story offered by broader Western culture and includes the myths of individualism, romance, and naturalism. The second is a warped Christian story offered by many churches. It includes the myths of legalism, sexual prosperity, and evil bodies. The third big story is what I'm proposing as a faithful biblical alternative in this book. It focuses on the gospel and its out working in our lives. Let me briefly unpack these three approaches to sex, marriage, and singleness.

What are bodies for? The overarching story of our secular age is one of liberty. The main command of secular sexuality is "You do you," using our bodies, sex, and relationships for self-expression and self-actualization. That is, bodies are for me to freely express who I am. I am free from any authority but myself. In contrast, authority is the overarching story of many churches and Christians. That is, God is the authority, so we should do what God commands. The first and greatest command of this approach is "Behave yourself." The core message about bodies and sex boils down to following certain rules from the Bible. Sexual purity, then, means sticking to these rules. This approach to bodies and sex often degenerates into legalism, where the focus is on me, not God, and what I do, not God's grace.

In contrast to the focus on authority and liberty, a powerful alternative lies at the heart of the gospel: fidelity. That is, a focus on God's covenant faithfulness. Sex and bodies are for living out the bigger story of the gospel, the story of God's faithful covenant love in the suffering body of Jesus Christ. We may not often use the word *covenant*, but Bible scholar Daniel Block argues that the concept of covenant is at the heart of Scripture. He defines a covenant as a "formally confirmed agreement between two or more parties that creates, formalizes, or governs a relationship."[6] In contrast to the me-centered focus of both individualism and legalism, this emphasis on covenant fidelity focuses first on God and God's character. He chooses us, he makes a covenant with us, and he is faithful in keeping his promises. As Tim Keller puts it, a covenant is "a stunning blend of both law and love. It is a relationship much more intimate and loving than a mere legal contract . . . yet one more enduring and binding than personal affection alone could make. It is a bond of love made more intimate and solid because it is legal. It is the very opposite of a consumer-vendor relationship, in which the connection is maintained only if it serves both parties' self-interest. A covenant, by contrast, is the solemn, permanent, whole self giving of two parties to each other."[7] We are his beloved, and he is faithful to us. We belong to him, and our identity flows from who he is for us, not who we can be for him or who we can be for ourselves. Seen from this angle, marriage and singleness give us different ways to focus on the same mission: embodying and pointing to God's faithful covenant love.

A second component of the overarching story of liberty is the myth of romance. For many people, part of expressing themselves means constructing their sexuality and finding a romantic partner (or partners) who complements and *completes them as a person*. In contrast to the myth of romance, the gospel promises something different: that we are now members of God's household. God's faithful covenant love toward us makes us members of his family. As such, we find our fulfillment not in romance or sexual prosperity but first in God and then in being given a meaningful place in God's family. The church family, the household of God, thus positions our smaller households (married and single alike) within God's work and mission in the world.

Within the church's story of authority, a similar romantic myth is at play: *prosperity-gospel sexuality*. This view says, "If you follow the rules and do what God says, you'll be blessed with a great marriage and a great sex life." So sex and bodies are part of a larger moral calculus where doing good means receiving blessings and doing wrong means receiving punishment. If we don't follow the rules, we will end up "impure" and ashamed; if we do follow the rules, we'll know God really loves us— because we followed the authority, behaved ourselves, and received the promised blessings. In contrast to the myth of sexual prosperity, we have to acknowledge that marriage is not merely an amazing reward for being good, but a road marked with suffering as we love our spouse with the love of Christ. Similarly, singleness is also a path of suffering, but it should not be the suffering that comes simply from lack or loneliness, but the suffering that comes from connection and solidarity with the body of Christ.

The third and final myth of the secular story of liberty is naturalism. According to this myth, sex has no inherent meaning, and bodies are nothing but *matter in motion*. Many people see this as a good thing because it means we each have the freedom to create and give meaning to our bodies and to sex. In essence, my body and sexuality become tools I can use to express my individual self. The myth of naturalism combines with individualism and romance to form the overarching myth of liberty. For broader Western culture, this is the path to true self-fulfillment and self-realization. In contrast to the myth of naturalism, the gospel says that our bodies are not merely matter in motion, but are in fact God's temple, dwelling place, home. Far from being raw physical matter, the body is "for the Lord" (1 Cor. 6:13), the place where God dwells and makes himself known to the world.

The third myth of the church story of authority is the story of evil bodies. That is, *the body is the enemy*. According to this myth, sex, sexual desire, or even bodies themselves are the source of sexual sin. The body is the enemy and must be defeated, broken, and brought into line. In contrast, the story of the gospel speaks to the immense goodness of bodies, so much so that the eternal Son of God assumes our humanity, including a physical body: "The Word became flesh" (John 1:14). Our salvation happens through the *body* of Jesus. His physical suffering, death, and resurrection are the basis for our salvation. Since this is true, we can ask ourselves, How does our embodied life in singleness, sex, and marriage embody the truth of God's faithful covenant love? This way of life embodies a mission and calling far bigger than churchly behavior management or secular self-actualization.

Ultimately, the secular story of liberty and the church story of authority both fall short. The focus on authority has not worked well inside or outside the church. We have essentially said, "Jesus is good news for your eternal life but bad news for your sex life." We have focused on God's no to sin rather than God's yes to what we should live *for*. We have tried to earn God's favor by keeping God's rules rather than living a life that bears witness to God's gracious rule in Christ Jesus. Even worse, our bad explanations for the purpose of bodies and sex reveal that we may have missed the plot of the gospel itself. When Christians fail to link a biblical theology of sex and bodies to the gospel, we tell a false story about God.

Because of this failure, Christians and non-Christians alike are enticed by how our broader culture answers the question, What are bodies for? The secular story of liberty seems more positive and life-giving than the body-bashing, legalistic, simplistic do-the-right-thing-and-you'll-be-blessed approach of many churches. But tragically, those who embrace this framework continue to miss out on the good news about bodies and sex the gospel presents. And we fail to see how that good news fits into the larger biblical narrative and our purpose in it. Whether we buy into the "Behave yourself" story of the Christian subculture or the "You do you" story of our broader secular culture, we fail to embody the gospel.

I am not satisfied with the options of authority or liberty. I'm sick of the shame that results from falling short in the story of authority, but I don't think a constant focus on pride from the story of liberty is a helpful corrective. I want a more compelling vision of sex and bodies than "Follow the rules." And I want a more compelling vision of sex and bodies than "There are no rules."

So, what *are* bodies for? They are for embodying the gospel, placing the good news of Jesus on display for the watching world. Our bodies are meant to be the visible image of the invisible God, making his faithfulness and self-giving love tangible to those around us. When we talk about a Christian view of bodies, sex, marriage, and singleness, we constantly have to ask, How does this tell the good news of who Jesus is? How does my body and what I do with it in terms of singleness, sex, and marriage become a symbol charged with meaning, pointing to the body of my faithful Savior, Jesus Christ? Of course, talk is not enough. The story you truly believe is not just about what's in your head; it's also in your body. Every body tells a story. The critical question I hope this book will help you answer is this: What story are you embodying?

PART 1

CHAPTER 1

WE ALL HAVE STORIES

When it comes to sex and bodies, we often focus on a set of specific questions and issues. Is same-sex marriage right or wrong? How should we think about transgender identities? Is pornography a problem or something to be normalized? Who cares if people live together before marriage? Is divorce and remarriage acceptable in some circumstances? What about alternative relationship arrangements, such as polyamory? The list goes on and on.

The problem with this approach, however, is that it fails to place our bodies within larger stories, whether that's the story of the Bible or the stories of our culture. Seeing the big picture is hard. The connections between our bodies and big stories are not always obvious. Issues and questions often arise unexpectedly and on a case-by-case basis. It takes time, intention, and work to think through how questions of sex, marriage, and singleness are related to one another and to the gospel. And even when churches do address these matters, they usually do so in sermons—monologues geared toward motivation and inspiration (not that there's anything wrong with that) as opposed to times of systematic teaching and dialogue aimed at cultivating and exploring good questions and answers.

Without taking the time to ask and answer complex questions, we risk pushing people away from Jesus and the church. That's what happened in the case of a former student and friend of mine. "The youth pastor at my church told me I couldn't serve in youth ministry anymore." This student was sitting in my office, sharing some of their story with me. After telling their youth pastor they were bisexual, by which they meant attracted to both men and women (*not* that they were romantically or sexually involved with anyone of any gender), this person had been abruptly uninvited to serve. As someone who wanted to follow Jesus and serve the church, where was this person supposed to go? They had taken the risk of confiding in a church leader, and the end result was being banished from service. No "Thank you for being courageous enough to share that with me," or "I would love to have coffee with you and talk about what you mean by being bisexual and how that connects with your walk with Jesus."

To be sure, there are numerous complicated questions here, but rather than someone taking the time to sit with this student to explore the connections between following Jesus and our bodies, this person experienced an abrupt cutoff. We need to take the time both to sit with those who are wrestling with these questions and to dig into Scripture in order to think through what it means to follow Jesus faithfully together. If we don't commit to this endeavor, people may end up alienated not only from the church but also from Jesus because of our failure to see and embody the connection between the gospel—the big story we claim to believe—and our everyday actions.

One example of this failure to connect bodies and big stories is the struggle to connect sex and bodies to Jesus and the gospel in any coherent way. As a Christian, I believe Jesus died and rose again to save me, and I also believe that I'm called to either celibate singleness or marriage with someone of the opposite sex. But how and why are these two linked? Most often, we can't really say, perhaps because we haven't been part of a church community that took the time to explore these matters. Or maybe we don't *want* to say what Jesus and sex have to do with each other! If we've been trained to think of sex and bodies as dirty and shameful, we need to keep them far away from Jesus. Or maybe we have been taught to avoid the topic, to see sex as highly private (like money), so we don't talk about how sex and Jesus are connected.

In this chapter, I will first explore how our bodies are embedded in broader stories about the nature of reality. These stories are embodied in daily practices and powerful symbols that reinforce either the stories of our culture or the gospel story.

THE STORY OF YOUR BODY

Every body tells a story. Whether a soldier sacrificing his own body, a professional athlete developing her muscle memory day after day, a fashionista selecting just the right outfit, a mother carrying a child in her body, or a Jewish rabbi hanging bloody and broken from a cross, we all embody a story about the nature of reality. Do our bodies matter, or is matter, in the end, meaningless? Will shame or pride or grace have the last word? What is love? Who is God? Who isn't he? Is there even a god at all? The way we live—what we do with our bodies—gives us clues to how we might answer those questions.

Paraphrasing Aristotle, theologian Allen Verhey asserts that "every ethos implies a mythos."[1] In other words, the patterns of daily living (ethos) imply and embody a larger story or narrative (mythos) about reality. The stories that shape our view of reality are not just what we think or believe; we participate in them and tell them through our bodies. This isn't a voluntary decision we make at a certain age. Even if we don't realize it, our bodies are already formed by the cultural stories we encounter daily. What we do with our bodies reveals what we believe

5

is at the heart of reality. So we have to step back and ask, What view of reality is inscribed in my body?

Through this lens, we can start to think about the body and sex, or at least start to ask questions about how specific actions or habits (ethos) connect with a bigger story about reality (mythos). If I regularly view porn, what is the larger story about bodies, people, and God that I'm telling with my body? If I am single and celibate, what does refraining from sex say about the bigger story I'm part of? If I'm in a relationship with someone, is marriage even necessary? If I am married, how should I think about my commitment to my spouse? And what do children have to do with sex and marriage? Is any of this in any way linked to the gospel, the story of God's faithful covenant love revealed in the body of Jesus? These are big questions, but ones we seldom stop and ask. All too often, our life simply operates on autopilot.

For the last thirteen years, I've taught college students, and I would often pose this question the first day: "How did you get here?" The question is somewhat disconcerting because it's ambiguous and a bit invasive. Some students took it as a basic question about mode of transportation— commuter students drive and on-campus students walk. Others went big and took it as a question about their life journey: What led them to a college where they ended up taking this class?

My answer to this question for my students is twofold: They got here mostly on autopilot, and they're here because something is drawing them. Let me explain. Most human life is lived on autopilot. And that's a good thing. Neuroscientists point out that if we had to stop and think hard about every action and decision we made, we would be exhausted before we ever left home. So my daily routine, like yours, is largely done on autopilot. I get up; get dressed; get a cup of coffee; eat a bowl of cereal; help get the kids up, dressed, and out the door to school; and then get myself to work, where I again operate mostly out of habit and routine.

Of course, I had to learn each practice and action for all of this to become routine. Take driving, for example. When I first started learning to drive in my dad's yellow Chevy Luv stick-shift pickup, I was conscious of every single step I had to take just to get ready to drive: Sit down. Buckle up. Adjust mirrors. Insert key. Step on the brake and clutch. Check for traffic in front, back, left, and right. Put just the right amount of pressure on the gas while easing up on the clutch, all the while continuing to check mirrors, getting ready to shift from first to second. Suffice it to say that this sequence of events frequently ended with me stalling out because of a combination of nerves and a failure to execute the proper sequence in exactly the right way. Now, however, I can drive home in a state of apparent semi-consciousness, aware of the arguments I'm listening to on sports talk radio or NPR but unable to tell you if I've stopped for red lights or properly yielded while turning left on green ones.

As psychologist Timothy Wilson puts it,

> The mind operates most efficiently by relegating a good deal of high-level, sophisticated thinking to the unconscious, just as a modern jumbo jetliner is able to fly on automatic pilot with little or no input from the human, "conscious" pilot. The adaptive unconscious does an excellent job of sizing up the world, warning people of danger, setting goals, and initiating action in a sophisticated and efficient manner.[2]

In other words, we need autopilot to function, and there's nothing wrong with that. But sometimes, particularly when the computerized controls of autopilot are compromised or mistaken, we become aware that it can lead us astray and do damage. We need to stop, step back, and ask ourselves again, "How did I get here?"

The second and deeper answer to this question is "because something drew me here." Admittedly, this sounds a bit mystical to my students, most of whom are waiting for the nitty-gritty of the course syllabus and assignments. But it's true. If they are at a college, it's because it somehow fits with a vision of the good life that draws them. Maybe they figure a decent middle-class American life is impossible without a college education, so they'd better get that degree so they can get that job and paycheck. The American Dream is drawing them.

For others, perhaps, college is a chance to engage big ideas, to ask big questions, and to think big thoughts. These students value the time and space college provides to get a handle on these weighty matters. For still others, college might be an opportunity to gain knowledge, skills, and attitudes that will enable them to better love God and neighbor, however that might look in terms of a future job or service opportunities. If they're sitting in a college classroom, *something* drew them there.

The thing that draws us, though—even through major decisions like a college, job, or spouse—often operates on the autopilot level. Let me give another example. I got my license when I was 16 because I had to drive as soon as possible. Many 16-year-olds today aren't drawn (driven?) to do that.[3] Why? Is it because 16-year-olds in the 1990s had an innate desire to get their licenses and drive, whereas 16-year-olds in the 2020s don't? No. The thing that draws us to act in certain ways is often instilled in us by our broader culture. In other words, my autopilot is not just *my* autopilot. Our culture cultivates a shared autopilot. It has built-in assumptions that shape us to adopt similar values and actions. It's one thing if I personally have a habit or routine that's on autopilot—especially if I intentionally choose it—but it's something quite different when an entire culture is drawn to something.

Every once in a while, however, something disrupts our familiar stories, making us question whether we need to reevaluate our cultural and personal autopilot. Is it taking us where we want to go? Is our autopilot embodying the gospel or some other story in our lives? In these moments when we switch to manual control, we have an opportunity to make big decisions about what is drawing us to the places we want to end up—and what story we're living out.

WHAT'S THE STORY?

What story is the *true* story of the whole world? In the last few decades, Christians focused primarily on our intellectual belief system, using terms like *worldview* in a very heady way. More recently, this focus on intellect and belief has been put in the broader context of a storied way of life. For example, James K. A. Smith points out that our culture's stories capture our hearts through the routine practices of our bodies.[4] He focuses on the story of consumerism, which enthralls us by the common but significant practice of going to the mall (at least for those of us of a certain age). According to Smith, a trip to the mall is not an intellectual message about the value of consumer products. It is a sensory onslaught that invites us into a story about the good life. At the mall, we are presented with sights, sounds, smells, and symbols that convey the powerful message that we express and discover ourselves in and through the products we buy. Although certain stores in the mall offer different identities via their clothes (Hollister versus Hot Topic), every store presents us with a unified vision of the good life: You are what you buy.

The stories and worldviews of our culture are more caught than taught. For Christians, who see our calling as bearing witness to the gospel, our beliefs and lives must align. In other words, we have to ask, Do our lives embody the story we say we believe?

Although any worldview may include an intellectual component, our actual worldview cannot be gauged simply by what we say we believe. To clarify this distinction, Steve Wilkens and Mark Sanford use the helpful terms *confessional belief* and *convictional belief.*[5] A confessional belief is what we say we believe, whereas a convictional belief is what our life reveals we actually believe. As they put it, "Our behaviors are the stage on which we play out our stories."[6] In other words, beliefs are always embodied.

It's not just that we're playing out stories we believe through our behaviors. That way of putting it overemphasizes the agency of the individual in choosing what stories we participate in. It's more accurate to say that these broader cultural stories are playing themselves out in and through us. Because of this, Christians need to be on guard not merely against false ways of thinking but also against ways of living that embody false stories about God and reality.

When our confessional and convictional beliefs are out of alignment, it's not always because we have consciously chosen to embody a story other than the gospel (though sometimes it is). We don't generally go through life thinking, *Hmm, today I think I'll buy into consumerism or embrace individualism or be an avid fan of nationalism.* Instead, our cultural stories capture our hearts and bodies so we act in ways more congruent with a non-Christian story than with the biblical story.[7] Through cultural autopilot, these stories choose us as much as we choose them. As Wilkens and Sanford summarize, "We are more likely to absorb them through cultural contact than adopt them through a rational evaluation of competing theories. These lived worldviews are popular philosophies of life that have few intellectual proponents but vast numbers of practitioners."[8] So we absorb a story about reality (*mythos*) through the practices and symbols of everyday life (*praxis*) in our culture, and the ethos of our everyday life embodies the story we *truly* believe about the deepest reality.

EMBODYING THE STORY: EVERYDAY PRACTICES

So how can you identify someone's worldview? How do you know what story they truly embody? You could ask for a belief statement, but a better option would be to look at someone's routines and everyday practices.[9] Two different worldview "tests" help us differentiate between confessional belief and convictional belief (praxis). First, if we focus on confessional belief, we might be tempted to ask questions about someone's doctrinal stance on a variety of issues. This is the angle taken by the organization Worldview Weekend, which used to have an online true-false test with statements such as "The Bible should be our foundation for all our beliefs, actions, and conduct" and "A good person can earn his or her way to heaven if their good deeds outweigh their bad deeds." These are fine questions to ask, but do they tell you what someone's *convictional* beliefs are? Probably not.

Contrast this with a second, very different worldview test that one of my professors, Sylvia Keesmaat, shared with our class. It included questions such as "How many of your neighbors do you know well?" "How involved are you in your neighborhood?" "How often do you go to the weekly worship gathering at your church?" "How is your main living space set up in relation to entertainment technology?" and "How much sleep do you get each night, on average?" This test digs into how we structure the rhythms and routines of our everyday life. It asks, What story are we actually embodying in our everyday praxis?

Let's use a concrete example: sleep. We see the interplay of confessional and convictional belief even in a basic question about how much sleep we get. The Bible indicates that my patterns of sleep and rest say something about my faith in God. For example, Psalm 127:1–2 emphasizes God's work as the foundation of any work we do. Verse 2 speaks strongly to me, tempted as I am toward workaholism at all hours of the day and night: "In vain you rise early and stay up late, toiling for food to eat—for he grants sleep to those he loves." Scripture also repeatedly emphasizes a Sabbath rhythm as a way of life for God's people to physically and spiritually rest in him. If I am repeatedly and willfully getting less sleep than I should, it may reveal a deep heart issue: a failure to trust God for my survival, identity, and wellbeing.

Of course, there are many legitimate reasons people might get less sleep than they need, reasons that have nothing to do with a lack of faith in God's provision: a struggle with insomnia, a third-shift work schedule that disrupts normal patterns of sleep, or the need to work long hours to make ends meet. Nevertheless, I may get less sleep than I should because I lack faith. This then manifests itself as working too hard or being unable to shut off my mind because of stress, worry, and anxiety about things left undone or things I'm planning to do. Something as basic as my sleeping patterns embodies a story about reality.

EMBODYING THE STORY: SYMBOL

The stories we embody are themselves embodied and communicated to us in powerful symbols and images that incorporate us into the story they tell. Mary Midgley draws out the way that our foundational stories (what she calls "myths") are interwoven with key symbols: "Myths are not lies. Nor are they detached stories. They are imaginative patterns, networks of powerful symbols that suggest particular ways of interpreting the world."[10] Symbols embody stories. How exactly does this work?

The controversies caused by Jesus are prime examples. Often we portray Jesus's conflict with the Pharisees, Sadducees, and other groups primarily as doctrinal conflicts. But it's more accurate to see them as conflicts around "networks of powerful symbols," as Midgley puts it, that embody a certain way of "interpreting the world" and what God is doing in it.[11] Jesus's words and actions in relation to the temple serve as a great demonstration of the power of symbols.[12] The temple was the central reality of Jewish life. God's promise in the Old Testament was to dwell among his people in the tabernacle and subsequently the temple. Exodus and Leviticus make it clear that God's dwelling place is holy and that those who serve him as priests must be holy. To that end, they were strictly following the guidelines that God had set up in order to make sacrifices and maintain a right relationship with God on behalf of his people. The temple was the symbolic center of Jewish life; it stood at the heart of their unique identity as God's people and thus their relationship with God.

With this in mind, we can begin to grasp why Jesus caused such an uproar. In Mark 11, we see two back-to-back stories that help us understand the power and controversy of Jesus's symbolic action. As he goes to Jerusalem, Jesus encounters a fig tree that is not bearing fruit. He curses the tree, saying, "May no one ever eat fruit from you again" (11:14). Jesus then goes to the temple, drives out those who were buying and selling there, and disrupts the normal functioning of the temple for a time. Quoting Isaiah 56:7, Jesus declares that the temple has departed from God's intentions for it. Afterward, Jesus and his disciples encounter the cursed fig tree, and it has withered from the roots. What is Jesus doing here? How should we understand this passage?

The way these stories are placed in the Gospel of Mark helps us see that Jesus's words and actions in the temple parallel his words to the fig tree: Jesus is symbolically cursing the temple. Like Jeremiah, Ezekiel, and many Old Testament prophets before him, Jesus warns that God's judgment is about to fall on Jerusalem and the temple. But he doesn't just do it with words; he does it by shutting down the temple for a time, symbolically pointing to God's judgment, which will shut it down in a more permanent way. It's precisely this symbolic action that provokes the chief priests and teachers of the law to look for a way to kill Jesus (Mark 11:18). He had acted in a deeply symbolic way against the central symbol of Jewish life, and those who were most deeply invested in that symbol could not sit idly by.

Controversies around powerful symbols are as much a part of our world as they were in ancient times. A prime example comes from the world of sports. In 2016, San Francisco 49ers quarterback Colin Kaepernick ignited controversy when he chose to kneel rather than stand during the pregame national anthem. Kaepernick's decision was rooted in his desire to protest police brutality and injustice toward racial minorities, particularly in light of several well-publicized deaths of people of color at the hands of law enforcement officers.[13] My goal here is not to debate the merits of what Kaepernick was saying or the means by which

13

he said it, nor is it to unpack the complex issues of race, history, and justice surrounding his message and his means of communicating it. But I do want to draw attention to the immense power symbols and images wielded in this controversy.

First, note that the point of controversy revolved around a symbol and ritual—the American flag and national anthem—not merely a set of intellectual arguments. According to the legal code surrounding the flag, the American flag symbolizes "a living country and is itself considered a living thing."[14] As such, there are strict rules about how to display the flag, treat the flag, salute the flag, and if necessary, dispose of the flag. Such strict routines and rituals are all part of the "networks of powerful symbols" that reinforce the myth/story of America.

To reflect on the power of this symbol and ritual, try the following thought experiment. In your head, put yourself in a local sports venue. Perhaps it's a minor league baseball or hockey game or a Friday night high school football or basketball game. Imagine the public announcement to rise for the national anthem, but you keep sitting. What kind of social pressure or anxiety would that create? What would people around you do? What kind of looks or remarks would you expect? When you imagine that scenario, what do you feel in your body? Anxiety? Stress? Whatever rational explanation you might give for staying seated—even if it's medical—the social pressure would be real, and you would feel it in your body. Why? Because honoring the flag during the national anthem is a powerful ritual and symbol that embodies a story that goes to the heart of American identity. Our symbols make us who we are because they embody the story of which we are a part, and our bodies are taken up into these stories and become powerful symbols that reinforce them.

A second and equally significant aspect to note is how and why Kaepernick's actions were perceived so negatively by many people. People were not upset by his words; in fact, most people for or against Kaepernick's actions probably couldn't quote a single statement he made about his actions. Rather, the power and controversy revolved around his bodily action. It was controversial because, like the controversy between Jesus and the chief priests, this symbolism highlighted two contrasting stories in American life. From Kaepernick's perspective, his bodily actions embodied a story of dissonance between American beliefs and ideals—liberty and justice for all—and what was happening on the ground—racism and unjust police action. For others, however, Kaepernick's actions were troubling because they placed a fundamental question mark beside the story they believe about America.[15]

Though some people might agree with Kaepernick that there is a problem with systemic racism in America but argue that his actions were not the best method to raise awareness, others might tell the story of America as though racism and racial injustice are unfortunate aberrations on the fringe of the American story. Through that lens, racism may be worth challenging but not in the highly symbolic way Kaepernick did. His actions suggested racial injustice is woven into the heart of American identity and history, and that is a story many people cannot accept about America. Whatever your view of Kaepernick, his actions were controversial because in one symbolic action, he embodied a story that was profoundly different from the dominant cultural story many Americans embrace.

In this book, I'm suggesting something similar about sex and bodies: The Christian story is not merely an intellectual story but one that is embodied in a variety of practices, including worship, prayer, and fellowship. When we tell and show this story in our sexual ethics, whether in single celibacy or faithful monogamous marriages, it disrupts the autopilot praxis of our dominant cultural stories. Our bodies powerfully symbolize and communicate the gospel story that stands at the heart of reality. To be clear, it's not just that our bodies are simply pointing to something else, but also that our bodies themselves are the symbols that offer up a certain interpretation of reality to the watching world: that we are called to embody the gospel in our sexuality, singleness, and marriage.

CHAPTER 2

EMBODYING THE GOSPEL IN A SECULAR AGE

We embody the gospel in a particular time, place, and culture, not in a vacuum. If we are going to communicate the gospel of Jesus accurately, we have to know not only the Bible but also our culture. This is Communication 101. Know your audience. Know what resonates. You can speak and embody truth all you want, but the job of a good communicator is to craft the message in a way that will be heard accurately and in the best possible light (which doesn't necessarily mean people will like or accept it).

As contemporary American Christians, then, we must ask, What are the main characteristics of our time, which philosopher Charles Taylor calls a "secular age"?[1] If we understand the key features of our secular age, we'll better grasp the cultural stories embodied in the overarching secular story of liberty, why the church story of authority often fails to resonate, and how the gospel story of fidelity can offer a more beautiful, compelling picture of what the Bible says about sex and bodies. We'll also be able to better see why our age presents both a challenge and an exciting opportunity for communicating our faith by embodying the gospel in our singleness and marriage. So before diving into the particular myths of our secular and church cultures, I want to devote this chapter toward better understanding the cultural context of our secular age and why a lived apologetic—embodying the gospel—is a better strategy than others Christians have tried in the recent past.

A SECULAR AGE

People use the term *secular* in all kinds of ways. In his book *A Secular Age*, philosopher Charles Taylor notes that this term is sometimes used to refer to political structures that do not have an official state religion (as in the United States). The country might have a solid percentage of religious people in it, but the actual structures themselves do not have an official religion. In that sense, it is secular. Another way *secular* can be used is to refer to the general decline of religious belief and practice.[2] Modern Europe is largely secular in the sense that religious believers make up an increasingly small minority of the population.

Taylor's third definition, though, focuses on what he calls conditions of belief. He asks, What makes belief in the Christian God seem almost natural in the year 1500 (in Western cultures) but almost impossible in the year 2000? As a philosopher and student of culture, Taylor is not focusing primarily on theology but on the intellectual and cultural framework that has shifted dramatically over the last 500 years. To get a better sense of the contrast between previous eras in Western culture and our current secular age, it's helpful to think about the sharp contrast between then and now. Here, then, is a brief overview of the story Taylor tells.

Once upon a time, (some) humans looked around them and saw a world of God's creation. They saw meaning and purpose in matter around them—the trees and rocks, stars and skies—speaking to the grandeur of God. Matter was infused with meaning, and mundane material like bread and wine could be taken up on a higher plane, acting not merely as a sign of transcendence but as the real presence of and link to the transcendent God. They even saw meaning in suffering, insofar as the parts of the world that didn't make sense were a sign and pointer to One whose ways are higher than our ways. There was an end goal to life, a purpose beyond mere physical wellbeing or human flourishing: worship of and communion with the triune God. This purpose was often achieved not in spite of suffering, but in and through it. In fact, self-discipline and self-control were good and necessary to live a truly good *human* life. In sum, this culture was saturated with a sense that the lives and stories of its people were embedded in a much larger story: the story of God and the gospel, the medieval church, and the divinely appointed monarchs.

Within that framework, they saw their lives and reality as permeable, for though they believed the natural and supernatural were distinct, they also recognized that these two worlds were constantly interacting with and affecting one another. In premodern Western culture, it didn't take a great deal of intellectual energy to believe this. The everyday practice and symbols of their lives reinforced and told this story at every turn, making belief in this view of reality "natural" for many. Taylor points out, however, that no matter how natural it may have been for them then, this view is anything but natural for us today.

A secular age, according to Taylor, is a world in which belief in God has been reduced to one option among many. For our purposes, we need to draw out three dimensions of our secular age that will give us a brief sketch of the cultural stories we'll look at later and how they are linked to our views of bodies, sex, marriage, and singleness.

One key dimension of the secular age is what Taylor calls "the immanent frame."[3] By that, he means we have constructed a world and culture that operates without reference to anything transcendent, whether that be the Christian God or any other god. In other words, as we go through the routine habits of everyday life—checking our iPhones, shopping, work, school, and so on—nothing assumes a transcendent reality. The immanent frame is not necessarily anti-God (at least overtly). It's just that we act as though we don't need God for anything. In our view of reality, we live in a closed universe in which natural explanations account for everything we experience. Reality—including ourselves—is simply matter in motion. We'll explore this dimension further in chapter 11.

A second key dimension of our secular age is what Taylor calls "the buffered self."[4] The buffered self is closely connected to the immanent frame, a view of reality that is closed to anything beyond the physical or material. This is illustrated in a recent conversation I had with someone who had recently stayed in India for several months. When I asked her about the difference between the cultures of the US and India, she noted that in India she didn't have to do any work to get people to believe in some kind of spiritual reality. The real question or issue was which gods, spirits, or forces were most powerful and what people had to do to be on the right side of this spiritual reality. This way of looking at things is what Taylor refers to as a much more "permeable" view of the self. Those in present-day India or the premodern West see themselves in the midst of spiritual realities and forces beyond their control. In contrast, secular cultures like much of present-day North America or Europe find it hard to believe there *is* a spiritual reality in the first place.

The buffered self is therefore "safe" from the influence of demons and God alike. The challenge for the buffered self, though, is that our identity is not something we receive—whether from God, tradition, family, or religion. Rather, the self is a project of self-invention and self-creation (although this self is largely created through the purchase and use of consumer goods to position ourselves within society). In other words, we don't go to church to receive our identity from God; we try to create a sexual and/or gender identity that truly captures our authentic self. We look to a romantic relationship and significant other to define and create our authentic self. This self-expression is central to how we understand our sexuality: We construct our self-identity by exploring which sexual identities and behaviors feel authentic to each of us as individuals. We'll explore this further in chapter 3.

Finally, a third element of the secular age entails striving after a "sense of fullness," as Taylor puts it, something that brings a true sense of fulfillment, that makes us say, "You complete me."[5] This might sound suspiciously like some sense of God or religious transcendence, but that is not what Taylor means. To be sure, Christians would claim that only communion with God brings a true sense of fullness. As Augustine puts it, "Our heart is restless until it rests in you."[6] Taylor's point, however, is that many unbelievers strive to be the kind of people for whom this life is full and enough. For them, Christianity is an unrealistic pie-in-the-sky hope—an illusion. Instead, real fullness can be found within the immanent frame, within a life constructed from pursuing this-worldly flourishing.

So when we are faced with questions about meaning and the struggle and despair of the human condition, the exclusive humanism of a secular age looks for a sense of fullness in a wide range of sources, including romance.[7] From a Christian perspective, it is tempting to jump right to a critique of romance as a secular idol that cannot fulfill our deepest desires. And while I think that's true, Taylor's point is more nuanced: Many people structure their lives around things like romance (and career, technology, politics, etc.) and genuinely see them as offering the possibility of a sense of fullness when they live into them with their best authentic selves.

CHRISTIANS IN A SECULAR AGE

How should Christians live and engage in a secular age? One of the features of a secular age, according to Taylor, is that neither religious belief nor exclusive humanism has won the day.[8] Instead, we're all constantly navigating a potential crisis of belief. The religious believer is tempted to doubt their faith. Likewise, the secular person must wrestle with the "temptation" to believe and answer nagging questions like, What if there's more? What if there is a God, and the sense of fullness and fulfillment I'm looking for can only be found in him? As James K. A. Smith puts it, "The doubter's doubt is faith."[9] Taylor summarizes the dilemma faced by religious believer and nonbeliever alike: "We cannot help looking over our shoulder from time to time, looking sideways, living our faith also in a condition of doubt and uncertainty."[10] As a result, belief and unbelief have reached an intellectual stalemate. If we're fair and honest, Taylor asserts, we recognize that intellectual arguments and evidence both for and against God have significant merit.[11] Despite hundreds of books that make a strong intellectual case for God's existence, a sizable percentage of the US still doesn't believe in God, including many people who are intellectual giants in their own areas of expertise. It's not that either believers or nonbelievers are stupid or ignorant. Rather, there are compelling intellectual cases that can be made for both positions, and there are limits to what rational argumentation can do to sway people.

I have seen these limits vividly displayed in numerous discussions (in person and on social media) when it comes to discussing issues relating to the COVID-19 pandemic, mask wearing, and vaccines. Why do some people seem predisposed to accept vaccines without question, whereas others seem to refuse them at all costs? I know some would argue that the former group is "rational" while the other is not, but the matter is more complex than that (and I say that as someone who got vaccinated as soon as it was available). Why do I accept my doctor's advice on anything? Why do I accept "the science" on any issue?

Philosophers like William James point out that there are numerous factors in decisions like these, including a desire to be—and be seen as—a certain kind of person (a modern, with-it kind of person or a rebel who doesn't go along with the government or the medical establishment).[12] The average person getting a vaccine has almost no knowledge of how it works but accepts it on a doctor's authority and an assumption that the vaccine is less risky than the disease itself.

Similarly, for many who refuse the vaccine, they are swayed not so much by intellectual arguments alone but by the belief that acceptance of a vaccine and/or vaccine mandates is going to erode personal medical autonomy. They may listen to political and medical authorities who question the necessity of the vaccine and operate with the assumption that the disease is less risky than the vaccine.

Part of the reality of a secular age is the two worlds of religious believers and unbelievers coexisting side by side, with some good reasons on both sides, but without a decisive knock-down intellectual argument that propels one side to victory. Both sides have their takes on reality, and both are plausible (in the sense that people do believe them). Within this intellectual stalemate and the lived reality of a secular age, religious belief and unbelief are constantly threatening to destabilize each other.

From a Christian vantage point, then, the key questions in a secular age are these: How can I best communicate the good news of the gospel within this framework? How can I destabilize the unbelief of my neighbor so they come to truly believe and know that Jesus loves them? How can I be a channel of the Spirit's work to create the "doubter's doubt" that would lead them to faith? In short, how do I embody the gospel in such a way that the normal stories of our secular age—individualism, materialism, and romanticism—are questioned? Let me start by describing three strategies that are insufficient on their own, particularly for the current context of our secular age.

RATIONAL ARGUMENTATION

First, we should not try to compel people to belief through rational argumentation alone. The Christian faith is reasonable, but the approach of some Christians in the modern era was to try to make belief in God the inevitable conclusion of a logical argument. In essence, we tried to intellectually force people into belief. We thought if we could construct an airtight argument and give the best possible answers to any questions, we would convince people of the intellectual truth of God. But we need to be careful of converting people to a faith that is grounded ultimately in reason and rational argumentation rather than faith in Christ. As people of faith, we should be able to give good reasons for what we believe and why. But if we convert people to a logical conclusion rather than to Jesus himself, they may walk away from the faith when a seemingly stronger argument comes along from another side.

In contrast to an exclusively intellectual model, which is mostly ineffective in our current cultural context, Justin Ariel Bailey points out that we need to reimagine apologetics.[13] Rather than trying to compel people to faith, Bailey suggests that our call is to embody the beauty and resonance of an authentic Christian life. Rather than constructing logical arguments to force belief, Bailey's approach is about "provoking desire, exploring possibility, and casting an inhabitable Christian vision."[14] Nonetheless, the intellectual approach is important as part of a holistic, full-bodied approach to communicating the good news of the gospel. Our witness must flow from a coherent, authentic life that is rooted in the gospel's appeal to our imagination and sense of beauty, not only an appeal to intellect and logic.

A DISJOINTED GOSPEL

A second insufficient strategy is the way we've often separated the good news of the gospel from sexual ethics. At this point, you might be thinking that making an appealing, beautiful case for a biblical sexual ethic may not seem possible. Maybe this is because discussions of sex have sometimes been loaded with guilt and shame, so the last word we would use to describe the sex talk is "appealing" or "beautiful." Maybe this is because we sometimes associate sex with pulpit-pounding dos and don'ts. There's not much beauty and winsomeness in a drill sergeant shouting in your face.

We preach grace, but when it comes to the Christian life, we often slide into a focus on clear-cut rules: *The gospel is how I get saved, but rules are how I conduct my life.* In my experience, most Christians struggle to connect the Bible's teaching on marriage, sex, singleness, and bodies to the big story of the Bible and the gospel at the heart of that story. And while there may be a beauty to the gospel, when we talk about sex and bodies, we often start talking about God's rules or design. Starting with Genesis 1–2 is great, but it has to be connected with John 3:16 and the big story of the Bible, a story that can be hard to grasp. We struggle to make a biblical, imaginative connection between the gospel and sexual ethics. Because of this, Christian sexual ethics are usually seen as unappealing to the surrounding non-Christian culture. Some Christians might say, "Well, of course a Christian way of life is not going to appeal to a sinful, non-Christian culture." I agree that the path of following Jesus is not going to instinctively appeal to non-Christians (and perhaps even to Christians). Often, however, Christians fail to convey the beauty of the gospel in a compelling way.

Let me illustrate. Jackson Pollock's paintings are not exactly easy to understand. Initially, his paintings look like someone just spilled and splattered paint all over the canvas. This is the kind of art where you might hear people remark, "This is art? My four-year-old could do that!" For those of us who like some kind of clear subject matter, Pollock's paintings are frustrating. You have to become familiar with a bit of art history and technique to understand what he was doing and why. As that becomes clearer, you can see the coherence and beauty in his art, even if it doesn't fit your art preferences.

But what if, instead of putting Pollock's work into the larger context of art history and technique, I cut up a copy of one of his works into pieces and scatter them all over the floor? Will that make it any easier to appreciate? On its own, the painting may be difficult to understand, but presented in an incoherent, chopped-up way, there is almost no chance of appreciating it on its own terms.

In a similar way, Christians have often unintentionally defaced the beauty of the gospel and how it is linked with what we do with our bodies. Many of us Christians cannot see the big picture ourselves. We cannot connect a Christian view of sex and bodies to Jesus or show how a Christian view of singleness and marriage embodies the gospel. All we've ever witnessed are the scattered, chopped-up elements of sexuality, so that's all we have to offer other people. We must develop the imagination to see, the language to tell, and the desire to live out and embody the gospel. This approach will resonate more than attempts to argue someone into following Jesus.

CULTURE WARS

A final strategy to avoid is that of the culture wars. Winning a culture war is much different from bearing witness to Jesus. Christians are called to engage every culture, but the approach of many American Christians—especially when it comes to questions of sex and marriage—has been to fight political and legal battles *instead of* focusing on the deeper fight that is not against flesh and blood but against the principalities and powers of this age. We have been fighting for a definition of marriage to be enshrined in the American legal code while failing to disciple people in our own churches on these matters with biblical and pastoral clarity. As a result, many people raised in the church cannot answer basic questions like, What are bodies for? What is sex for? and What is marriage for? Nor can they link the answers to such questions with Jesus and the gospel. We have tried to gain the political world and have lost our missional soul.

To be clear, I am not saying Christians should be politically disengaged or uninterested in the broader culture's definition of marriage. Rather, I am saying that our top priorities should be discipling Christians and cultivating a culture that points to God's good, beautiful, and true intentions for marriage and singleness, not political action. Jonathan Leeman puts it well when he contends that "the picture that Scripture offers is less cultural warrior and more ambassador . . . [Ambassadors] are not just trying to win a war; they're trying to represent a whole other kingdom."[15]

In a similar vein, James Davison Hunter points out that American Christians have become so focused on the culture wars and politics that they have tragically reduced a robust faith to one more interest and identity group on the American political landscape. In contrast, he argues that Christians are not called to "change the world" but to be a faithful presence, living out God's ways in the midst of a culture that does not.[16] What God does with that faithful presence may vary widely in different times and places. Sometimes a culture may be radically changed thanks to the leaven of gospel people; other times it may react violently and harshly. But we measure our success based on our faithfulness and fruitfulness, not on our ability to grab the levers of power and make culture and history move the direction we think they should go.

LIVING QUESTIONABLE LIVES

So what should we do? Rather than trying to communicate the gospel through one of these insufficient strategies, our calling is to put a question mark next to the stories of our secular age through our strange way of life and our readiness to explain how that life stems from the gospel and Jesus. In other words, we proclaim the gospel in both deed and word through a way of life that embodies the gospel. As Michael Frost notes, Christians are called to evangelize primarily by living "questionable" lives.[17] He observes that we often view evangelizing through the lens of a bold evangelist preaching the gospel on a street corner or an old-school door-to-door evangelist, asking people if they know where they'll spend eternity. Or maybe we view an evangelist as someone constantly talking about Jesus to their unbelieving friends, family, and coworkers. Through that lens, most of us feel guilty and insufficient, like we're not measuring up to our evangelistic mandate.

However, Frost points out that Scripture makes a clear link between a life of discipleship and evangelism: As we follow Jesus and live differently, our way of life will prompt curiosity and questions from the watching world. At that point, we are called to be ready to "give an answer to everyone who asks you to give the reason for the hope that you have" (1 Peter 3:15). Frost contends that we as Christians need to be ready to "speak about Jesus conversationally when questioned about how they deal with suffering, or why they spend their vacation serving the poor, or why they've opened their home to refugees, or why they're fasting during Lent, or why they've made career choices that allow them to contribute to the greater social good."[18] I'd add to that list one more item: why we live lives of celibate singleness and faithful one-man, one-woman marriage as part of the family of God.

To be honest, though, most of us have not been taught how to connect our sex lives with Jesus and the gospel. When my unbelieving friends in high school and college asked why I didn't have sex, I had no clue how to answer in a way that took them to the heart of the gospel: Jesus. But this is exactly what we need to do. We must embody the gospel story with our sex lives, and we must be able to explain how what we do with our bodies—including our sex lives—is linked directly to the story of what Jesus does with his body: the gospel.

A DISTORTED GOSPEL

But there's a complicating factor. Our secular age is, in some ways, too familiar with Christianity and the Christian view of sex and bodies. So if they hear any talk about "saving yourself" for marriage, Christians speaking in favor of marriage between a husband and wife, or anything else associated with a Christian view of bodies and sex, they are likely to respond with vigorous accusations of Christians being repressive and oppressive. In the face of this, we might be tempted to get defensive. But I suggest an alternative strategy: When someone accuses Christians of doing a lot of harm through our sexual ethic, the best initial response is to say, simply and honestly, "I agree."

If we're honest, we must acknowledge that we have often talked about sex and bodies in a way that not only is unhelpful and harmful but also has distorted our view of God and the gospel. Rather than embodying the gospel, we have often warped it. You'll discover in the chapters that follow a few ways in which Christians have done this. Truly embodying the gospel in our secular age will mean, on the one hand, telling and embodying a story that contrasts with the secular age. But it also will mean, on the other hand, telling and embodying a story that renounces the distorted stories we Christians have told about sex and bodies.

PART 2

CHAPTER 3

THE MYTH OF INDIVIDUALISM

"You Do You"

E very body tells a story. This is true not just for Christians but for the broader culture as well. Many people recognize that there have been dramatic shifts in practice around sex, bodies, marriage, and singleness thanks to the sexual revolution. But the sexual revolution wasn't simply about sex. It was about the underlying stories about reality our culture tells and embodies. Many people assume sex before marriage is normal and permissible, but few can articulate how that practice is tied to a particular story about the nature of reality and our place within it. Just as Christians often struggle to articulate how our sexual ethics are tied to the larger story of the gospel, non-Christians also struggle to articulate how their sexual ethics embody three central myths that make up what I call the big story of liberty: the myths of individualism, romance, and naturalism.

Several years ago, Russell Brand, a comedian and TV show host known for his promiscuity and drug use, shocked the world by going on a rant about a mainstay of our culture: pornography.[1] Brand has a regular political comedy web series, *The Trews*, and in the context of addressing the release of the movie *50 Shades of Grey*, Brand aimed his wit and vitriol toward the accompanying issue of pornography. He shared his own experience of porn addiction from a young age, when porn was still primarily a print phenomenon. He derided the way Western culture sees porn as a harmless practice (one example that comes to mind is the *Friends* episode "The One with the Free Porn," which certainly normalizes and makes light of porn consumption).

Citing scholarly research and his own personal testimony, Brand walked through the damaging effects of porn, including voyeurism, objectification of people, the mistaken attempt to validate masculinity through porn, seeing women as mere trophies to be pursued, and fear of true intimacy. Noting that we are still on the front end of a massive social experiment where "icebergs of filth" are digitally accessible in almost every home, Brand put a huge question mark beside the Western culture's porn autopilot and pointed out the devastating physical, emotional, and relational effects of this commonplace practice. Some media outlets responded to Brand's rant with support; others dismissed his concerns outright. But all seemed shocked that a public figure like Brand would even question something so prevalent and passively accepted in our culture. We need to be able to see the bigger picture, the link between everyday acts and the larger stories that our culture embodies.

There are several reasons Christians need to recognize the link between the embodied practices of our secular age and the foundational stories they symbolize and in which people participate. First, seeing this link can help us think through some of the genuinely good insights these stories may have. Some forms of naturalism can make us appreciate the goodness of the body, some elements of individualism dovetail helpfully with a biblical view of the dignity of each person, and some forms of the story of romance remind us that we are created for community and connection. We need not deny the elements of truth or goodness found in these stories. That is, these stories take something relatively good (bodies, the individual, romantic love) and make it the ultimate good, idolizing it in place of God. Just like carving a literal idol out of a tree (see Isa. 44) doesn't mean the tree itself is evil, so turning something good into an idol reveals the sinfulness of our hearts, not the inherent badness of the thing we're idolizing. (I'll elaborate more on this idea in chapter 8.)

Second, despite some helpful elements in each story, we also need to recognize that these stories cannot be simply added on to the biblical story. At a fundamental level, the stories told by individualism, romance, and naturalism are not compatible with the story of the good news of Jesus. In order to live out the gospel faithfully, we need to resist not only the intellectual view of the world presented in these stories, but also the symbolic power of these stories, which are embodied in our culture's views and practices surrounding bodies and sex.

Christians may embody these secular stories intentionally or unintentionally. On the one hand, many Christians have been disenchanted (and understandably so) with a so-called "Christian" view of sex and bodies that is actually a warped view of God and the gospel. They therefore intentionally embrace these secular stories and the practices that accompany them. In other cases, however, Christians may unintentionally adopt and adapt the practices or views of these secular stories without fully realizing what they are doing. They may be on autopilot, simply going along with normal cultural practice, without seeing that they are embodying a different story from the gospel.

But we need to assess whether what we do with our bodies (our convictional beliefs) aligns with what we say we believe (our confessional beliefs). To faithfully embody the gospel, we need to resist not only the warped Christian stories that have been handed down, but also the way the stories of our secular age warp our witness. If our ultimate goal is to bear witness to the good news of Jesus, that will involve a holistic way of life that understands and integrates every part of who we are—including our bodies and sexuality—for the sake of that mission.

Finally, we need to see the link between these stories and particular views and practices of sex, bodies, singleness, and marriage in our culture. Often, Christians focus on particular topics and the ethical questions surrounding them, such as sex outside of marriage, cohabitation, same-sex marriage, polyamory, birth control, or others. This is not bad, but it often keeps us from understanding the root story that guides how we think about such matters. These underlying stories are crucial to grasping why our culture operates the way it does. Why does same-sex marriage seem so obviously right to so many people? Why is pornography normalized and widespread? Why does polyamory seem like an increasingly viable option for so many? To answer these questions, we must understand the foundational stories of naturalism, individualism, and romance.

We need to carefully attend to our own practices and views so we can be faithful to Scripture and consistent and coherent in what we teach and practice. For example, if we embrace a view of marriage and divorce that is rooted in individualism or if we place a high value on marriage because we are rooted in the story of romance, we are not embodying the gospel. We dare not critique the broader culture for specific practices that go against Scripture while still embracing the root stories that inform those practices.

WHAT'S THE STORY OF INDIVIDUALISM?

Perhaps no story has saturated our culture like the story of individualism. We absorb this story through the entertainment industry, it drives our political discourse, and it's central to how we think about education and economics. It's no wonder that the way we view sex, bodies, marriage, and singleness would be shaped by this story. In fact, many of the hot-button controversies in our culture, including questions about same-sex marriage, transgender identities, and alternative romantic relationships like polyamory, are rooted not simply in ideas about sex but also in the long history of Western individualism, a story that is centuries old but has profoundly affected our views of sex, marriage, and singleness in the last several decades.

Who are we? According to the story of individualism, we are individuals striving to be free. I discover who I truly am by looking inward and then authentically expressing my true inner self in my outward interactions with the world. But we don't often step back and ask, What exactly is an individual, and how does individuality affect how we perceive reality?

Because individualism is so ingrained in our culture, it can be difficult to recognize that the story told about who we are as individuals is merely one way of looking at the world. That is, the individual is a powerful social and cultural construct, and we must recognize it as such—not to dismiss or undermine it, but to properly think through how this basic assumption about who we are affects everything, including our sense of self and our views of sex and bodies.

Psychologist and philosopher Jonathan Haidt summarizes our individualism in a memorable way with the label "WEIRD morality," an acronym that stands for "Western, educated, industrialized, rich, and democratic" morality. What is a key characteristic of WEIRD morality? According to Haidt, "The WEIRDer you are, the more you see a world full of separate objects, rather than relationships."[2] That is, generally speaking, WEIRD people identify who they are primarily through their own characteristics, preferences, and accomplishments, whereas non-WEIRD people tend to identify themselves through relationships and connections.

As political theorist Patrick Deneen notes, American and most other Western democratic political structures assume the individual is the basic building block of human society and existence.[3] When we define ourselves as individuals, we think about ourselves first not as members of a family, dwellers in a specific geographical place, or adherents to a religious tradition. Rather, we think about ourselves as a stand-alone, self-sufficient individual, someone with rights and desires who is disconnected from others and only enters into relationships in order to live out those rights and fulfill those desires. That is, a core dimension of being an individual is freedom—freedom from others imposing their will or desires on me, and freedom to be who I want to be. This is not something that has to be argued for in our culture; it is the fundamental and universal assumption. American politics runs on the autopilot of individualism.

The story of individualism is powerfully embodied in key cultural symbols, including America's foundational political documents. For example, it is built into the Declaration of Independence and, as such, drives our political discourse and the way that we as Americans (Christians and non-Christians alike) think about ourselves.[4] According to the Declaration, an individual is a political entity endowed with "inalienable rights," including life, liberty, and the pursuit of happiness. Each of us is a rights-bearing individual with the basic right to life. An essential element of our life is that we have political liberty, the freedom to pursue happiness as we define it. This way of viewing society, at least on the popular level, sees our world as a collection of individuals. Each individual has some definition of how they understand the world and what it means to seek happiness and the good life. Society as a whole and the political structures that exist serve to reinforce and protect the rights of each individual to pursue their own understanding of the good life.

Of course, there are limits to this liberty, and those limits relate to preserving the life, liberty, and pursuit of happiness of other individuals. We justify laws and limits to our liberty on this basis. For example, although limiting my speed while driving might seem to infringe on my freedom to get where I'm going as soon as I possibly can, driving too fast can be reckless and dangerous to other people (and to myself). If I cause an accident due to fast driving, it's quite possible that I would infringe on the liberty and pursuit of happiness of others, if not their very lives. Even our intense political debates and disagreements are driven by our fundamental agreement around the liberty of the individual. Although progressives and conservatives disagree about how best to maximize individual freedom, they disagree so vehemently because they are fighting about the best way to achieve the same goal: maximizing individual freedom.

For example, debates about abortion are often framed in terms of individual freedom, pitting the mother's freedom of choice against a child's freedom to grow and live. Debates about gun rights and gun control pit the individual freedom to bear arms against the individual freedom to be safe in public spaces. While those on different sides of these debates disagree with each other, they often agree on the foundational starting point of debate: individual freedom.

From a biblical and Christian standpoint, this is not a neutral or natural way of looking at the world, but a particularly modern way of viewing the nature and purpose of human life. To grasp the basic storyline of individualism, it's helpful to briefly consider two philosophers who have shaped this way of living and thinking and how they answer key questions about the world.

Who are we? What's the problem with the world? Jean-Jacques Rousseau provides valuable insight into how individualism answers these questions. A key figure in the development of the story of individualism, Rousseau lived in the 1700s. His autobiography, *The Confessions*, opens by putting the story of individualism on display with a testimony about his own ability to know and reveal himself to his readers. Though this way of speaking might sound familiar to us now, Rousseau's individualistic way of narrating his life was unique for his time. In the opening lines, he states,

> I have resolved on an enterprise which has no precedent, and which, once complete, will have no imitator. My purpose is to display to my kind a portrait in every way true to nature, and the man I shall portray will be myself.
>
> Simply myself. I know my own heart and understand my fellow

man. But I am made unlike any one I have ever met; I will even venture to say that I am like no one in the whole world. I may be no better, but at least I am different.[5]

This way of telling his own story assumes that Rousseau has a full knowledge of who he truly is on the inside and that this knowledge of his inner self is, in many ways, unquestioned and unquestionable by those outside him. He "knows his own heart" and thus expresses and communicates externally what he is internally. Rousseau answers the question "Who am I?" with this answer: I am an individual, unique in my being and in my knowledge of myself.

The story of individualism is reinforced through later philosophers, including the existentialist Jean-Paul Sartre. Sartre explains how individualism sees humanity with a helpful analogy.[6] According to Sartre, if I see a pair of scissors, I can ask, "What is that?" and "What is that for?" Someone can answer, "It's a pair of scissors, and it's made for cutting things." I know what it is, and I know its purpose. I can know this because it has a maker and a purpose.

According to the atheist Sartre, when it comes to humans, no one can answer the second question, "What are we here for?" There is no creator to tell us what we exist for, what our purpose is. Because there is no one outside or beyond ourselves to define us, we cannot really answer the first question, "Who or what are we?" We exist, but it is up to us to define ourselves and the reason for our existence (hence the name *existentialism* for this strand of thinking). The definition of who or what we are is not something that can come from outside any of us, but must come from inside each one of us as we embrace our own path of self-definition and self-creation.

With this framework, we can now answer the question, "What is the problem with this world?" For individualism, the problem is anything outside yourself that tries to define who you are and what your purpose is. According to Sartre, when you let something outside of you control your destiny or self-definition, you are living an "inauthentic" life. The problem is that others—family, tradition, religion—try to tell you who you are and who you are supposed to be. Philosopher Charles Taylor sums up this focus on authenticity: "Each one of us has his/her own way of realizing our humanity, and . . . it is important to find and live out one's own, as against surrendering to conformity with a model imposed on us from outside, by society, or the previous generation, or religious or political authority."[7] In other words, you do you.

This story of individualism is not just an abstract way of looking at the world; it is embodied in the key stories, symbols, and practices of our culture. We learn it not in discussions of political theory in college classrooms or Bohemian coffee shops but in much more powerful ways and at a younger age. It's proclaimed, sung, and represented in the core storylines of many treasured Disney films.

In the first *Frozen* movie, we see this expressed in Elsa's hallmark song "Let It Go," in which she renounces her role as queen and the people's unfair expectations. In responding to admittedly unjust reactions to her unique powers, she sings a praise song to expressive individualism: Let go of all the things outside yourself that would define you (including right, wrong, and rules) and embrace who you authentically are.

Another poignant example comes from *The Little Mermaid*.[8] In this movie, the mermaid Ariel is dissatisfied with many things about her life: her role in her society as a princess; her father, King Triton's, commands; and even her own nature and body as a mermaid. She longs to be part of the human world. This desire leads her to make a deal with Ursula, the sea witch, to try to gain the love of Prince Eric. Her actions lead to a series of cascading catastrophes that nearly destroy her, as well as her father and Prince Eric. Yet the movie resolves in a way that suggests all this was worth it for Ariel to achieve what she wanted: freedom from her role in Triton's kingdom, freedom from obligations that came with that role, and even freedom from the limits of her mermaid body as she is transformed into a human. Ariel's goal is liberty, and nearly any cost is worth it to achieve that goal.

This message is seen especially clearly when contrasted with the original tale of *The Little Mermaid* by Hans Christian Andersen. In that story, when the little mermaid approaches the sea witch about being transformed into a human, the witch warns, "I know what you want. It is very stupid of you, but you shall have your way, and it will bring you to sorrow, my pretty princess."[9] Unlike the Disney version, the mermaid ultimately fails in her quest to win the prince's love, and the story ends with her dying by dissolving into sea foam. The contrast between the overarching messages could not be starker: The original story warns against overstepping your limits and wanting to be something you are not, whereas the modern Disney version applauds and affirms a near-limitless pursuit of your own self-definition and self-creation. As the character Sebastian summarizes, "Children got to be free to lead their own lives."[10] The original version shows that "You do you" leads to death; the Disney version says that "You do you" is the only real path, no matter the cost.

The message is clear: Be authentic. Don't let anyone else define you or tell you who you are. When you listen to your heart and inner self, you'll find yourself and discover your place in the world. In this way, the powerful songs and stories of Disney show us the story of individualism: unique individuals overcoming obstacles to be their true selves. Like them, we are unique individuals who need to listen to our inner voices, not messages or people external to us who might offer a different account of who we are or the purpose of our lives. The story of individualism is assumed in our economics and education; built into our everyday discussions and decisions; and written into the music, movies, and TV we consume. Through political practices that construct and reinforce the individual as the central figure of history and through the messaging of Disney's billion-dollar media empire, the story of individualism is deeply embedded and embodied in our culture.

EMBODYING INDIVIDUALISM: SINGLENESS AND CONSENT

So what are bodies and sex for according to the story of individualism? To express and actualize your unique inner self. Although he is speaking of a Christian view of sex, what Christopher West says applies to the story of individualism and the sexual revolution: "Sex is not just about sex. The way we understand and express our sexuality points to our deepest-held convictions about who we are . . . the meaning of love, the ordering of society, and the mystery of the universe."[11] According to the story of individualism, bodies and sex are for authentically expressing our own individuality, whether that is in singleness or marriage or some other romantic arrangement and relationship.

The story of individualism strongly shapes how we see singleness. Many stay single precisely because marriage or commitment to some other person means letting someone else or some other relationship define you. Singleness means freedom and freedom of choice to be who I want and to be with who I want without any long-term ties.[12] Singleness means I'm free to be me and to do what I want. Singleness allows me to maximize my freedom of expression. As the character Carrie Bradshaw in *Sex and the City* puts it, "Being single used to mean that nobody wanted you. Now it means you're pretty sexy and you're taking your time deciding how you want your life to be and who you want to spend it with."[13] For that reason, our culture often highly values singleness over marriage, seeing marriage as a choice that restricts freedom. Of course, singleness also (so the story goes) means that I'm free to have sex with anyone I want, with or without commitment. Within this individualistic framework, a central ethical standard is consent.

Consent is a central practice for contemporary sexual ethics because it is rooted in the story of individualism. Though precise legal definitions of consent vary, consent is seen as "an informed, affirmative, conscious decision by each participant to engage in mutually agreed-upon sexual activity."[14] Particularly in light of the recent #MeToo movement,

41

individuals, activists, and legislators alike have raised awareness about the centrality of consent, focusing not simply on whether someone said no to unwanted sexual advances, but on the need for all parties involved to actively say yes.[15] I want to be clear: Consent is a good thing. Consent recognizes our dignity and freedom as God's image bearers and that sexual union is fundamentally distorted when it is not consensual. But is consent all you need? That is, can consent alone sustain a sexual ethic? No.

Consent plays a crucial role in the sexual ethics of our secular age because it is rooted in the story of individualism, as well as naturalism (which we'll address in more detail in chapter 11). Let me unpack that. For the stories of individualism and naturalism, sex doesn't mean anything in and of itself. Because we are nothing but matter in motion seeking to express our individual selves, the crucial question to establish whether sexual activity is legitimate is this: Does a person consent to this sexual encounter? If so, then it is morally permissible. If not, then it's not.

Though someone might want to push someone into sexual activity without their consent, this would violate the core tenet of individualism that each of us has the right to determine what sex means and what we are willing to do. Individualism plus naturalism says I can do whatever I feel comfortable with and truly expresses my authentic self in a way that is true to me. But individualism also says that I have to give others the same right of self-determination. I should not allow another person's desire or self to overrun my own comfort level and preferences, and neither should I overrun anyone else's comfort level and preferences.

For the story of individualism, sex is whatever you make of it. One person may see it as a deeply personal and romantic encounter to be taken very seriously, whereas another may see it as a one-time recreational encounter to be taken very lightly. And the same person may see it two different ways, depending on the time, circumstances, and partner. If sex has an inherent meaning beyond myself, then I have to ask whether I'm being faithful to that meaning, which may be bigger than both people involved. But according to the story of individualism, a person only needs to ask, Does the other person consent to this encounter at this time? Again, consent is good, but it is not sufficient to sustain a healthy and whole approach to sex in our culture. What if instead of asking, "Do I consent to this?" we asked a deeper question: "To what persons and actions should I give my consent?"

How we answer this question affects those around us, though individualism seeks to suppress this. Part of the story of individualism is that my sex life is my business and no one else's. What I consent to is up to me; it's my body and my choice. The problem with this way of thinking, however, is that sexual ethics are always communal. The communal nature of consent was highlighted in a story regarding comedian Aziz Ansari that broke in the midst of the #MeToo movement. The initial stories that generated the #MeToo movement were clear situations of misconduct. But many people found the story involving Ansari, cocreator and star of the show *Master of None*, to be more complicated.[16]

A woman identifying herself as "Grace" wrote a post for the website Babe titled, "I Went on a Date with Aziz Ansari. It Turned into the Worst Night of My Life."[17] After meeting Ansari in Los Angeles, Grace reconnected with him in New York a short time later. They went out for dinner together, then returned to his apartment. While there, they engaged in sexual activity that made her uncomfortable. According to her account, she sent both nonverbal and verbal cues to express her reticence, which Ansari either did not receive or did not acknowledge. As the Babe post summarizes: "The night would end with Grace in an Uber home, in tears, messaging her friends about how Ansari behaved."

This account became a kind of Rorschach test, provoking mixed reactions in the ongoing conversation about sexual ethics. Was this an example of sexual assault or just social awkwardness and miscommunication? Some see Ansari as the latest in a long line of abusers. Others believe Grace's story is not at all abuse, going so far as to call her accusation "the worst thing that has happened to the #MeToo movement"[18] since it began. A key concern in the debate about this incident was consent: Was the activity consensual or not? But this again raises a deeper question: Is consent really all you need?

Think about the question this way: Why did Ansari feel comfortable with how things were proceeding while his date did not? Most likely he'd had previous encounters with women who consented to moving very quickly into a variety of sexual activities that Grace found uncomfortable. Based on his experience, was he justified in perceiving his date as consensual? Perhaps. Was she justified in feeling uncomfortable and used? Absolutely. At the very least, this thought experiment helps us realize that anytime we consents to something, it inevitably has a broader impact than on just two people.

Our sexual encounters might not become national news like Ansari's, but someone's consent or level of comfort is always interpreted through the broader communal mores around sex. In a sense, every woman who previously consented to being treated in this way by Ansari played a part in that encounter. And Ansari's own consent to treating women as nothing more than objects of pleasure and letting himself be treated as a trophy to be claimed ("I was with Aziz Ansari!") played a part in the encounter as well.

As much as we might like to think of sexual ethics in general or consent in particular as something that's up to each individual, it just doesn't work that way. Sexual ethics are always communal. What two people do in the privacy of their own space inevitably affects others, not just themselves. A radically individualistic notion of consent is an insufficient basis for sexual ethics because it fails to see the ways we are all interconnected, an interconnection that the story of individualism cannot fully account for. Individualism tells a false story not only about sex but also about who we are and how we are connected to one another. The notion of sex as a private, personal matter disconnected from other people is just as false as the notion of the individual as a stand-alone, disconnected entity.

EMBODYING INDIVIDUALISM: SEXUAL IDENTITY

The story of individualism also lies at the heart of sexual identity. Once upon a time, there was no such thing as sexuality. Such a statement seems confusing at best and perhaps downright false, at least from our cultural perspective. The term *sexuality* is quite vague, even if broadly used, and many use it to describe a natural reality that is true for all times and places. I'm not saying we are not sexual beings, but the way we think about our "sexuality" is rooted in how we think about sexual identity, using terms and concepts such as *gay, straight, bisexual,* and more. In other words, our concept of sexual identity is rooted in the story of individualism. As Jenell Williams Paris puts it,

> Sexual identity is a Western, nineteenth-century formulation of what it means to be human. It's grounded in a belief that the direction of one's sexual desire is identity-constituting, earning each individual a label (gay, lesbian, straight, etc.) and a social role. Perceived as innate and as stemming from inner desire, sexual identity has to be searched out, found, named, and expressed in order for each person to be a fully functional and happy adult.[19]

The commonplace terms we use to mark sexual identity, such as *gay* or *straight,* are not themselves timeless terms that reflect the natural and obvious experience of everyone or every culture. Rather, they are products of the story of individualism, and their constant use reinforces the story of individualism in which they are embedded and on which they depend.

As Paris notes, studies in anthropology show that same-sex relationships take on a variety of patterns, including relationships based on age (in ancient Greece), gender roles (in South America, the Caribbean, Mesoamerica, and the Mediterranean), and even profession, including entertainers, prostitutes, and religious specialists (in some Native American and ethnic groups in Borneo, Siberia, and the Philippines).[20]

Though many of these cultures have examples of same-sex sexual activity and relationships, the contemporary Western category of "gay," which generally implies exclusive same-sex attraction in an egalitarian relationship, is absent. This helps us see that individualism and sexual identity are interdependent concepts.

This connection between sexual desire and identity helps us see why the Christian vision of sex is offensive to the story of individualism. A key part of personal growth and development is coming to define who I "really am" in terms of my sexual desires and practices. Those desires and practices are then seen as a core part of my identity. This focus on identity has led us to an interesting place. For the story of individualism, the act of sex means nothing outside of whatever meaning I give it, but my sexuality means everything. As a result, if I as a Christian tell someone (straight, gay, or bisexual) they should not have sex with someone (of the same or opposite sex), the offensive nature of that prohibition is not really about sex. Rather, I am telling someone they can't act out of and express their true self.

According to the story of individualism, though, any prohibition that tells someone not to be and express their true self is an act that genuinely harms people. That prohibition flies in the face of the call to self-invention and self-creation, which are the goals of individualism, and so it is to be rejected as not just wrong but dangerous and harmful.

Does this mean we ignore or reject completely the categories of sexual identity? No. Because our culture is saturated by the story of individualism and the categories of sexual identity, those categories possess real power. For that reason, we can't ignore them. They shape everyone in our culture, including Christians. Furthermore, these categories may sometimes be useful, helping us describe or understand ourselves and the world in certain ways. Just because they are particular to our culture doesn't mean they are totally wrong or unhelpful. Every culture generates concepts and practices that may have some good dimensions and some flawed ones. So we need not completely reject these categories simply because they are specific to our time, place, and culture. Every culture has categories and ways of being in the world that must be tested to determine what is useful and what is not, what is compatible with God's intentions for his world and what is not.

Here again, Paris is helpful, emphasizing that our task is "learning to use sexual identity categories strategically (which sometimes means not using them at all), instead of being (ab)used by them when they tell us who we are, what we're worth and with whom we should associate." Our goal, she continues, is "understanding cultural categories but not living by their power."[21] What does it look like to do this in a wise and winsome way?

One clear example is Greg Coles's testimony in *Single, Gay, Christian.*[22] All three of those terms come loaded with certain meanings and connotations in our culture and in Christian circles. For many, *single* means alone and lonely, *gay* means you're a man having sex with other men, and *Christian* means you're backwards and a bigot. So why does Coles embrace all three of these descriptors? To understand what these words mean and how Coles uses them, you have to enter into his narrative (which I highly recommend).

In various ways, he acknowledges that these terms can be limited and restrictive. Nevertheless, in telling his own story, he uses all those terms strategically, in ways that clarify how these words revolve around Jesus rather than around the common (mis)conceptions of what these words must mean. For him, *single* doesn't mean lonely but part of the family of God, *gay* doesn't imply sexual activity but an orientation, and *Christian* means a beloved child of God. In embracing but redefining the way many people hear those terms, he serves as a great example of Paris's call to understand and use the terms of our culture without living by their power. If Christians use terms like *straight* to describe themselves, they would do well to take cues from Coles about the need to clarify how their use of that term differs from what is considered normal for straight people in the broader culture.

47

So the story of individualism is embodied in how our culture lives in relation to singleness, consent, and sexual identity. Who are we according to individualism? We are individuals on the path to increasing freedom as we live into our unique selves, especially in our sexuality. This story claims to free us from all external sources that would tell us who we are and what we should do: "You do you." This story is central to the big story of liberty. In contrast, the gospel tells a fundamentally different story, not a story of self-sufficient liberty achieved but a story of grace-dependent identity received.

CHAPTER 4

THE STORY OF GOD'S COVENANT FAITHFULNESS

"You Belong to Jesus"

Whereas the story of individualism calls us to embody and express our unique self, the story of the gospel calls us to embody the story of Jesus, pointing to the faithful covenant love embodied in his crucified and resurrected body. The gospel is the story of God's faithful covenant love. The reality of God's gracious covenant is crucial for helping us think through how we understand ourselves.

WHO ARE WE? PEOPLE WHO BELONG TO JESUS

What does it mean to be in covenant with God? As I mentioned at the outset, it means that God takes the initiative in bringing us into covenant relationship with him.[1] This relationship isn't a temporary or consumer-minded relationship, but one where God makes promises and calls us to respond as faithful covenant partners. But we don't enter or stay in this covenant by what we do. In contrast to the story of individualism, it is not about generating our identity and self but about receiving our identity and self in relationship with God and the covenant people of God.

This does not mean that constructing my identity and self is solely passive and that I have no part to play. But in contrast to the story of individualism, my identity and self are first and foremost a gift to be received rather than an outcome to be achieved. As question and answer one of the Heidelberg Catechism puts it, "I am not my own but belong, body and soul, to my faithful savior Jesus Christ."[2] This is identity by grace through faith: "You receive you." Our union with Christ is the source of our ultimate identity. This covenantal way of looking at the self is crucial to grasp if we are to think through how we are called to embody the gospel in marriage and singleness. It also puts a fundamentally different spin on our notion of authenticity.

Theologian Justin Bailey points out that our quest for authenticity and self-realization can be seen as either a narrow, self-focused pursuit or a broader, deeper pursuit to clarify our place as an individual within the larger sweep of reality.[3] This distinction is helpful. The authenticity of individualism stems from a mistaken view that we invent and create ourselves. This is self-invention. The second kind of authenticity comes from discovering one's self as part of a larger reality and narrative. This is self-discovery, not in the sense that I am creating myself, but rather that the self I am discovering and living into is, at root, a gift and call from God.[4] This identity produces a sense of rest that comes from not having to strive after constant self-invention, but instead receiving the good news that we are who God says we are. Rooted in God's gift of my life and self, I then respond to God's call to live into who he is calling me to be. God is not an obstacle to authenticity but rather the possibility of my true authenticity, which stems from my response to God's love and faithfulness.

To ground ourselves in this covenantal way of living and thinking, it helps to see an example of a self that is constructed in relation to God. The fourth-century theologian Augustine serves as a helpful example, answering the questions "Who am I?" and "What is the problem?" very differently from individualism. Augustine's narrative of his own life in his *Confessions* serves as a stark contrast to *The Confessions* of Rousseau noted earlier. Whereas Rousseau begins his confession with a bold proclamation that he will fully reveal his true self to the reader, Augustine begins his confession with a series of questions to God about both God and Augustine's knowledge of God. In other words, far from being the self-assured narrator who understands all things, Augustine needs help from outside himself to grasp and understand his own self.

As he begins telling the story of his own life, Augustine starts with who he was as a baby and young child, noting that his description of himself comes not from himself but from what he's been told by others. In saying this, Augustine is intentionally reinforcing the reality that our self is not self-constructed. Even in understanding my own life and story, I have to rely on those outside myself to narrate it. Again, this stands in contrast to the story of individualism, which says that only I can truly tell the story of my own life. For Augustine, that story will always be constructed in relationship—to other people and ultimately to God. Who am I, according to Augustine? I am a creature of God, dependent on God's revelation of himself and myself to understand who I am.

But Augustine identifies a challenge in this. The problem is not external but internal, a problem of confession. For Augustine, the idea of confessing—either the truth about God or the truth about his own self and his struggle with sin—reveals the limits of his own self-knowledge. Can he tell the truth about his own story and about his struggle with sin? It would seem not, for the nature of sin is to be self-deceptive, thus warping his ability to even see and understand who he is and why he does what he does. Furthermore, as a finite, limited being, Augustine acknowledges the limits of his self-knowledge. Thus, far from being transparent to his readers or his own self, Augustine confesses, "I cannot myself comprehend all that I am."[5] The main problem or obstacle is not in the world out there, but in his own limits and especially his own sin.

Augustine thus points his readers to the truth: Knowledge of my self is not an achievement but a gift of God. Only when he encounters the gracious God of Scripture can Augustine tell the story of his true self, which is in relation to God and whose very existence is a response to God's gracious gift of life and redemption. His confession of his true self thus involves humility and dependency, virtues that are scandalous to the story of individualism. Whereas expressive individualism typically sees external sources of the self as hindrances to the actualization of the self, Augustine realizes that true knowledge of himself is impossible apart from God.

This points to an even deeper truth about Augustine (and us): Just as his knowledge is dependent on God, his very being is utterly dependent on God. Far from being the stable center of the universe, as the story of individualism would have it, Augustine recognizes that he is radically dependent, and his identity and self-understanding are gifts that God is calling him to live into.

This self can know both God and self only at the foot of the cross. Here we see the reality of our sin and waywardness, the result of our attempt to construct reality centered on ourselves: Jesus, our Savior, crucified for us. At the cross we see the reality of God's faithful covenant love, God's unwillingness to let us stay in our self-enclosed kingdom that leads only to death: Jesus, our Savior, giving himself completely for us. This scandalous claim that we don't belong to ourselves but are called to embody God's faithful covenant love profoundly shapes how Christians tell the story of the gospel with their bodies in singleness and marriage.

EMBODYING THE GOSPEL: WEDDING VOWS

How can Christians embody the gospel in our secular age? How do we respond to the notion that consent is all you need? That it's normal to live together, get married, and get divorced, all for the sake of striving to construct and express my true self? That marriage and singleness alike are life projects centered on me? That monogamous marriage is but one form that the pursuit of self-realization can take? These are complex questions with numerous possible angles and answers. And while Christians often grapple with them on a theoretical level, it's often harder to imagine how we actually shift our practices so key symbols of our life point to Jesus and the gospel.

One key symbol we should reconsider is the practice of weddings. One practical way to counteract the story of individualism with the gospel would be to start having wedding ceremonies within the context of a church's worship service. In other words, place weddings right in the middle of our weekly Sunday worship services in a way that shifts the focus from the story of individualism to the way marriage is meant to embody the gospel. This practical but unusual step would powerfully embody the gospel and form a stark contrast with how the story of individualism has shaped not only our weddings but also how we think about marriage and singleness.

How could churches make this shift more possible? People often like to get married in a place that is beautiful, so some churches might need to acknowledge that the physical appearance of their sanctuary could use some attention, even appointing someone in the congregation with an eye and passion for design to help with improvements or special decorations for the occasion. I'm not saying that churches have to look like a contemporary wedding venue, but they might benefit from considering the role of beauty not only in a special ceremony like a wedding but also in the weekly worship of God.

How would this fit or merge with a regular church service? I can imagine pastors struggling to juggle a wedding plus all the regular responsibilities of a Sunday service. But if all the parties involved recognized that the wedding is meant to be a worship service (and already is seen as such in the liturgies of many church traditions), it would not be "one more thing" added into a regular service but would serve as the church's weekly Sunday morning worship service, including Scripture, songs, and a sermon. And the wedding itself would be a highly charged symbol of what Christ-centered marriages already show in their everyday life and praxis: that Christian marriage is sustained and sustainable only by the grace of God and the community of disciples, the church.

A few years back I mentioned this idea to one of my friends who pastors in an urban Cleveland neighborhood. His response surprised me: "We actually did this recently!" He went on to tell me about a couple from their church who celebrated their wedding with their church family on a Sunday morning, with a church potluck that followed. Although it lacked some of the frills of a more expensive wedding, my friend spoke enthusiastically of the joy and celebration that the bride, groom, and whole church family experienced. He also reminded me that many of our expectations come primarily from our wedding industrial complex and are relatively recent developments, luxuries that most families in his neighborhood couldn't afford anyway, no matter how or where they got married.

Such a shift in the time and place of wedding ceremonies would help Christians and non-Christians alike better see a properly biblical view of marriage. How so? First, this practice would highlight the uniqueness of the Christian view of marriage. What Christians mean by "marriage" is not necessarily the same as what the broader culture means, a fact that Christians and non-Christians alike often miss. In the wedding ceremony, vows are made that, if truly understood, involve a call to die to yourself in order to truly become one with your spouse. The goal is not seeking the freedom to express yourself, but using your freedom to serve, as God gives you the grace to serve and love your spouse. This is not something we can do on our own. In that sense, Christian marriage is not "natural." It is not something that can be achieved on the basis of our strength and work. As the disciples in Matthew 19 recognize, this kind of faithful covenant love is exceedingly difficult, so much so that it causes them to exclaim that "it is better not to marry" (19:10) due to the high demands of love.

Since marriage is meant to embody the union of Christ and the church, our wedding ceremonies should be less about our unique, individual self-expression and more about what we share: the recognition that God in his grace has reached out to us and called us to follow him and embody his faithful covenant love in this relationship we call marriage.

This need not negate the unique stories represented and celebrated by each couple. However, by putting wedding ceremonies within the worship service of the church, we would clearly communicate that the story of this particular couple makes sense only within the story of God's faithful covenant love for us. By anchoring the wedding ceremony within our rehearsal of that story in worship, the marriage would be grounded in something far bigger and greater than itself: the gospel. Our stories—and marriages—are called to embody and be taken up into the story of Christ's love for us.

By placing the wedding ceremony in a worship service, we also would see more closely the link between faithfulness, consent, and the gospel. The gospel is the story of God's faithful covenant love, embodied in the body of Jesus. If what we do with our bodies is meant to embody the love of God in Jesus, then the question is not merely whether we consent to something, but whether we consent to something that faithfully embodies the faithful covenant love of the gospel. When thinking about the nature of consent, then, the question is not merely whether someone consents to a particular sexual encounter (and it's crucial to recognize that, even within marriage, consent to each particular sexual encounter is necessary), but whether we are consenting to the practice of sex in a way that is inscribed into the self-giving, faithful, covenantal story of the gospel. In other words, Jesus's own body reveals that true freedom entails faithfulness to God's call, not simply freedom to do whatever I want. When I know the faithful love of God, I freely and faithfully bind myself to a path of self-giving love toward my spouse.

This gospel-centered view of marriage and consent reframes how we understand one of the main goals of individualism: freedom. For individualism, consent equals freedom. If I choose it, I have made a free choice. For the gospel, freedom involves not merely the ability to choose but the strength to choose the good. True freedom is not merely freedom from external constraint but freedom from the sinful interior motives that would cause me to choose something that doesn't align with the gospel and therefore my truest self—the self redeemed to walk in newness of life. This is not merely freedom *from* external forces but freedom *for* choosing what is good, what truly embodies the gospel.

This view of freedom is captured well by Wendell Berry in his essay "Sex, Economy, Freedom, and Community." He asks, "What must we do to earn the freedom of being unguardedly and innocently naked to someone?"[6] This a very different question from that of individualism, which views freedom primarily as permission to take from or do something to someone. This freedom, however, never attains a place of fidelity, a place of trust. In this way, mere mutual consent masquerades as freedom, but it is not the freedom of covenantal nakedness, a complete self-giving and transparency that comes with the promises and actions of the faithful care of one's spouse as one's beloved. This authentic freedom comes only as one embraces the covenantal reality of sex and marriage.

Berry answers his own question about how we attain the freedom of true faithfulness, saying, "We must make promises and keep them. We must assume many fearful responsibilities and do much work. We must build the household of trust."[7] This way of looking at things sheds new light on why Christians have emphasized that marriage vows should precede sexual union: Marriage vows are the proper form of consent. They recognize the true covenantal meaning of sexual union as complete, faithful, self-giving love.

In this way, marriage vows consent to seeing your spouse as a full person to be loved, not just a body or person to be used. They are a full person made in God's image and thus worthy of respect, dignity, care, and fidelity. Marriage vows also affirm that our bodies have meaning and worth. Sex and bodies are not for mere recreation or self-expression, but are taken up into the story of God's faithful love for us, embodied fully in Jesus. These words faithfully affirm that what is going on in sexual union is not only physical but also deeply personal and covenantal. Marriage vows are a form of consent that acknowledges that the end goal is embodiment of the gospel in the marriage, not merely a one-time physical encounter.

To be clear, I'm not saying that marriage vows are a blank check for consent and that spouses don't have the ability to reject sexual advances from their spouse. Rather, I'm drawing attention to the way marriage vows place any and all sexual encounters within the bigger story of the gospel (which is precisely why it's so important that vows are not seen as a blank check allowing a spouse to adopt a self-serving posture toward sex and consent). In this way, marriage vows call us not to a self-fulfillment found through mere self-expression or actualization but to a fulfillment that comes from participating in a larger story, as embodied signs of and witnesses to the gospel.

Think about how this connection between consent and the gospel shapes us to answer the question, "Why should I wait until I am married to have sex?" The complete gift of your body in sex speaks to the complete gift of your self to your spouse. If you are ready for that kind of faithful, self-giving love, then you are ready for the marriage vows, which consent to love and be loved in that way.

This understanding of consent, marriage, and fidelity should form the character of Christians to stand out in our culture, in part because it is truly human and humanizing. In contrast, an ethic that is linked only to consent will end up dehumanizing others. In other words, the character of people formed by the story of individualism, with its focus on consent alone, will ultimately be deformed insofar as it does not treat them as people to be loved but as objects to be used.

The question of to whom and to what we consent is linked to the question of character. By character I mean the reality that we as people are shaped over time to act in ways that are either virtuous or vicious.

We are not just free-floating individuals who can act any way at any time. Rather, how we act and what we value are shaped and formed so that our moral character is a kind of second nature, a way of acting and behaving that flows from whether previous choices we have made are virtuous or vicious, good or bad. We act in line with our character. We do not just flip a switch and go from behaving in a self-centered way to making wise, other-centered choices. Human behavior doesn't work that way. And here is the issue: We have created a sexual culture where it is normal for people to consent to being treated and treating others as mere objects to be used for their own pleasure, whether physical, emotional, or relational.

Even someone as seemingly innocent as the beloved (but fictional) coach Ted Lasso illustrates the way we turn people into objects to be consumed. In season 1 of *Ted Lasso*, after Ted has a one-night stand with a woman (a scene I'll come back to later), he's feeling guilty that he had sex with someone with whom there was no commitment. His friends tell him it's no big deal, and ultimately he's cheered up by the question, "Was it fun?" The message is clear: If it's fun, do it. If everyone's okay with it, it must be okay. This scene stands out because treating people *as people* is a hallmark of Coach Lasso, part of what makes him unique and endearing. Sex, however, appears to be the exceptional area of life where it's okay to see someone as an object to be consumed rather than a person to be respected and loved.

Someone might object that if someone wants to consent to essentially be seen as an object to be used and not a person to be loved, it is their right to do so and to express their sexuality that way. But the paradox is this: The more we consent to being treated as mere objects and treating others in that way, the more we will create people who do not actually value consent. We can consent to living in such a way that we end up devaluing consent.

If I see someone as an object to be used, I am not seeing them as a whole person. Now, someone can consent to being treated simply as an object, a means to another person's end goal, and not as a whole person. For example, I'd argue that consenting to a one-night stand or one-time sexual encounter is consenting to being an object in another person's striving for self-expression and self-fulfillment. But an object is not a person. An object is something to be used and then set aside once its purpose has been served.

Further complicating things, one doesn't need consent from an object as one does from a person. So even if I recognize that consent is important, the more that others consent to being treated as objects, the more my character is shaped to see other people as mere objects, not as full persons. In this way, our emphasis on consent can create a sexual culture where it is normal to dehumanize people, seeing them as nothing but objects. And if we see people as objects, we tend not to value their consent. So, paradoxically, if we consent to dehumanizing, objectifying practices, we shouldn't be surprised that our culture undermines consent even as we preach it.

This should concern us, especially when we consider the pervasive problem of sexual assault on college campuses, where 26.4 percent of women and 6.8 percent of men experience rape or sexual assault.[8] Certainly, an emphasis on consent is desperately needed! But we need to recognize that a remedy of consent *alone* can't fix our cultural problem. Thus, the Christian practice of marriage vows as the proper form of consent is not merely about marriage, but is instead a crucial way that our character is shaped to see the whole person, in sexual ethics and beyond, in the light of the gospel—not as an object to be used but as a person to be loved.

Let's return to the symbolic practice of using weddings in our worship services. This practice would emphasize that it takes a church to raise a marriage and remind spouses that marriage is not an end in itself but one path of discipleship alongside singleness. Divorce is so prevalent in our culture in part because it is merely an extension of the logic of individualistic marriage. In other words, if someone gets married with the goal of self-realization, there's a good chance they are going to get divorced for the same reason. In contrast, by putting our weddings in the midst of our communal worship services, we emphasize that Christian marriage is possible only within the context of Christian community.

This is part of the broader truth that the Christian life is sustained by fellowship not only with God but also with the family of God. God's sustaining grace for spouses flows through the reality of Christian sisters and brothers who walk alongside them, sustaining, challenging, and encouraging them as they embody God's faithful covenant love in marriage. As David Matzko McCarthy puts it, "When two are bound together, they are more deeply bound in the household of God."[9] Because of this, it makes sense that our weddings would take place in the context of our actual Christian community. While it's fine to have extended family and college friends celebrate the wedding day with you, it is crucial to make wedding vows surrounded by the folks who are going to walk with you in the day-in, day-out journey of marriage.

Some wedding liturgies even invite those present to make vows to the couple, asking, "Will all of you witnessing these promises do all in your power to uphold these two persons in their marriage?"[10] When we include this question in the wedding ceremony, it emphasizes that the marriage is not self-enclosed or self-sustaining. Rather, marriage is a covenant that takes place within the context of God's covenant community, the church.

As such, putting weddings in our worship services also reminds us that this new marriage and family is not an end in itself, but is anchored in and oriented toward the kingdom of God. This is one way the church can confront the epidemic of divorce produced by the story of individualism. The solution to widespread divorce is discipleship, not "family values" that often emphasize marriage and the family as self-enclosed relationships but don't challenge the core symbols and praxis of the story of individualism. In the New Testament, marriage and the family have value (alongside singleness) because they are one mode in which discipleship is embodied in everyday life, not because they are an exalted state of existence.

The Bible does not urge us to "focus on the family" but to "seek first the kingdom of God," recognizing that all other good things, including good marriages and families, will come as offshoots and byproducts of that, not as ends in themselves. As McCarthy points out, the New Testament contains little to no exhortation on the particulars of what it means to be a "good husband" or "good wife" (especially when compared to current Christian books).[11] Rather, what we find is a call to discipleship, as in Matthew 5, where followers of Jesus are urged to be reconciled to one another, to discipline our eyes and hearts not to lust, to discipline our words and be faithful to what we have said, not to retaliate when others wrong us, and to love our enemies. This is the path of discipleship that makes it possible to follow Jesus's words about marriage and divorce (Matt. 5:31–32). Jesus's words about marriage make sense only within the context of a life of discipleship within a community oriented by God's kingdom.[12]

Thus, putting weddings in the context of the worship service would be a highly symbolic move that would help to encapsulate the way in which Christians already, God helping us, put our marriages in the context of the community of disciples, the church. Although it's certainly possible to do the latter without embracing the former, the former would be a powerful way to symbolize and embody the gospel before a watching world.

This symbolic practice might provoke deeper questions. What if an even stranger wedding is on the way—a marriage of heaven and earth, of Christ and the church, a wedding banquet with Jesus at the center of all our worship and praise? Could it be true that I am not alone, striving to freely define and invent myself? Is there a God who offers me belonging and rest? Though God offers us this rest, we turn now to another story offered by many Christians, a story of trying harder to do better and be better on our own strength: the story of legalism.

CHAPTER 5

THE MYTH OF LEGALISM

"Behave Yourself"

E very body tells a story. The broader culture is rooted in the story of individualism, "You do you." In one sense, legalism and individualism are opposites: Individualism prizes liberty; legalism prizes obedience. From another angle, though, legalism is a mirror image of individualism, because legalism is a myth that subtly centers us on ourselves and what we can accomplish. The story of legalism says, "Behave yourself." It constructs a self based on behavior.

When Christians and non-Christians alike think about Christianity, sex, and bodies, they generally think about following the right rules about when to have sex and with whom. Endless youth group hours are spent delineating exactly what is allowable and what isn't. Some kiss dating goodbye altogether to avoid any hint of breaking the rules, while others strive to maintain their moral code by becoming downright Levitical in outlining precisely what kind of kissing, touching, and caressing *are* allowed before marriage. The message is clear: Behave yourself and you will be good enough. You will have constructed a self that is worthy of God's approval and others' applause. This is not just a story about sex; it is a distorted story about God that passes itself off as gospel truth.

WHAT'S THE STORY OF LEGALISM?

Who is God, according to the distorted story of legalism? What's the problem, and what's the solution? Legalism focuses on the rules, the dos and don'ts commanded in the Bible—especially the don'ts. Often, legalism ends up adding extra rules as well, just to be sure that we stay in line. I grew up in fairly legalistic church circles. How do you know you're a Christian? I remember one saying that circulated the halls of our Sunday school: "Christians don't drink, smoke, or chew, or run with girls who do." (Imagine my confusion when I later read a C. S. Lewis book and could scarcely see the author's face through the cloud of smoke in the picture on the dust jacket!)

The Bible college connected with our group of churches carefully monitored students' music choices, occasionally holding "raids" on students' rooms to see if they had any music that didn't fit the school guidelines (such as having excessive drums). The hair length and facial hair of male students were carefully monitored to avoid "the appearance of evil" (by which I assume they meant hippies from the '60s). Those are more extreme examples, but the general tenor of legalism was an undercurrent in our church circles. Good Christians are people who behave themselves. We show up for both Sunday services and Wednesday night. We wear the right clothes. We definitely don't have tattoos. We look respectable. We do what's right and avoid what's wrong. We honor our parents. We don't have sex outside marriage. We don't steal, kill, or cheat. Looking back, I realize that our motto seemed to be, "They'll know we are Christians by our good behavior."

The Bible is indeed filled with laws, commands, and instructions from beginning to end. Good portions of the Pentateuch, the first five books of the Bible, are devoted to God's law. Later in the Old Testament, the prophets hammer the people of Israel repeatedly because of their failure to obey God's law. And although some might see the New Testament as focused solely on grace, not law, Jesus gives numerous clear commands and expectations for his followers. The Sermon on the Mount does not relax the expectations of the law; it heightens them. Jesus calls not merely for external conformity to God's law, but for an internal righteousness that surpasses that of the scribes and the Pharisees. Furthermore, the letters of the New Testament are filled with clear instructions and commands for the first-century church. Many of the commands throughout the Bible are easy to spot and straightforward to apply today (though not all, particularly some in the Old Testament).

Given that such laws pervade Scripture, what's the problem with legalism? Isn't doing what God says a key part of the Christian life? To answer this, we need to see that the issue is not just the presence of biblical commands but also the broader theological framework of legalism, which distorts how we understand sin, grace, the gospel, and the character of God. In other words, legalism warps our view of the biblical story and the God revealed there. Legalism also distorts the biblical story in a subtler way by focusing on the very real problem of sin but framing it in a twisted way. So how does legalism define sin? What's the problem?

For starters, legalism views sin primarily as "breaking the rules."[1] This view of sin is connected to our view of God. The story of legalism portrays God primarily as the divine lawgiver who tells us what to do. God is not so much a loving Father, but judge, jury, and executioner, waiting to see if we're living up to the standards he has set down.

This is a view of God that starts with Exodus 20, not Genesis 1 (or even Exodus 1). The god of legalism is a god whose love is dependent on our ability to measure up. This is true especially when it comes to sex and bodies. Rather than giving any deeper account of how sex and bodies are connected to God's life-giving love in creation and redemption, the god of legalism stays at the level of behavior, giving us the list of rules to follow in order to uphold this god's design for sex and bodies. In this way of thinking, if we fail to follow the rules, God will punish us, and if we keep the rules, God will be happy and reward us. In this way, legalism roots our relationship with God in our ability to fully follow the rules and constantly keep God's commandments.

A central problem with legalism, then, is that it doesn't actually take sin seriously enough. On the surface, that might seem like a strange claim to make because a legalist is always on the lookout for rule violations. However, legalism doesn't take sin seriously enough because it focuses primarily on behavior modification, not heart transformation. A good biblical doctrine of sin recognizes that sin is fundamentally a heart problem, disordered desire and love, not a behavior problem. Legalism says, "Get your act together," whereas the Bible says, "Your heart needs healing." The former is far easier than the latter. Let's unpack this distinction between law and love with help from Augustine.

For Augustine, to be human is to love.[2] God creates out of love for us and all creation, and as his image bearers, we are fundamentally wired to love. This love was meant to manifest itself in all our relationships: with God, other humans, and all creation—all the good gifts that God pours out on us. But this love was also meant to have a proper order, so to speak.

God intends us to love things according to the kind of thing it is. For example, we're meant to love God *as God should be loved.* And we're meant to love any creatures of God (say, my backyard chickens[3]) as they should be loved. On the one hand, if I were to love a chicken with a love that I should show to my child, you'd likely recognize that something was off. If I set aside a bedroom of my house for my chickens, spent most of my evenings hanging out with them, and opened a college savings account for them, you might conclude that my love was disordered. I'm treating a pet the way I should treat my child. In Augustine's terms, if I'm not loving something according to the kind of thing it is, my love is disordered. On the other hand, if I were to abuse an animal or treat it as something to be used solely for my benefit without regard to its wellbeing (a concern food ethicists might raise about the treatment of chickens in our culture), then I would also be loving it in an improper way. Again, my love is disordered.

Another way to look at sin as disordered love is to recognize that sin loves something good in the wrong way, wrong context, or wrong proportion. Probably the easiest example to identify here is the way I am frequently tempted to love myself above God. I'm taking something good (myself) and giving it an absolute value, even above God. When I do this, I'm tempted to see God as someone I can use to further my own agenda for my life and ignore when I don't feel that he benefits my own plans. Within this framework, it's helpful to see that sin is me taking something genuinely good—like a desire to feel secure, or to be known, or to have purpose—and exalting it to a higher place than I should. In other words, sin is idolatry.

When we are engaged in idolatry, though, it generates a problem that Augustine summarizes this way: "You [God] have made us for yourself, and our heart is restless until it rests in you."[4] In saying it this way, Augustine recognizes that it is only when we love God as our supreme love—when we put him first—that we can truly be satisfied. Any other good thing, while good, is something we can lose and thus must work ever harder to hold on to (health and wealth are two good examples). If we try to cling to these good things, we will always be restless, never finding what our hearts long for. In this way, a proper view of who we are—desiring beings created to find fulfillment in God—gives us a deeper and more complex account of sin and goodness than legalism, which views sin merely as breaking the rules.

If the problem, according to legalism, is breaking the rules, then the solution is to behave yourself. Be good enough. Follow the rules. Fight whatever in you is telling you to disobey and bring yourself into line with the rules. From the perspective of the gospel, this approach is problematic. This story is about me just as much as the story of individualism. Though God is the divine lawgiver, I'm the hero of the story. I behave, so I belong. I'm good enough. My identity is rooted in myself and what I can accomplish. In many ways, this is a baptized version of "You do you," an approach that is ultimately self-reliant and self-glorying. Christians who live into this story embody the law, not the gospel. Unfortunately, though, this law never actually cuts to the heart, but always stays at the level of behavior. Because legalism wrongly identifies the root problem as behavior, its solution—"Behave yourself"—fails to get to the heart of the matter.

EMBODYING LEGALISM: "THOU SHALT NOT"

One way legalism shows up in Christians' discussion of sex is in how so many of its rules start with "thou shalt not." "Thou shalt not commit adultery." "Thou shalt not have sex outside of marriage." The list goes on. In other words, the focus is on the "no" of the law, not on the broader but positive questions "What are bodies for? What is sex for?"

We know to say no. But many of us don't know why, nor do we know what to say yes to. If you were raised in a legalistic environment, you may know *what* to do (and not do), but you likely were not taught *why*. That is not an environment that can produce spiritually mature Christians because following Jesus is conceived primarily as following the rules. This ignorance shows up in a big way in one of the central debates around sexuality in the last forty years: same-sex relationships and marriage.

I'm not going to treat this topic fully now, but here I want to note a significant point: Both those who do and those who do not affirm same-sex relationships often fixate on prohibition (thou shalt not) texts like Leviticus 18:22; Romans 1:24–27; and 1 Corinthians 6:9–10. Now, I get why those verses are crucial to wrestle with and think through. We have to ask what exactly is being commanded. What is being prohibited? That's a legitimate exegetical exercise. But I want to note that much of this debate happens without engaging passages that speak more directly about a positive, constructive view of sex and marriage. For example, Genesis 1–3; Song of Songs; Matthew 19:1–12; 1 Corinthians 7; and Ephesians 5:21–33 all speak to questions like, What is marriage? What is sex for? What is marriage for? When we discuss what is commanded or prohibited, we need to place those commands within that larger framework.

However, for many legalistic churches, the "thou shalt nots" are the place to start. It makes sense, then, that many advocates for (and opponents of) same-sex marriage never really engage passages like Genesis 1–3 and Ephesians 5:21–33. Rather, they think that if they can prove that the prohibition passages aren't prohibiting *all* forms of same-sex relationships (especially consensual, monogamous relationships), then that's all there is to address. In other words, the legalists who are against gay marriage and those who affirm gay marriage both adopt the same approach to reading Scripture.

Legalism gets further complicated by the fact that we often pick and choose which commands to fixate on. For example, we might focus on commands against sexual immorality but mostly pass over those against greed. We might focus on the need to attend church regularly (Heb. 10:25) but ignore God's call to share with those in our church who have financial needs. Because it's so hard to be thorough and consistent in keeping all God's commands, legalistic Christians are often susceptible to charges of picking and choosing which of God's commands they want to follow.[5] Given the reality of our own sin and struggle, our theology of "no" often rebounds back on us in the end.

EMBODYING LEGALISM: CHURCH DISCIPLINE AS PUNISHMENT

"We can't let your dad come back to church because we can't compromise the purity of the church." I never imagined I'd find myself hearing these words. Two well-respected leaders of my church were explaining why my dad (and my family) were now outcasts at the church where he had been pastor for over a decade. A couple of weeks before, while studying for finals during my first year of college, I received a phone call. The tone of my mom's voice on the other end of the line took my breath away even before she told me what was wrong. In my gut, I knew that something had happened that would change my life forever. She told me that my dad, who was also the pastor of our church, was having an affair with another woman and that this had come to light when my family was visiting me at college the past weekend.

The church leaders reacted swiftly. They changed the locks on my dad's office door and gave my family six weeks to move out of the parsonage, our home for the past 13 years. Though I heard her words, my mind struggled to wrap itself around the news that my family and my church family—the fabric of my life to that point—were falling apart and would never be the same. I was 19, studying to be a pastor and follow in my dad's footsteps, but now I was on the brink of losing everything I had known, including my faith.

Since then, God has given me eyes to see that these two well-meaning leaders were doing the best they could to explain why my dad—and really my whole family—were no longer welcome as part of the church. That doesn't mean they were right. But I understand what was driving them. They pointed me to 1 Corinthians 5, where Paul says the church should not associate with "sexually immoral people" (v. 9) and that those who sinned sexually should be judged and cast out from the church community (vv. 12–13). In their minds, my dad had crossed a line. Even though my dad repented and asked forgiveness from my mom and our whole family, what he did could not be undone.

The church board and congregation felt deeply hurt and betrayed, and understandably so. They trusted my dad, and he failed them. Nonetheless, in my family's time of deepest need, the message from my church family was clear: You haven't behaved, so you don't belong.

Because of my dad's sin, our whole family was guilty by association. The rules had been broken, so we were no longer welcome or loved.

In contrast, church discipline that is rooted in God's grace (rather than legalism) is not merely for the sake of punishment for breaking the rules, but for clarity about sin and the repentance and restoration of those who are not walking in line with Jesus. If we are simply trying to punish people, Paul says, we risk pushing truly repentant people to despair and, in that way, colluding with Satan in their destruction rather than with Jesus in their repentance and salvation (2 Cor. 2:5–11).

My own experience stands in contrast with how I saw a different church handle a similar matter. When pornography was discovered on their pastor's computer, they exercised discipline in a loving way aimed at repentance. This pastor was removed from his position, but this church and denomination had people and resources to come alongside both this pastor and his grieving wife and family and enable them to process what they were going through and move forward. Rather than simply cutting them off as punishment, this church and denomination had structures in place to exercise discipline in a way that kept the big picture of the gospel at the forefront of that process.

After my family's experience, as you might imagine, I was left wondering if any of the stuff my church taught me was real. *If my church family has rejected us, has God rejected us? Who is Jesus really? Has he cast us out too? Does his love endure when our ability to follow the rules doesn't? Do I really believe any of this Christianity stuff, or should I just walk away from it all?* The god of legalism was a harsh master, and if this really was the biblical story, I was sure I didn't want it.

My own faith was saved, by God's grace, by digging into the story of Scripture and the heart of the gospel, where I encountered a Jesus who introduced me to a different God from the god of legalism. This God loved me *before* I could do anything. This God made promises and kept them, not because of my good behavior, but because of his faithfulness. This is the God of the gospel.

CHAPTER 6

THE STORY OF GOD'S COVENANT FAITHFULNESS

"God Keeps His Promises"

The stories of individualism and legalism ultimately revolve around me. I need to express myself. I need to behave myself. In contrast, the story of the gospel revolves around what Jesus has done for me. My identity comes not from what I can do or be, but in being loved by Jesus. In God's mercy and grace, I am de-centered from my place but caught up in God's larger story and mission in the world.

As we turn again to the gospel, we have to ask, What's the story? Who is God? Who are we? As we ask those questions, we'll see how the story of God's faithfulness to his world and people is embodied in sex and marriage. In other words, marriage and sex itself are caught up in the story of God's covenant faithfulness. Whether we're trying to behave or express ourselves, the fundamental mistake of individualism and legalism is making sex and marriage about us and refusing the larger drama, the story to which they point.

WHO IS GOD? THE COVENANT GOD OF THE GOSPEL

Legalism not only warps our understanding of sin; it also warps our understanding of the character of God. As I mentioned in the previous chapter, the Bible contains all kinds of commands. But too often we fail to see how those commands are embedded in the broader biblical narrative. It's only when we back up and take a wider view of the biblical story that we begin to understand *why* God calls his people to a certain way of life.[1] When we do this, we can see how those commands come in the context of God's covenant with his people, emphasizing that our relationship with God is always about God's grace and faithfulness toward us—not primarily about what we can do for God or in relation to God.

God's commands make sense only when we realize how they are rooted in God's grace. It's worth acknowledging stereotypes of the Old Testament God. Many people believe he's angry, judgmental, and ready to throw thunderbolts at a moment's notice toward anyone who gets out of line. But close attention to the Old Testament reveals a God who is overwhelmingly gracious. He is "the compassionate and gracious God, slow to anger, abounding in love and faithfulness, maintaining love to thousands, and forgiving wickedness, rebellion and sin" (Ex. 34:6–7).

Numerous examples show that this isn't just God's talk but also his walk. When God's people engage in a constant cycle of stupidity and idolatry in the time of the judges, he doesn't abandon them, but provides leaders to deliver them. Despite wicked king after wicked king, God is patient with the children of Israel, sending prophets to warn them for literally hundreds of years before sending the Assyrians and then the Babylonians to judge his people. God's grace and patience are exactly why the prophet Jonah *doesn't* want to go warn the Assyrians in Nineveh, Israel's enemies. When God shows his grace and patience toward these pagan people, Jonah gets upset: "This is exactly why I tried running away! I knew this would happen. I knew you were gracious and compassionate, slow to anger and abounding in love. Just kill me now, God!"

When I became a parent, I had a whole new appreciation for the grace, patience, and faithfulness of God. God's grace and faithfulness extend from generation to generation, but some days when I'm around the house, I can hardly make it to lunch! God makes promises and keeps them based on his covenant faithfulness, even when we show ourselves to be faithless. But before we briefly unpack the big story of God's covenant faithfulness, we must tackle the question, What is a covenant? This will be significant not only for understanding the big story of the Bible, but also for understanding how marriage and sex are themselves covenants that point to God's covenant with us.

Bible scholar Gordon Hugenberger defines *covenant* as "an elected, as opposed to natural, relationship of obligation established under divine sanction."[2] Hugenberger unpacks this definition by distinguishing four essential ingredients in the Old Testament understanding of covenant: (1) a relationship (2) with a nonrelative (3) involving obligations (4) established through an oath.[3] In other words, covenants are made by parties that do not have natural obligations to each other. Parents and children are understood to have obligations to each other by definition of their relationship, so it would be strange for a parent to say, "I will make a covenant with my child to treat them as a child should be treated, and I will take on myself the task of providing for their food, clothing, and shelter, as well as other essential needs that they have." Those obligations are usually considered inherent to the parent-child relationship. No one needs a special covenant to establish that relationship. In contrast, a covenant forges a new relationship of responsibility where none previously existed. The act of making a covenant brings that new relationship into existence.

Hugenberger also highlights that a covenant has to be established by an oath that often takes a twofold form: words and actions. In the process of making a covenant, the two parties would outline the promises and/or the nature of the relationship being established. In that context, they would invoke a deity to act as their witness and to judge them if they failed to live out their commitments to the other party. These words are crucial to forming the covenant, but they are not the only ingredient. Covenant terms are usually accompanied by physical actions that either complement the words or, in some cases, even replace them as "oath-signs" that in effect seal the covenant between the two parties.[4] These actions are not merely symbolic in the sense of representing something else (such as the words of promise). Rather, they effectively seal the covenant, bringing the new relationship into existence and forging a new reality.

One example of a covenant sign and seal that took place in biblical times and still continues today is the physical action of shaking hands (Ezek. 17:18; Ezra 10:19).[5] Another key example of an oath-sign is the practice of sharing a meal.[6] For example, when the elders of Israel ate a meal in the presence of God in Exodus 24, this was likely seen as ratifying the covenant God made with Israel at Mount Sinai (Ex. 20). In order for there to be a covenant, you need both words and symbolic actions that bring it into existence.

Now that we have this background that clarifies what a covenant is, let's turn to some key scenes in the biblical story, all of which help us see the priority of God's grace and faithfulness. Let's start with the Ten Commandments, the most famous biblical commands. To understand these commands and how they are rooted in God's grace and faithfulness, we have to flash back to three key scenes in the biblical story that come before Exodus 20 (where the Ten Commandments first appear). If we don't look at what comes first in this story, we will completely miss the proper context of these commands and so end up distorting the purpose of the commandments and the God who gives them.

The first scene is Genesis 12. In Genesis 1–11, we see God's creation of the world and humanity's catastrophic fall into sin, pride, and violence. This is the wide-angle backstory of the whole world, which narrows down in Genesis 12 to the story of one man and his descendants. In Genesis 12, we read that God calls Abram and Sarai out of their home country and promises them four things: a place (land), people (a great nation), privilege (I will bless you), and purpose (all peoples on earth will be blessed through you).[7] In essence, God's response to the catastrophe of human unfaithfulness—to God, to other humans, and to creation—is to call Abram's family as his set-apart people in a world that has gone astray.

But here's the key: The covenant that God makes with Abram, his family, and his descendants is rooted in God's grace. In other words, God doesn't single out Abram and his family because they are morally or spiritually superior. God doesn't decide to act faithfully toward Abram and his family because they have shown themselves to be a cut above other families in the region of Mesopotamia. No, the text is clear that there is nothing inherently better or distinctive about Abram and his family compared to other people. They are chosen because of God's grace and God's commitment to be faithful, not because of any kind of superior behavior.

This notion is underscored a couple of chapters later in Genesis 15, a passage that seems strange to our modern sensibilities. In this text, God makes a covenant with Abram through a ritual ceremony involving a number of animals cut into halves (literally cutting a covenant). Usually when this kind of covenantal ceremony happened, the two parties of the covenant would walk between the pieces of the animals to show that they were both active parties to the contract, kind of like a contract today that includes signatures from both parties. However, this covenantal ceremony is different. Only God passes between them. This covenant relationship is rooted in God's action, God's movement toward Abram, God's faithfulness. It's not based on what Abram did, is doing, or will do. In other words, it's an unconditional covenant—a covenant of grace.

So the first thing to know about the God of this covenant story is that he is full of grace. He doesn't wait for us to get our act together. He comes to us. He enters into a faithful covenantal relationship with us rooted in who he is, not what we can do.

The second scene is Exodus 3. God's people are slaves in Egypt, and in slavery they are multiplying and thus fulfilling God's promise to bring forth a people, a nation, from Abraham (formerly Abram). But they do not have their own land, a home to live out God's ways in God's world. In that context, God calls Moses to be a prophet and a mouthpiece of the deliverance that God will bring to Israel. He reveals himself as "I AM WHO I AM," the God of Abraham, Isaac, and Jacob (Ex. 3:14–15).

As he reveals himself as deliverer and redeemer of Israel, though, it is significant for us to see that this redemption does not depend on Israel getting their act together and following God's commands. God doesn't show up, give his people the Ten Commandments and the law, and say, "*If* you keep these commands, *then* I will be your God and you will be my people. *If* you keep my commands, *then* I will send plagues on Egypt to deliver you and fulfill my promises to Abraham." No! God first graciously delivers his people because of his faithfulness to his covenant, which is rooted in God's character rather than his people's performance.

If it's true that God makes a covenant of grace with his people, then does it mean God doesn't care what his people do? Instead of a legalistic self-righteousness, can they indulge in a sinful free-for-all? Some people raised in legalistic systems of Christianity do just this; they end up rejecting legalism for a cheap grace that says, "God forgives, so I can do whatever I want!" This issue has surfaced throughout church history in a variety of ways.

One example is the Antinomian Controversy in colonial Massachusetts. The antinomian (anti-law) position was ultimately rejected because it seems to say that the grace that forgives sin ultimately excuses or gives the Christian permission to sin. I sometimes hear this position among friends who advocate for same-sex marriage, saying something like, "We're all saved by grace, so who am I to judge?" (I don't hear this question much when it comes to sins like racism or greed.) I love their focus on the fact that we are all sinners in need of God's grace, but this kind of approach misses the fact that God not only gives us saving grace, forgiving our sins, but also gives us sanctifying grace, empowering us by his Spirit to love God and neighbor in the concrete ways he spells out in Scripture. In fact, the apostle Paul, the champion of grace, calls Christians "slaves to righteousness," bound to Jesus and to faithful, obedient living as Spirit-filled people (Rom. 6:15–23).

To avoid swinging the pendulum from legalism to licentiousness (license to sin), we need to understand another scene: God's encounter with Israel in Exodus 19 at Mount Sinai *before* he gives them the law. God reminds them he has faithfully and graciously delivered them: "You yourselves have seen what I did to Egypt, and how I carried you on eagles' wings and brought you to myself." He then calls them to respond in faithful obedience to him and says, "Although the whole earth is mine, you will be for me a kingdom of priests and a holy nation" (Ex. 19:4–6). To understand God's commands to us, we have to unpack these two phrases: "kingdom of priests" and "holy nation." Let's take the second one first.

When God calls Israel to be a holy nation, he is highlighting that they are set apart. The true God has revealed himself to them and redeemed them from slavery. In that sense, they are set apart not because of their action, but because of God's grace, faithfulness, and action toward them. But this set-apartness is also meant to come through in how they live, conducting their lives in a way that is different from the surrounding nations. In their worship, they are called to serve the one true God. In their relationship toward their Israelite neighbors, they are called to do justice and show love in a variety of practical ways, from using just weights in their buying and selling to watching out for their neighbors' animals to caring for the poor and needy. In their relationship to the land, God's creation, they are called to treat it with care, giving the land rest on Sabbath days and years, and restoring lost territories back to families in the Year of Jubilee.

Why does God call his people to this way of life? We've established that it is not in order to be in a covenant relationship with him. That has already happened on the basis of God's grace. This is where the phrase "kingdom of priests" comes in. A priest is a mediator between God and people. Now, if you know something about the Old Testament, you know that some specific people—descendants of Aaron, Moses' brother—functioned as priests in Israel, offering sacrifices and being a set-apart group within Israel to perform these key tasks of worship as mediators between God and humanity.

But Exodus 19:6 talks about the entire people of Israel as a kingdom of priests. All of God's people were meant to be mediators between God and the surrounding nations who would observe their life together. God's people were called to live in a unique way so others who did not know the true God would see their life together. In seeing that holy, set-apart way of life, these nations would see the true character of God shining like a light from his people. They were called to follow God's commands and instructions because it would lead to flourishing in God's world and reveal the true character of God to the watching nations. They would embody the story of God's faithfulness and grace in a way that would cause others to see the reality of who God is.

Unlike the covenant with Abraham, in which Abraham did nothing but trust God, this covenant with Moses and the people of Israel has conditions and calls for a response: a faithful way of life. If they are faithful to God, it will lead to life. If they are unfaithful, it will lead to death and destruction (Deut. 30:15–20). But the conditions of this covenant with Moses and the people are embedded in the larger covenant with Abraham, so even when God's people are judged for their unfaithfulness, this does not nullify the fact that they are still God's people. God's faithfulness is the first and last word on who they are.

The storyline of the Old Testament, as you likely know, is of God's purposes moving forward even though his people fail to carry out the mission he gave them. In the imagery of Isaiah, God planted them as a vineyard to bear fruit that would be for the healing of the nations, but the vineyard did not yield good fruit. God looked for them to bear the fruit of justice but instead saw bloodshed and violence. He looked for them to bear the fruit of righteousness but instead heard cries of distress that went up from their sinful and oppressive way of life (Isa. 5:7). God in his grace had set Israel apart to point to the one true God, but the sin that afflicted the Gentiles was also present in Israel. The ones who were supposed to be the solution had the same problem as everyone else.

One of the central images of God's covenant relationship with his people is the covenant of marriage. In the Prophets, God repeatedly uses marital imagery to highlight Israel's unfaithfulness to God in violating his covenant. In other words, idolatry is adultery, covenant infidelity to the faithful covenanting God. The basic storyline of God and Israel is that of a marriage gone wrong:

- God entered into a marriage covenant with Israel, and Israel initially responded as a loving bride (Jer. 2:1–3; Ezek. 16:8–14).
- Despite God's love and care, Israel was unfaithful to that marriage covenant and became a prostitute (Jer. 3:1–3; Ezek. 16:15).
- Israel's infidelity and adultery led them into all kinds of idolatrous sins like those of the surrounding nations, including arrogance, greed, gluttony, and indifference toward the suffering of the poor and needy (Ezek. 16:48; 22:6–12; 23:5–27).
- God calls his people to return to him, their faithful husband who still wants to respond graciously (Jer. 3:14).
- Even though God's people will be punished for their sin, God will not abandon his covenant with them. He will atone for their sins and establish his everlasting covenant with them (Ezek. 16:59–63).

The storyline of this marriage, with Israel's unfaithfulness and God's fidelity, is the story of the book of Hosea, in which the prophet Hosea and his wife, Gomer, embody the story of God and Israel. The word of the Lord comes to the prophet Hosea and tells him to marry an adulterous wife, just as Israel has been an adulterous wife to God (Hos. 1:2). Like Gomer, Israel will experience judgment and servitude because of their infidelity to their covenant with God.

But that is not the last word on their covenant relationship. God promises that he will not abandon his covenant people, using the central image of marriage to describe the work he will do: "I will betroth you to me forever; I will betroth you in righteousness and justice, in love and compassion. I will betroth you in faithfulness, and you will acknowledge the LORD" (Hos. 2:19–20). In other words, God was not going to abandon his marriage covenant with his people, but would instead work to bring about covenant fidelity in his rebellious bride.

Because of his grace and faithfulness, God doubles down on his commitment to God's people, the nations, and his creation. Through prophets like Jeremiah, Ezekiel, and others, God promises that he will continue to be a faithful covenant God. He will forgive the sins of his people. He will also give them what they need to respond faithfully to the covenant he has made with them: an intimate knowledge of who he is that comes from having new hearts that are made alive by God's Spirit. God's forgiveness and restoration, along with our new hearts, flow from the climax of God's covenant with his people: the embodied life, death, resurrection, and ascension of Jesus Christ.

Jesus is the Messiah, which means "anointed" or chosen for a particular task. What is that task? In his humanity, Jesus is the faithful covenant partner that God has been looking for. Adam could not do it. Abraham and Israel received God's unconditional covenant of grace, but they were faithless while God was faithful. In his life, Jesus offers himself up as a living sacrifice through the way he lives. His words and actions reveal the Father, and his humble obedience takes the place of Adam's prideful rebellion. Here at last is the faithful covenant partner God has been looking for. In his death, Jesus bears and bears away the covenant curses associated with Israel's disobedience. God does not abandon his plan or his people. Rather, God forges a new covenant with them, a covenant that continues the grace-filled covenant with Abraham and fulfills the conditions of the covenant with Moses.

Jesus is the true Israel, God's faithful covenant partner, who responds with perfect faith and obedience, as humans should to the one true God. This new covenant is made in the actual body and blood of Jesus Christ. The cross is the place where this covenant is made, and the resurrection of Jesus Christ is God's validation that it lasts forever. He himself is our peace, the covenant embodied, so we are reconciled with God, and Jew and Gentile are brought together in the body of Christ.

How do we fit into this story? How does the church today continue this story? When Jesus ascends to the right hand of the Father—to his rightful place of authority, honor, glory, and power—he pours out his Spirit on his people. And what is the result? Through the proclamation of the gospel and the work of the Spirit, people are "cut to the heart" (Acts 2:37). This language harks back to Deuteronomy 30:6 and God's promise to do a work in his people, to mark his covenant not just on their external bodies (as in circumcision) but also in their hearts. It is also covenantal language, the language of "cutting" a covenant. The Holy Spirit is the covenantal seal, the connector between the resurrected, glorified body of Jesus Christ and us, and the Holy Spirit empowers us to do what we cannot do in our own strength. Any good works that we do are because of God's gracious empowerment, making us alive and able to respond faithfully by the power of his Spirit.

This understanding of the work of the Holy Spirit reframes how we understand the biblical call to holiness and obedience to the way of Jesus. When we go back and read the Sermon on the Mount, we see that this is not "hippie" Jesus. This is not "live and let live" Jesus. Jesus lays out a way of life for his followers that exceeds the righteousness of the scribes and Pharisees. Is this legalism or moralism? Definitely not! Jesus can call his disciples to a *higher* standard than the Old Testament law precisely because they have the full personal presence and power of the Holy Spirit. Because his followers live from the power unleashed by the work of Christ and the presence of the Holy Spirit, they can be a faithful kingdom of priests and a holy nation.

Now, does that mean the church is perfectly faithful to Jesus? By no means. Yet, it does mean that we have the power of the Spirit, who enables us to live a life of continual repentance and spiritual growth. Our life together is a light and witness to those around us of God's covenant faithfulness in the sacrifice of Christ and the gift of the Spirit. Our testimony to the gospel is not our moral perfection, but our continued proclamation of the finished work of Jesus and our constant need for his Spirit to work in us so that we can repent daily and respond faithfully to his covenant faithfulness.

How does understanding this story of God's grace and covenant faithfulness shift our view of God's commands and call us to a holy life of obedience? If we look at God's commands in the context of God's covenant with his people, we can see them through the lenses of witness/ mission and gratitude rather than performance. The lens of witness and mission helps us see that the goal of living out God's ways in God's world is not solely for the sake of me and my relationship with God. Rather, it is for the sake of revealing who God is to those who do not yet know or acknowledge him.

Furthermore, the lens of gratitude helps us see that following God's ways is not the measure of whether we can be in relationship with God (as in legalism); rather, following God's ways reveals whether we truly and gratefully understand the gracious, faithful character of the God who has already redeemed us in Christ and placed us in relationship to him by the work of the Spirit.

EMBODYING THE GOSPEL: SEX AND COVENANT FAITHFULNESS

So what does any of this have to do with sex and marriage? The most famous of all Christian rules about sex is "Thou shalt not have sex until marriage." But why? Usually the best answer people can come up with is something like "Because the Bible says so" or "It's God's design." But why link sex and marriage in this way? Our contemporary culture sees it as dangerously repressive, and even many Christians, in practice at least, see it as something from an outdated era, especially with the average age of marriage now hovering around the late 20s and early 30s for most people. Many Christians simply see this as a law to be followed without questioning or even understanding. But remember: Every body tells a story. And the gospel is the climax of the story of God's faithfulness, embodied in the very body of Jesus. If we understand that and see marriage through the biblical lens of God's covenant faithfulness, then we can begin to see that sexual union actually makes a particular kind of covenant: marriage.

How does marriage embody and display God's covenant faithfulness? As we saw earlier in this chapter, the entire biblical story is the story of God's covenant faithfulness. His persistent faithfulness and love are revealed supremely in the gospel, the good news that, in Jesus, God is faithful to his covenant with his people and world.

How does this inform the Bible's view of marriage and sex? From this covenantal viewpoint, it's not just that you should "save sex for marriage"; it's that sex *is the covenant act of bringing a marriage into existence.* Sex is the symbolic act that makes (and renews) a covenant, the "oath-sign" that makes promises with a symbolic action. In other words, when you have sex with someone, you are making a covenant with them.

Why is this way of thinking foreign to us—even to Christians—in our day and age? When I was in college, I was part of a group of high school and college students who went into local public schools, along with an educator from the local pregnancy resource center, to do abstinence education. We would do some skits, share a bit of our personal stories, and interact with students. We weren't necessarily overt about our faith and sometimes tried to translate our biblical rationale into practical reasons for abstinence as well, noting things like STD prevalence and teenage pregnancy. We got a mixed reaction from the classrooms we visited, with most students looking like they wanted to simply escape the whole conversation.

I must admit, though, that my understanding of sex and marriage at that point was pretty much the legalistic model: Have sex when you're married; don't when you're not. The notion that sex was a covenantal, marriage-making activity was foreign even to us good church kids. The idea that our faithfulness in sex and marriage was meant to be taken up into the bigger story of God's faithfulness to us was totally missing. Yes, Jesus saved us. Yes, we knew we should save sex for marriage. But we didn't see any connection between eternal life and our sex life, between God's covenant faithfulness and marriage.

Plus, in our culture, we tend to see marriage primarily as a mental or emotional act, one that involves how we think, how we feel, or the verbal vows we make to someone. We often have a low view of our bodies, which I'll discuss more in part 4. For now, suffice it to say that Scripture takes our bodies very seriously. In sex, our bodies tell and embody a story. Having sex with someone says, "We two are now one. I commit my whole life and self to you, with all that I am and all that I have." Scripture sees sex as a covenantal act that unites a man and woman for life. Don't take my word for it, though. Let's look at Scripture to see how it speaks about the covenantal story of sex.

Genesis 4:1 is one of the first places where the Bible refers to sex, and the way it does so is significant. The Hebrew word used in this passage is *yada*, which in older translations is often translated as "knew," as in "Adam knew Eve his wife; and she conceived, and bare Cain" (KJV). For years, I assumed this was just a polite euphemism for sex. I mean, the Bible can't just come right out and say, "Adam and Eve had sex," right? But contemporary translations often translate *yada* in a way that clarifies what is going on for contemporary audiences.[8] The NIV translates it, "Adam made love to his wife Eve," and the NLT translates it, "Adam had sexual relations with his wife, Eve." (I guess today you *can* just come right out and say it.) All of these translations do a fine job communicating the main point of what happened in slightly different ways. But the original Hebrew word here has connections we can't see just by looking at our English Bibles: *Yada* is a covenant word.

Why does the Bible use the word *yada* when it talks about sex? Let's back up a bit and look at where else we see *yada* in the world of the Old Testament. One of the main contexts for covenants in the ancient world was between rulers (often called the "suzerain") and the people they ruled over (often called "vassals"). In those covenants, the two parties often used the term *yada* to convey that they "acknowledged" or "recognized" each other as covenant partners.[9] Sometimes they even used this word in the process of first establishing a covenant between two covenant partners. This is different, though, from what I hear as an English speaker when I hear the word "know."

I think about it primarily in terms of intellect or cognition, as in "Do you know the capital of Michigan?" or "Did you know that Michael Jordan is the greatest basketball player of all time?" But when used in relational contexts in Scripture, *yada* isn't primarily about mental cognition. Rather, it refers either to a covenantal relationship or to sex.[10] More broadly speaking, to know, acknowledge, and recognize someone in this way is to establish a covenant with them or to behave in a way that acknowledges the covenant that has been established. And the fact that it is used in reference to sex helps us see that sexual union is a specific instance of making a covenant. It's a covenantal act.

Several texts illustrate the covenantal use of *yada*, where it is used specifically with reference to God and Israel. These texts help us see that this *yada* (knowing) is not just about cognition but also about covenant. This is how Amos 3:2 talks about God and his covenant with Israel. As in Genesis 4:1, older English translations use the word "know" in this verse, which again sounds a bit confusing to us: "You only have I known of all the families of the earth" (KJV). Of course God is all-knowing, so why does this verse say that he knows only Israel? Once we realize that *yada* is a covenant word, the meaning of this verse becomes clear. More contemporary translations highlight that the point here is that God chose Israel as his covenant people and entered into this unique relationship with them: "You only have I chosen of all the families of the earth." That is, God chose to enter into this unique covenantal relationship with only Israel. He "knows" Israel alone, not in the sense of mental cognition but in the sense of covenantal recognition.

We also see the covenantal use of *yada* when the Bible talks about Israel's covenant response, whether faithful (they know, recognize, and acknowledge God) or unfaithful (they do not know, recognize, and acknowledge God). For example, Jeremiah 22:16 talks about the covenant faithfulness of King Josiah in contrast to Shallum, Josiah's unfaithful son. In speaking of Josiah, Jeremiah says, "'He defended the cause of the poor and needy, and so all went well. Is that not what it means to know [*yada*] me?' declares the LORD." As Hugenberger puts it, "It seems clear from such a text that 'knowing' God is more than a matter of mere cognition!"[11] That is, in defending the cause of the poor and needy, King Josiah is acknowledging Israel's covenant obligations before God and behaving in a way that knows, recognizes, and acknowledges who God is and who King Josiah is called to be as kingly representative of Israel.

With this covenantal background, let's return to the idea that sex is a covenant-making act by returning to Hosea. Hosea 2:20 is a key passage that interweaves the concepts of covenant and sex. Remember that the story of Hosea is all about his faithful covenant love to his wife, Gomer, even when she is unfaithful. This story is an embodied story of God's faithful covenant love to his people, Israel. In Hosea 2, we hear God's promise that he will be a faithful husband and that, one day, his people will be a faithful wife: "I will betroth you to me forever; I will betroth you in righteousness and justice, in love and compassion. I will betroth you in faithfulness, and you will acknowledge [*yada*] the LORD" (Hos. 2:19–20). This passage uses the language of sexual union—the covenantal consummation of marriage—to talk about God's covenant with Israel. Of course, this is a metaphor. But the metaphor works because God and

Israel are in a covenant, just as a husband and wife are in a covenant. And the use of *yada* here reinforces that sex is a covenant act of knowing and acknowledgment.

Let's bring together what we've learned about *yada* and covenants. To *yada* someone is to know/recognize/acknowledge them as a covenant partner to whom you are bound. This can be a broadly covenantal term, but it's also used to refer more specifically to sexual union. This means that "the act of sexual union by itself is constitutive of marriage."[12] In other words, sex is a covenant-making, marriage-making act. It is the embodied "oath-sign" that says with body language what our words say in a marriage ceremony: "I take you to be my wedded husband/wife, to have and to hold from this day forward, for better, for worse, for richer, for poorer, in sickness and in health, to love and to cherish, till death do us part, according to God's holy ordinance; and I pledge myself to you."

So what is sex for? It makes a marriage, uniting a man and woman in a lifelong covenant of faithful love that is meant to be an embodied sign and symbol of God and his people, Christ and the church. Bodies that engage in sexual union are meant to be telling a self-giving story of faithful covenant love. When a man and woman have sex, they "know" one another in a full-bodied, covenant-making act that points to the covenant that God in Christ has made with us.

PART 3

CHAPTER 7

THE MYTH OF ROMANCE

"You Complete Me"

The story of romance holds out the promise of an ideal soulmate, a significant other who will love us for the unique individual we are and bring to our life a sense of fullness and completion. Although we work hard to establish and form who we are as an individual, the story of romance says that something is missing, something is not quite complete. Only when we find "the one," so the story goes, will we have a true sense of fulfillment as we share life with our true love.

Those who are of a certain age will remember the 1996 movie *Jerry Maguire*, the story of a sports agent who, at the height of his career, recognizes that his sought-after work achievements and carefully cultivated macho identity are not enough. In the movie's most famous scene, Tom Cruise gives an impassioned speech to his estranged wife, played by Renee Zellweger, about how his accomplishments have left him empty and lacking because he hasn't been able to share them with her.

At the pinnacle of this speech, he declares the basic credo of the story of romance: "You complete me." The story of individualism can leave us with a sense that we're missing something. We do our best to create our authentic self and make something of ourselves through who we are and what we accomplish. But at the end of the day, we need a soulmate, a romantic relationship that serves as a safe harbor, a place where a person can know and be known, can be seen and loved for who they are, and can find emotional and relational stability in a world that often changes in the blink of an eye. Thus, when we find the one, we will be complete.

According to the story of romance, who are we? To answer that, we have to see how the story of romance is linked to the story of individualism. On the surface, the two stories might seem to contradict each other. Individualism implies a focus on the individual, independent of anyone else, whereas the story of romance implies a focus on relationship, a sense of dependence on or connection with others.

For the story of individualism, I am an independent self. I don't need anything or anyone else to define me. Anything that tries to define me outside of me is an obstacle to be overcome in my quest for autonomy and authenticity. On the other hand, though, as I seek to become a truly authentic person, aligning my life with my sense of who the "real me" is, I am looking for validation that the self I'm creating is indeed good. Where does that validation come from? The story of romance proposes that I have a "significant other" or "soulmate" who can provide what I need to experience the fullness of life: validation and confirmation that I, as a unique individual, am seen and loved. In this way, the stories of individualism and romance are complementary.

Within the story of romance, sex has a particular function: to express one's intimate connection with and exclusive love for one's soulmate. Philosopher Caroline Simon points out that the story of romance may talk about sex in terms that overlap with Christianity to some degree, seeing sex as "sacred" and as a gift to be saved for someone "of profound significance."[1] The story of romance may thus emphasize fidelity and monogamy as a key aspect of one's relationship. Importantly, however, those themes are rooted not in the story of God's faithful covenant love for us but in the romantic notion of a soulmate. Whereas God is committed to us forever because of his faithfulness and love in Christ, romantic commitment is contingent: "Commitment lasts for as long as romantic love lasts."[2]

Thus, within the story of romance, sex and marriage are symbols of one's commitment to another person rather than the result of one's commitment to another person. What's the difference? It might seem small, but it's not. For the story of romance, sex and marriage symbolize an underlying commitment. If that commitment goes away, then it's totally valid to end the marriage, since marriage was merely a symbol of something: "I married you *because* I was committed to you" (but now I'm not). In contrast, the story of the gospel holds out a different view of marriage and commitment: Marriage and sex are promises, a committing of oneself to a spouse. In other words, "I'm committed to you *because* I married you, because I have sex with you." This view of commitment and faithfulness is fundamentally different from the story of romance, which is always contingent on the underlying romance to sustain the relationship.

Within the story of romance, what's the problem? The problem is that I'm lacking something, missing a specific need. The story of romance denounces many need-based reasons why people in past eras or even in different cultures today might get married. For example, many people get married because it's an economic necessity or for the pragmatic purpose of uniting two families or for the sake of sheer survival. These reasons, according to the story of romance, are bad (or at least lesser) reasons to get married.

This attitude is summarized well by one respondent to a CNN article on the "marriage apocalypse," their term for why fewer and fewer people are considering marriage. According to this respondent, "Marriage should be for love, not a matter of expectations, routine, and everyday practicalities."[3] This emphasis on romantic love as the true meaning of marriage probably seems obvious to most of us, but it's worth noting that this is not a universal story about the meaning of marriage and life. We should also note the contrast in the story of romance between romantic "love" on the one hand and "expectations, routine, and everyday practicalities" on the other. Within the story of romance, true love has nothing to do with the routines and habits of everyday life together.

This kind of relationship—rooted in romantic love alone—is what sociologist Anthony Giddens refers to as a "pure relationship." His definition of that term is crucial to how our culture views sex, bodies, marriage, and any kind of romantic relationship. It has nothing to do with the conversation around sexual purity. Rather, as Giddens defines it, a "pure relationship" is "a situation where a social relation is entered into for its own sake, for what can be derived by each person from a sustained association with another; and which is continued only insofar as it is thought by both parties to deliver enough satisfactions for each individual to stay within it."[4] In other words, a pure relationship is completely voluntary and has no obligation or goal other than the emotional satisfaction that stems from the relationship itself. In other words, it's most definitely *not* a covenant.

In contrast, there are a variety of relationships, including family relationships, where the goal is not merely emotional relationship. For example, parents have a relationship with their children, but the relationship is not completely voluntary (in one sense), and the relationship doesn't exist merely for its own sake but for the care and wellbeing of the children. Young children need their parents in order to survive. It is not a "pure relationship," but one characterized by necessity.

The goal of these labels is not to condemn either form of relationship but rather to try to get clear insight about how our culture works. As Giddens points out, this rise of the "pure relationship" is a historical and cultural development that we mostly take for granted as a fact about how marriage and romantic relationships are supposed to work. In contrast, he points out that it is a peculiar historical and cultural development of modern Western culture. It is one story, but not the only possible story, about love, sex, relationships, and fulfillment. Thus, for the story of romance, the problem is not that we need to get married, in the sense that it's a necessity for economic, social, or survival reasons. Rather, the problem for the story of romance loops us back to a problem of identity that is connected to individualism.

Remember that, for individualism, my goal is constructing and creating a life that is uniquely authentic to me. I'm trying to be true to myself. Within this framework, the problem isn't necessarily some kind of physical or sexual lack; it is an emotional, relational, and personal lack. It is about a close, perhaps even spiritual, encounter between two people. In this encounter (perhaps "love at first sight" or "true love's kiss") of two souls, "the flawed individual is made whole."[5] In this way, the story of individualism often finds its completion and fulfillment in the story of romance. As Giddens puts it, the romantic "quest is an odyssey, in which self-identity awaits its validation from the discovery of the other."[6] I can tell the true story of my self only when I discover and receive affirmation and love from my soulmate, the one who provides the missing piece that completes the picture of who I am as an individual.

So what's the solution to that problem? The story of romance bears a striking resemblance to the biblical story—with an important difference. As John Calvin points out, knowledge of God and knowledge of our self go together.[7] As we come to know who God is, we come to see and understand who we are more truly and clearly. Thus, to tell the story of who I truly am, I need to see and know God as the one who is my Creator and Redeemer, the one who truly fulfills and completes me. A Christian theology of marriage is built upon this knowing of God, according to Giddens, in which the "mystical unity" between a man and woman in marriage becomes a sign of and pointer to the unity we have with God through Jesus Christ. He also notes, however, that the modern world offers a strikingly altered story of romance here: Rather than God being the "significant Other" through whom we come to know who we truly are and find fulfillment, the romantic significant other becomes the one through whom we come to know who we really are and find fulfillment.[8]

The modern story of romance places more weight on one person than a biblical theology of marriage. This might seem surprising, given that, as we've explored in a variety of ways, marriage is a sign of Christ and the church. Marriage signifies something centrally important. But a biblical theology of marriage should never portray a person's spouse as their "everything." The story of romance, however, places a singular weight on one's significant other. As marriage therapist Esther Perel puts it, "We come to one person, and we are basically asking them to give us what an entire village [or, I would add, God] used to provide: give me belonging, give me identity, give me continuity, but give me transcendence and mystery and awe all in one."[9] In other words, as David Zahl sums up, "We want to marry a Savior."[10]

This desire for a savior, a soulmate, someone to complete us, explains why marriages are so hard to sustain in our era of romance. In the story of individualism, divorce is often the natural outcome of a story that emphasizes self-expression and self-actualization. Likewise, in the story of romance, divorce is the natural outcome of a story that emphasizes that there is a soulmate out there who perfectly and fully completes us.

Once you've accepted the myth of a soulmate, it gets harder and harder to see your spouse—in a marriage that consists mostly of daily expectations, routines, and practicalities—as "the one." Rather than disbelieving the story of romance, though, we question whether our spouse is *truly* the one. We may even become cynics, then, about romance or the possibility of actually finding our one and only. The song "From Above" by Nick Hornby and Ben Folds is a great example of this, as it affirms that we have soulmates but laments that there is no guarantee of actually connecting with "the one."[11] In other words, the more tightly we hold to the story of romance, the less likely it seems that any actual living, breathing person can hold up under the weight of expectations put on them by that story.

Tragically, I saw this in a friend's marriage. My wife and I met with her around a year after she had gotten married in a romantic, all-the-frills wedding. She shared the numerous challenges she and her husband had faced over their first year and dropped the bomb that she was seeking a divorce. She shared that she had seen red flags in their relationship even before they got married but moved ahead in part because of what seemed to be the story of romance: Just get married and your happily ever after will work itself out. It didn't. Thus, the modern epidemic of divorce and temporary relationships is not somehow a sign that "romance is dead." Rather, this epidemic is itself the natural result of the story of romance, which looks for love in all the wrong places, seeking a Savior where there's only another sinner in need of Jesus.

EMBODYING ROMANCE: *THE BACHELOR*

Where is this story embodied and displayed in our culture? One prime example is the long-running reality show *The Bachelor*. This show features one man with numerous women vying for his affection and attention. (Or in its sister show, *The Bachelorette*, one woman with numerous men.) Each episode includes various dates and drama between the contestants as the competition escalates. Shouting matches, name-calling, and cryfests are common as contestants take out their frustration on their competition (with whom they are forced to live during this time). And sometimes the competition doesn't work out like it's supposed to, with the Bachelor rejecting the two finalists (Brad from season 11) or changing his mind and dumping the winner for the runner-up a couple months later (Jason from season 13).

This show reinforces the contrast between romance and everyday expectations, routines, and practicalities. Kutter Callaway points out that *The Bachelor* displays and perpetuates the story of romance.[12] (He also reveals the staggering percentage of young adults—94 percent!—who say they "want their marriage partner to be first and foremost a 'soul mate.'")[13] The bachelor or bachelorette and the various contestants are pulled out of the normal routines of their everyday lives to encounter each other in a made-for-TV setting, complete with luxurious accommodations and unique dates that would likely never happen in real life. This setting reinforces the idea that the first and primary connection is an emotional connection with a unique individual, divorced from their daily life, work, family relationships, and neighborhood. The question of compatibility is entirely emotional/relational, with no bearing on other things, such as whether the two people live near one another, work well together in everyday settings, or even have the same fundamental beliefs. *The Bachelor* thus embodies and reinforces the idea that true romance happens in a "pure relationship," and true love happens when two soulmates meet each other in a romantic oasis.

EMBODYING ROMANCE: SAME-SEX MARRIAGE

Same-sex marriage is one of the most contested issues of our day, though the legal and cultural battle seems to have been clearly won by proponents of same-sex marriage. Many people, Christians and non-Christians alike, think of same-sex marriage as a fundamental shift in the way our culture looks at marriage and sex—and they are right, to some extent. And within the myths of naturalism, individualism, and romance, same-sex marriage makes perfect sense. Far from being an anomaly or a recent shift, the widespread approval of same-sex marriage in the last two decades is simply the logical step in a culture that has been steeped in the stories of liberty for the last two centuries. If we ask the question, "What is marriage for?" the answers provided by these stories give no reason to restrict marriage to a man and woman.

The myth of naturalism (which we'll unpack in more detail in part 4) says that we are matter in motion, that bodies themselves do not make a substantial difference in defining who we are. Thus, it makes perfect sense that male and female would be seen as interchangeable in marriage. A view of marriage rooted in naturalism necessarily includes same-sex marriage. The myth of individualism says that we are individuals, called to exercise our freedom and truly express ourselves in every arena of our lives, including marriage and sex. Thus, in the Supreme Court ruling in favor of same-sex marriage, Justice Anthony Kennedy affirms that the "right to personal choice regarding marriage is inherent in the concept of individual autonomy."[14] In other words, a view of marriage rooted in individualism necessarily includes same-sex marriage.

Finally, the myth of romance says that I find fulfillment in a romantic relationship that truly completes who I am as a person. Again, the romantic concept of marriage is repeated throughout the Supreme Court's ruling on same-sex marriage. As Justice Kennedy puts it, "Marriage is sacred to those who live by their religions and offers unique fulfillment to those who find meaning in the secular realm. Its dynamic allows two people to find a life that could not be found alone, for a marriage becomes greater than just the two persons. Rising from the most basic human needs, marriage is essential to our most profound hopes and aspirations."[15] For Justice Kennedy, marriage offers a "unique fulfillment" to a secular culture, making it "essential" to truly becoming who we are supposed to be. (Note that this secular story of romance excludes singleness as much as any Christian sexual prosperity gospel, which we will discuss in chapter 9.)

Further, Justice Kennedy argues that "the nature of marriage is that, through its enduring bond, two persons together can find other freedoms, such as expression, intimacy, and spirituality. This is true for all persons, whatever their sexual orientation."[16] What is marriage for? Finding and maximizing freedoms, including self-expression, intimacy, and spirituality. The myths of individualism and romance perfectly intertwine here. In summarizing the ruling in favor of same-sex marriage, Justice Kennedy declares, "Same-sex couples, too, may aspire to the *transcendent* purposes of marriage and seek *fulfillment* in its highest meaning."[17] In a secular culture that often fails to acknowledge anything transcendent, romantic marriage has become one of the few places left where we believe we can connect with something transcendent and find true fulfillment.

When we understand how same-sex marriage is rooted in the myths of individualism and romance, we can understand why so many in our culture would see Christians who are against same-sex marriage as committing a grievous evil. If you do not affirm gay marriage, then you are seen as robbing someone of the basic freedom to express and discover their true self while also depriving them of the opportunity to find the transcendence and fulfillment that come from a romantic relationship.

Furthermore, Christians who hold to the historic view of marriage (as between a man and a woman) often affirm the basic stories of individualism and romance in a variety of ways. For example, our sexual prosperity gospel is, in many ways, the story of romance with a Christian twist. Thus, we Christians should question our own consistency if we find ourselves espousing a view of heterosexual marriage that basically embodies the myths of individualism and romance while rejecting same-sex marriage that embodies those two stories more fully and logically.

EMBODYING ROMANCE:
COHABITATION, MARRIAGE, AND DIVORCE

Although many people still embrace the "you complete me" mantra of *Jerry Maguire*, it's clear that, in some ways, we're no longer in the '90s. Today, in many circles, the notion of marriage or even long-term commitment is on the decline. In its place is the continued rise of the "pure relationship," a relationship that is entered into for the benefits it brings, but also one that can be ended at any time if it is no longer seen as beneficial. In other words, "you complete me . . . for now." If the "you complete me" of the '90s is an equal parts mix of the myths of individualism and romance, "you complete me . . . for now" is the cocktail of three or four parts individualism and one part romance.

Cohabitation—living together before marriage—makes perfect sense within the myths of romance and individualism.[18] In an article in *The Atlantic*, journalist Lauren Fox notes that our culture sees it as "odd not to test drive a partner before marriage."[19] This mindset exposes the individualistic, consumeristic way we view relationships. Sure, we may be romantics, but we're also realists. After all, when I go to the car dealership, I want to test drive a vehicle. I want a 100 percent satisfaction guarantee. If it doesn't live up to my expectations, I should be able to take it back.

This view can masquerade as something psychologically healthy and enlightened, even in the process of divorce. So, for example, we may no longer "divorce" or even "break up" with someone. Rather, we use phrases like "consciously uncouple," as Gwyneth Paltrow did when she separated from and eventually divorced Chris Martin.[20] We "consciously couple" with someone because we think we can learn and grow in a relationship with them. And when it's time to "consciously uncouple," we don't get angry but recognize that we are "partners in each other's spiritual progress." You completed me for a time, and now it's time to move on. What's the problem?

Ironically, this approach to marriage values my individual growth but ultimately turns every other person into a vehicle to be used for my own (spiritual, relational, emotional) gain. It says, "You are valuable insofar as you contribute to the center of my life: me." As soon as someone hits a certain mileage or wears out their usefulness for this leg of the journey, there's nothing wrong with trading in and, hopefully, trading up. Within the myths of romance and individualism, people get divorced for the same reason they get married: to take the next step in finding and expressing their true self.[21]

Although this may appear more enlightened than a brutal divorce or angry separation, it raises a question: What kind of marriages are produced by the stories of romanticism and individualism? If partners test drive one another long enough—theoretically to make sure they end up with their "one and only"—they may feel confident that the other will maintain their end of the bargain. And so the two partners have a successful relationship, negotiating with one another to make sure that no one is ever so dissatisfied that they dissolve the relationship. But this reveals that the underlying question is not "Do you want a successful marriage?" but "What kind of successful marriage do you want?" Do you want a marriage in which you see your spouse as a vehicle to get you to your own destination of self-expression and self-realization (and vice versa), or one in which you see your spouse as a person you are called to love unconditionally, the way God in Christ loves us?

The sequence of cohabitation–marriage–divorce does not tell the story of God's gracious faithfulness and his willingness to love and serve us "while we were still sinners" (Rom. 5:8). We were incompatible with him. We were inconvenient for him. And yet he gave himself fully for us and to us. That is why the Christian vision of marriage involves the total commitment of each spouse to the other. Cohabitation and "conscious uncoupling" fall short because of the warped story they tell about God.

Marriage is not a contract but a covenant that points to the God who enters into a covenant with us. Spouses give themselves not because the other spouse has successfully upheld their end of the bargain, but because of God's deep love for them. Christian marriage is not sustained by compatibility or the rationale of the spouses heading into marriage; it is sustained by being rooted in God's empowering grace to love my spouse the way God loves me. If this is so, then no amount of "test driving" a future spouse can ever match the constant refueling that comes from the unlimited energy of God's other-centered love. The story of God's faithful covenant love must be embodied in the complete self-giving covenant of marriage. To do otherwise not only shortchanges ourselves but also misses our mission of embodying the gospel before a watching world.

EMBODYING ROMANCE: POLYAMORY

A further iteration of "you complete me" is the rise of polyamory, a romantic and often sexual relationship of three or more people.[22] Polyamory can take a variety of forms and include three, four, or even more people in the polyamorous relationship. Polyamory differs from polygamy in that it does not revolve around one person with multiple spouses, nor is there a defined commitment that applies to all polyamorous relationships. Those who advocate polyamory frame it in terms of the myths of individualism and romance: Some people find fulfillment and authentic self-expression through romantic and sexual relationships with multiple people. Some even argue that being polyamorous is a matter of sexual orientation or identity, like being gay or straight.[23] In any case, this is not a rejection of the myth of romance but a further expression of it. In other words, "you *and* you complete me."

Those unfamiliar with polyamory often see it as an example of an "anything goes" mindset, and that is certainly the case in some instances. However, it is important to understand those who practice polyamory on their own terms—not to justify polyamory but to understand the framework used by those who practice it. Against the "anything goes" accusation, advocates of polyamory often highlight the centrality of ethics for those who are thoughtful about the practice of polyamory, noting the importance of honesty and openness in these relationships.[24] Rather than just conforming to broader cultural expectations about singleness or marriage, polyamory requires a high level of open communication and ongoing work, because each polyamorous relationship is different and is constructed by the participants in that relationship to meet their individualized needs and goals.

I am not saying this somehow justifies polyamory; rather, paying close attention to the language used by polyamorists can help us see that our culture's practice of polyamory is simply an extension of how the stories of individualism and romance have shaped us. Polyamorous relationships are a prime example of what Giddens means by a "pure relationship"—there may be no cultural script for it, so those within it determine what the obligations, commitments, and expectations are. Just as each person in individualism "invents" themselves, so every relationship is an "invention" of the participants.

Whereas many Christians see polyamory as a prime example of a culture that has completely lost its moorings, I think it is more helpful to recognize that polyamory is simply the logical extension of the myths of romance and individualism. It is the normal and expected outcome of a culture steeped in the Declaration of Independence and Disney, where we are constantly told to pursue what makes us happy and to follow our heart. And if we're told that another person should "complete" us, when that other person inevitably falls short, it's not inconceivable that we might assume the problem is that we need two or more someones to "complete" us instead of just one.

The underlying rationale for polyamory is the same story that saturates more "acceptable" behaviors that underlie our practices regarding singleness, marriage, and divorce. In its strangeness, however, polyamory can helpfully awaken us to the way that romance and individualism undergird all other romantic and sexual relationships. The message is clear: Pursue whatever path you think will complete you. If singleness and sexual promiscuity (or celibacy) lead you to that sense of fulfillment and completion, that's fine. If monogamous marriage does, do that. If cohabitation or divorce does, go for it. If polyamory does, by all means, pursue it. While the forms of the relationships differ, the underlying myths remain the same: You do you, and seek whatever you think will complete you.

Rather than focusing solely on the questions surrounding topics like polyamory, cohabitation, and same-sex marriage, we need to go back to more basic questions: What is marriage for? What is sex for? What are bodies for? Too often, we start digging into Bible verses and weighing the reasons for or against gay marriage (for example) without stopping to unpack these basic questions and our unspoken and often unrecognized cultural autopilot that governs how we think and act. And given the way the story of romance has saturated our culture, we need to start with more basic questions: Where do I find fulfillment? Where do I find someone or something that will complete me? Those are valid questions. But they need very different answers from the ones given in the myth of romance.

CHAPTER 8

THE STORY OF GOD'S HOUSEHOLD

"We Belong to Each Other"

How does the gospel contrast with the story of romance? As we look at the story of romance, we need to think through the narrative it tells about fulfillment: Can another person or a romantic relationship "complete" us? On one hand, a good biblical answer is no, and we'll unpack Augustine's theology a bit more to explain that answer. On the other hand, a good biblical answer is also yes, though not in the way we might think. We'll explore Ephesians 5 to see the surprising biblical reason for this.

WHO ARE WE? PEOPLE WHO BELONG TO THE HOUSEHOLD OF GOD

The pastor and theologian Augustine knew what it was like to be on the move, looking for something or someone to complete and fulfill him. His *Confessions* narrate his search for fulfillment: in adolescent friendships that often led him astray, in sexual and romantic relationships, in his educational accomplishments, in climbing the ladder of a successful career, and in his philosophical quest to discover the ultimate truth about reality. In the process of telling us his story, Augustine forces us to ask ourselves an important question: What (or Who) are you really looking for? Augustine helps us see where the story of romance goes astray and why it can never truly deliver on its promises.

Who are we? As we saw earlier in chapter 5 on legalism, Augustine essentially says that to be is to love. In other words, as God's creatures, we are created from God's love and created with a desire at the core of our being that draws us out beyond ourselves, seeking ultimate fulfillment and joy. So the story of romance is right to see us as desiring beings, in search of true love. It's just that, as Augustine points out, we're looking for love in all the wrong places. He contends that there are basically two categories of things: God—who should be enjoyed and loved for his own sake—and everything else—which can be a source of joy and life to us only insofar as we recognize that they are creatures, not the Creator.[1] The problem, according to Augustine, is that no creature can bear the weight of glory, worship, and ultimate love. The biblical word for this is *idolatry*, elevating something created to the status of Creator.

For Augustine, idolatry isn't just wrong because it breaks God's law; it fundamentally doesn't work. It's an unsustainable way of life, leaving us always longing and never fulfilled. This is what he's getting at when he says, "You have made us and drawn us to yourself, and our heart is unquiet [restless] until it rests in You."[2]

Augustine doesn't stand as a cold, far-off critic of the story of romance, however. It's clear from his own story that he has walked this road: "In love with loving, I was casting about for something to love."[3] He can relate to a culture that is romantically unsettled, shifting from one person to the next, trying to find "the one" who truly fulfills us and quiets our restless heart. The problem with the story of romance, for Augustine, is not that it's looking for transcendence or fulfillment, but that it's fixated on another human person rather than the divine

Trinity, the three persons in one God, in whom we live, move, and have our being, and in whom alone we find true rest and fulfillment. It's God alone who can complete us, God alone who can bear the weight of being our ultimate love.

Finding rest in God alone does not exclude other loves, including the romantic and sexual love in marriage, but it fundamentally reframes them. Everything good is a gift from God. But everything that is not God passes away. That's the transient nature of what is finite. So if I fixate on anything, including a person, as my ultimate love and source of hope, I will be disappointed. Again, this is part of the nature of idolatry: I cling to something that, by definition, cannot endure because it is a mere creature and not the Creator. When I fixate on what is finite, I'm inevitably restless, because what I love doesn't last. As James K. A. Smith puts it, "The heart's hunger is infinite, which is why it will ultimately be disappointed with anything merely finite."[4] This doesn't mean that the finite is evil or bad. Far from it! Rather, it means we need to see every creature of God, including one's spouse, as a good gift from God.

This view fundamentally shifts the story of romance. When I recognize that my spouse is a gift from God, not God, then I will stop putting the weight of love and expectation on them that only God can bear. I won't look to them for my identity. I won't assume they can fulfill the deepest needs of my heart. I won't place my hope in maintaining a fever pitch of romance in our relationship. This also changes how we approach singleness. If romance is not where we find fulfillment and identity, then we shouldn't pressure single Christians to get married. We should acknowledge that pressuring them to do so is a subtle (and sometimes not so subtle) form of idolatry, a posture that claims we need another person to complete us.

But, some might ask, doesn't Genesis teach that "it is not good for man to be alone"? Granted, we shouldn't idolize another person or assume they can complete us in the way that God does, but isn't the Bible teaching us a scaled-down version of the story of romance, one where we should expect that marriage is the normal path unless we've been given a supernatural gift of singleness? Isn't marriage the solution to the problem of loneliness and being alone? No, and the discussion of marriage in Ephesians 5 shows us why.

In Ephesians 5:21–33, the marriage of a man and woman is shown to be a picture of the deeper reality of Christ and the church. When the text of Genesis speaks of husband and wife, Paul reads it with a deeper layer of meaning that connects to Christ and the church. Christ is the new Adam, a theme that emerges frequently throughout the New Testament. The church, then, is the new Eve. If this is true, then it is the family and household of God, not a spouse, that is the ultimate answer to loneliness. We as human beings, bearing the image of the Trinitarian God, are created for community.

We need other people in a variety of ways and at a variety of levels. The work of Jesus—our single Savior—was to form a new family around himself by his Spirit. The main biblical solution to our need for community is not marriage, but the family of God. That is why Psalm 68:6 says, "God sets the lonely in families," not "God sets the lonely in marriages." That is why the New Testament holds up singleness and marriage as equally valid paths for Christians. If marriage were essential to a full and complete human life, then it would be commanded as a necessity in Scripture. But it's not! What *is* commanded is a life of community and connection with the body of Christ, connected to God and to one another.

God's solution to the problem of loneliness and the need for connection is not a spouse, but the church, the new Eve. In this sense, we don't need others to "complete" us because God alone can fill that need. Yet because God is a relational God, he sets us in his family, a place where we are meant to know and experience God's love and care through the care of sisters and brothers in Christ. This is a place of true completion and fulfillment: that we know the love of Christ, which fills us "to the measure of all the fullness of God" (Eph. 3:19). As we are filled with his love, we are called to connect with and serve one another so we reach the "fullness of Christ" (Eph. 4:13). As we find our rest and fulfillment in Christ, we grow up as the body of Christ, embodying the fullness of his love in a world restlessly looking for a love that will satisfy.

EMBODYING THE GOSPEL: HOUSEHOLDS OF FAITH AND WORK

What does this look like in everyday life? The story of romance says there's nothing bigger than me and my romantic relationship. We are lost in each other, and the practicalities and necessities of everyday life have nothing to do with the euphoria of romance. In the midst of this story, Christians can focus our households on our shared work, both the good, everyday work of maintaining our households and the gospel work of making disciples.

This way of life includes both married and single Christians. A Christian household might be a nuclear family, with dad, mom, and kids. But there are numerous other options: several unmarried people sharing the same living space, a family plus one or more single people, or a mix of married couples and single people who choose co-housing as a living option for the sake of community and affordability.

For single Christians, singleness does not imply a solitary housing arrangement, and the households we form are meant to be characterized by shared work and shared mission. It's common for younger single people to live with others (especially in college), and the accountability and familial aspects of shared living space don't have to end at graduation. For married couples, this way of life recognizes that what binds us together in marriage is more than romance; it's shared work, a shared mission. A Christian household is thus not defined by a romantic relationship (or lack thereof), but by shared work and a shared mission in the world.

My friends Sam and Kristi are a great model of a Christian view of hospitality, housing, and shared space. They bought a house several years ago in our church's neighborhood. From the outset, they saw their home as a space to share and connect with others. They let another couple from the church, Gideon and Taylor, live in their basement, which they (Gideon and Taylor) did work to finish.

Sam and Kristi have had numerous folks live in their home over the last few years, some of whom are Christian and some of whom aren't. When Gideon and Taylor's family began to grow and baby Abigail came along, they ended up buying a home that they now share with another married couple and Taylor's single friend Jen. Though this form of hospitality and co-housing may seem foreign to the American dream, the rising costs of housing plus a Christian vision of hospitality combine to offer a different alternative, a household of shared faith and work.[5]

This focus on shared work and mission does not preclude romance as a dimension of marriage, but it rejects the way modern marriage unhinges romance from the practical love of everyday work. When you are first and foremost co-laborers in the gospel, as Paul often puts it, you have a shared mission and a shared Spirit that take you beyond the inevitable roller coaster of romance to the slow and steady work of God's kingdom. Let's examine how this notion of shared work and shared mission challenges the romantic version of marriage.

SHARED WORK

Households of faith are households characterized by shared work. This goes all the way back to Genesis 1–2. When God creates Adam and Eve, he puts them in the garden of Eden and commands them to be caretakers of the earth, tending the plants and animals in a way that faithfully images God's own caretaking and faithfulness (Gen. 1:26–31). In the beginning, there was work, and there was *shared* work between husband and wife, and it was very good. Marriage is meant to be a co-laboring, a collaboration of husband and wife in the good work given to them by God. From the beginning, then, marriage has been oriented beyond itself by the call to be culture makers and to care for God's good world. In contrast to the story of romance, which focuses on the relationship as an end in itself, to the exclusion of "everyday practicalities" (as we noted earlier in the previous chapter), marriage participates in God's call to cultivate creation and build culture through shared work.

Now, in our postindustrial culture, we often have a reductionistic view of work. We tend to identify "work" as paid labor that (usually) happens at a location outside the home. But as Kristina LaCelle-Peterson points out, this way of thinking that seems so natural now is relatively new to our time and place: "Before the Industrial Revolution in the late eighteenth and early nineteenth centuries, there was no 'traditional family,' if by that term we mean the husband going off to work while the wife stayed home. . . . In the agrarian model, everyone worked and everyone's labor was integral to the family economy. . . . No one was said to 'work' while the other 'stayed at home.' They *both* 'worked' and 'stayed at home.'"[6] In other words, husband and wife were co-laborers in their household economy.

In contrast, Wendell Berry points out that most of our contemporary homes are not places of active work but of passive consumption:

> According to the industrial formula, the ideal human residence is one in which the residers do not work. The house is built, equipped, decorated, and provisioned by other people, by strangers. In it, the married couple practice as few as possible of the disciplines of household or homestead. Their domestic labor consists principally of buying things, putting things away, and throwing things away. . . . In such a 'home,' a married couple are mates, sexually, legally, and socially, but they are not helpmates; they do nothing useful either together or for each other. According to the ideal, work should be done away from home. When such spouses say to each other, "I will love you forever," the meaning of their words is seriously impaired by their circumstances; they are speaking in the presence of so little that they have done and

made. Their history together is essentially placeless; it has no visible or tangible incarnation. They have only themselves in view.[7]

What the story of romance sees as a strength—"They have only themselves in view"—Berry sees as a serious lack, a way of life that is unsustainable precisely because it is self-enclosed and not oriented toward a life of shared work. This notion of shared work is radically different from the romantic form of marriage discussed above, the "pure relationship," where "expectations, routines, and everyday practicalities" supposedly have nothing to do with the relationship. I'm not suggesting that our marriage crisis can be solved by somehow going back to the past, that all households should be agrarian, and that if we all could just be like Pa and Ma Ingalls from *Little House on the Prairie*, life and marriage would be great. Too many Christians engage in that kind of magical and wishful thinking. But how can we shift out of this romantic, consumeristic, and passive mindset, and cultivate households that actually work?

To cultivate households and marriages that work, we first need to recognize that the root problem with the story of romance is its failure to properly define love, especially in relation to work. A broad biblical definition of love is always concerned with everyday practicalities. For example, the Old Testament law is summed up in the twofold command to love God and love your neighbor. What does it mean to love your neighbor? The law is very specific about that and digs directly into everyday practicalities: It means that you return your neighbor's straying animal (Deut. 22:1–3), it means that when you build a new house with a flat roof, you put railings around the edge so your neighbor doesn't fall off (Deut. 22:8), it means that every seven years debts are canceled (Deut. 15:1–6), and it means that you freely lend to those who have need (Deut. 15:7–8).

Love, broadly speaking, involves practical acts of everyday care. As Wendell Berry puts it, "Charity [or love] is a theological virtue and is prompted, no doubt, by a theological emotion, but it is also a practical virtue because it must be practiced."[8] Love works. That is, love seeks out the knowledge and skills necessary to work well in order to take care of one's household alongside one's spouse. This involves both an intellectual and a practical knowledge, and it is the opposite of romance insofar as it emphasizes long-term courage, consistency, and caretaking through everyday practicalities.

The shared work of love is a key element of the bond of marriage and any well-functioning household. As Berry puts it, "Good work is not just the maintenance of connections . . . but the *enactment* of connections. It *is* living, and a way of living; it is not support for a family in the sense of an exterior brace or prop, but is one of the forms and acts of love."[9] In other words, work isn't an external add-on to marriage and our households; it is an essential feature of what it means to practically love one another.

Part of the reason the story of romance doesn't work, then, is because it doesn't *work*. It doesn't recognize the practical dimension of love. Without that practical dimension of love, we become self-obsessed and consumeristic, constantly questioning whether this other person is truly my soulmate or really "the one." In contrast, true love stands shoulder to shoulder in the trenches of everyday life, partnering together in the shared work and mission of the kingdom of God.

THE WORK OF A HOUSEHOLD

So what does this look like? For starters, it's worth recognizing the obvious: Every household takes some kind of work to maintain. Most of us are not operating in an agrarian context. But food has to be prepared. Dishes have to be washed and put away. The house has to be cleaned. Clothes have to be washed, folded, and put away. If you have a yard, it has to be maintained. If you own a home, it has to be cared for in a variety of big and small ways. At minimum, spouses work together to perform the necessary work for the household to function.

Some tasks may be interchangeable, whereas others may become the purview of the husband or wife. Though it's not paid labor, this is good and necessary work, without which the household could not function. It is a collaborative effort: love works. The same holds true for a household composed of single people or a mix of married and single people. Co-laboring and some kind of division of labor are necessary for those households to function as well, and working through the practicalities of who does what is a great exercise in the practical nature of true love.

Another element of a household's work is hospitality, the welcoming of those outside the family into the daily life and rhythms of the home. One key way this hospitality is shown is in welcoming children into the family. As parents exercise hospitality and begin to welcome children into their home, it's clear that this monumental shift requires parents to be fully engaged in the work of caring for and raising their children. Not only is this view in the sense of constant feeding, diaper changing, bathing, and putting to sleep, but there is also the even greater work of nurturing a child's overall development, including their spiritual development.

Equipping children with everything they need, including a life of discipleship, is an immense task requiring a great deal of energy. Parenting is an amazing privilege, but it's also an overwhelming amount of work. (I have six kids ages 2 to 13, so I know what I'm talking about!) This good work requires parents to be intentional and collaborative with one another in shepherding and raising their children. Most families engage in the work of educating and training of their children to some extent, whether that's reading books or engaging in recreational activities. Some families embrace home-centered education, where one or both parents take on the role of planning and facilitating their kids' learning activities. In any case, welcoming children into the home takes the motto of "love works" to a whole new level.

Furthermore, a household of work also invites children into the joy and task of collaborative work, giving them chores and increasing responsibilities as part of the daily work of the household. Children become apprentices, gaining everyday skills and knowledge that equip them to practically serve other members of the household. In a world that often reduces the value of work to a paycheck or reduces vocation to a job, cultivating a household of work from the beginning allows children to see the breadth and goodness of work.

Households of work, though, may often include collaborative paid work as well. For example, small family businesses are often collaborative efforts where spouses and households work together, sometimes spanning generations, in order to serve their neighborhoods, communities, and cities. My friend Dave is a contractor who does great work and communicates well. As you might imagine, his services are in increasingly high demand. His wife and daughter both assist him with some of the administrative and office work needed to maintain his growing business.

When smaller family businesses get big, a community may benefit in a variety of ways. For example, the city of Grand Rapids, Michigan, where I live, has benefited from several family businesses that started small but have grown, including Amway (DeVos and Van Andel families) and Meijer retail stores. Even though "family business" evokes images of a mom-and-pop operation, these larger businesses clearly see themselves as key members of the community and, being philanthropically minded, have contributed to the city in a number of different ways, from underwriting large portions of hospitals and medical research institutes to funding botanical gardens and concert venues. In an increasingly connected world, our households can share our good work with others all around our country and globe in a variety of ways, whether it's producing arts and crafts; creating blogs, podcasts, or other forms of media; or partnering together in other unique ways to provide goods and services to our world.

When we think about the work and calling of raising kids who are disciples of Jesus, it's clear that many benefits can come from households of faith that are also households of hospitality. In other words, when families invite other Christians to live with them, whether married or single, they form a household of shared work and shared discipleship that benefits everyone involved. Kids see another example of what it means to follow and serve Jesus. Single Christians without children grow through the process of befriending, caring for, and discipling younger Christians. Parents learn how to co-labor with other Christians in the task of caring for and apprenticing kids in everyday discipleship, letting go of the notion that their children's faith is solely dependent on them.

We might stereotypically think of single parents in particular as needing extra help in the work of raising children, but their need for help from the broader family of God should be held up as a model for everyone, rather than a special case. I mentioned earlier my friends Gideon and Taylor, who model this hospitality and shared discipleship well. Their young daughter, Abigail, is blessed by the fact that they live in a co-housing model with another couple, Kevin and Kandi, and a single friend, Jen. Gideon and Taylor are Abigail's main caretakers, but she has aunts and uncles in the faith who are not just a presence in her life once or twice a week but are actually part of her household. This household embodies shared work and shared hospitality.

Our marriages and households can serve as mission centers for our jobs and careers outside the home as well. When we see our paid work as part of our larger calling to contribute to the common good in our world, then the whole household can participate and build each other up as we serve where God has put us. For example, if there are times when our paid work is particularly stressful and demanding, others might serve in additional ways in the work of the household to alleviate the stress and burden.

If we use an individualistic calculus, where we are constantly comparing who does what within the home without any broader sense of our work and service in the world, we risk treating each other's jobs as individualistic endeavors. In contrast, if we see all the jobs represented by household members as serving the common good of our communities, we will see ourselves as participating in a shared mission where we look for ways to support one another and send one another into our work outside the home with the strength and resources we need.

When we take a wide-angle view of work, we also might recognize that there's a good rationale for one spouse to stay home, if that is economically possible (and for many families, it is not). It takes a lot of work to make a household function, especially if kids are involved! So often men and women alike find their value in the work they do outside the home, but we fail to see the value in the work we do in our households. We need not pit the work we do outside our household against the work we do inside it. Rather, when we recognize the necessity and value of both, we can make honest decisions about where to allot our time and energy to accomplish all the work it truly takes for our households to thrive.

This wide-angle view allows us to see all the work a household needs to thrive and then make decisions accordingly. Sometimes we fall into the "traditional" stereotype (which, as we discussed above, isn't all that traditional), where the wife must stay home while the husband works outside the home. Or sometimes we fall into a more recent stereotype that says both husband and wife must have a career outside the home to be truly valued and affirmed. Both are equally unhelpful insofar as they fail to provide a wide-angle view of work that pictures husband and wife as co-laborers together, in their household and beyond. Rather than falling prey to either stereotype, we need to ask critical questions about the mission of our household and then make decisions accordingly.

THE MISSION OF A HOUSEHOLD

The most crucial question about our household is this: What is its ultimate mission? If households of faith are called to be households of work, then no work is more central than the task given to us by Jesus of making disciples. The call to follow Jesus is a challenge to "family values" and forces us to examine how we think about our marriages and families. If they are not oriented around following Jesus and the gospel work he calls us to, then they are idols that need to be dismantled. Thus, far from focusing on the family, Jesus calls us to fundamentally rethink the value we place on it.

For Jesus, family is radically relativized by the gospel: Our definition of who our true family is revolves around allegiance to Jesus and to the will of God (Mark 3:33–35). So we are bound together not only through the work that provides for our physical necessities, but also by the daily work of making disciples and living a life in service of Christ's mission in the world.

This is part of Paul's logic in 1 Corinthians 7:29–31. In the context of giving advice about marriage and singleness, he says that those who have wives should live "as if they do not" (1 Cor. 7:29)—strange advice for someone with a high view of marriage. But he's not saying husbands should ignore or abandon their wives. Rather, he emphasizes that so many things we devote our lives to are, ultimately, passing away. His point is to use those things wisely, rather than seeing them as ends in themselves.

This line of thinking applies to marriage. It is not the end goal for Christians. Marriage is oriented toward something beyond itself: the mission given to us by Jesus. Our purpose in the world is to share the good news of Jesus through our lives and words, and to make disciples who are committed to him. Thus, Christian marriages should be characterized by our shared work for the sake of the gospel.

What does that look like? For starters, we have to see our individual households as part of the household of God, mini gatherings of the body of Christ called to do the work of Christ every day of the week. The daily rhythms of the household should be shaped by the life of the body of Christ, the local church. Even if our household includes only our spouse and/or children, the daily work of our households is the work of the church: being devoted to the apostles' teaching, fellowship, breaking of bread, and prayer (Acts 2:42). We don't do this to the exclusion of our broader church family, but out of recognition that following Jesus is a matter of daily discipleship. Therefore, we need daily teaching, prayer, fellowship, and breaking of bread together as husbands and wives, parents and children, if we are to grow in our faith.

This also means our daily and weekly schedules need to revolve around the broader household of faith, the church. We are dedicated to teaching and learning, fellowship, breaking of bread, and prayer with the broader body of Christ. This includes not merely participating in the regular worship services of the church, but also opening our lives and homes to other members of the body of Christ from Monday to Saturday. Making disciples of our own children or of others beyond our household cannot be accomplished in one day per week. God calls us not only to good work but also to the good works that Jesus prepared in advance for us to do, the service to the body of Christ that is the calling and ministry of every Christian.

My wife, Sarah, is an amazing model of caring for others' children, not just her own. Our friends Eric and Julie's youngest daughter, Kate, who is the same age as our oldest daughter, had some bad experiences at her school, including bullying, and needed to look at other schooling options. Sarah homeschools our three oldest kids and readily volunteered to include Kate as part of that, if that seemed like the best option for a midyear schooling change. To be honest, I was a little hesitant to add another person to the mix (even though Sarah is the one who does virtually all the work of teaching). But Sarah's commitment to the larger household of God was evident in her commitment to teaching and discipling Kate.

Another key part of this shared gospel work for spouses and single people alike is identifying and encouraging one another's strengths and gifts and coordinating our lives so that our work for the sake of the gospel is at the center of our life together. So we might ask, What gifts and abilities does my spouse and/or roommate have? How can I encourage them to grow and develop their use of those gifts for the sake of God's kingdom? What life decisions and priorities do we need to make so our gifts can be fully used in the body of Christ? In a similar way, a key part of the work of parents is to ask, How can I teach and train my children to know God's deep love for them and, from that love, to serve God's mission in our household, our neighborhood, our city, and the world? Those without biological children should ask themselves the same question regarding other young people in the faith. These questions can serve to direct our focus to the way God wants to use us as coworkers for the sake of the gospel.

In a world driven by the story of romance, married and single Christians alike can live "questionable" lives by building households of faith where love works. Our very act of building these households of faith should give the world pause. What is it that drives this way of life? Why do Christians find joy in the everyday work of maintaining life? Why is your family so focused on the life of the body of Christ? Why is your home a place of hospitality, welcoming those who do and don't know Jesus? As we live questionable lives in which love works, we will point to the One in whom our souls find rest, the One whose work of love has made us members of God's household.

CHAPTER 9

THE MYTH OF SEXUAL PROSPERITY

"Your Best Sex Life Now"

While our culture is often caught up embodying the stories of romance, our Christian subculture often embodies the story of sexual prosperity.[1] We've looked at the story of legalism, which emphasizes following the rules of God the divine lawgiver. If you fall short of the rules, you end up in a place of shame and guilt. But what if you think you did good enough? What if you do keep the rules? Then what? That's the story of the sexual prosperity gospel, a story of moral cause and effect. Do the right thing, and good things will happen to you. Stick to the rules, and you will be rewarded. Follow God's guidelines for sex, and you will get your best sex life now.

If you push the right buttons, God the lawgiver becomes God the blessing dispenser. Like the previous false "Christian" stories we've examined, this one is often implicit in our views and practices around sex, singleness, and marriage. But this story distorts not only how we think about sex and bodies, but also how we tell the story of God and the gospel.

WHAT'S THE STORY OF SEXUAL PROSPERITY?

In her book *Pure*, Linda Kay Klein relates the story of Muriel and Dmitri.[2] They met their first day of Bible college, and according to Muriel, she knew that "he was the man God had for me to marry" by the end of the first week of school. Following a popular path for that time, the couple decided not to even kiss until they were married. Perhaps in part because of this, the couple raced through a quick engagement toward marriage and sex, going so far as to have their wedding at 9:30 a.m. so they could have sex earlier in the day. Reflecting on the mixed messages about sex, Muriel points out that sex "was what everybody talked about, in the negative. But then supposedly once it was in marriage it was supposed to be this amazing celebration."[3] It wasn't. An awkward kiss during the wedding ceremony was a foretaste of things to come. A wedding night that didn't go as planned turned into four months of failed attempts at intercourse.

Their story might be more extreme than some, but it is not unique. At the Christian college I attended, as couples began to marry, there were a number of side conversations, indirect but clear: For a couple of virgins, sex isn't an easy, stupendous experience right off the bat. In contrast to all the overblown stereotypes of the "wedding night," having sex at all (not just having great sex) might take some work and a learning curve. Not everyone's story is the same, but for Muriel (and many others), her church had taught her that the most important thing in life was to remain pure before marriage. If she did that, she would have an amazing marriage and sex life. What happened when that turned out not to be true? Muriel is blunt: "To me, it meant there was no God."[4]

The story of the sexual prosperity gospel promotes a false view of God and the gospel in several ways. One way it distorts the character of God is by fixating on God as the dispenser of divine blessings. It focuses on key blessings and promises in the Bible, urging Christians to claim those blessings and promises for their lives. Now, I want to be clear: The Bible does include a wide variety of blessings and promises that God makes to his people. But we often distort those blessings and promises by pulling them out of context so they fit a narrower version of what counts as a blessing or promise rather than reading them in context so we can see the fullness and richness of God's blessings and promises. To see this more clearly, let's reflect briefly on probably the most famous verse taken out of context in the last couple of decades.

Jeremiah 29:11 contains these words of blessing and promise: "'For I know the plans I have for you,' declares the Lord, 'plans to prosper you and not to harm you, plans to give you hope and a future.'" This is God's Word. But how do we interpret this word of promise and blessing? One of the most common mistakes is to read this verse without paying attention to the larger context in which it occurs. When we ignore the context, we read this verse as written first and foremost to us, not to Jeremiah's original audience, so we tend to interpret it as applying directly to our circumstances. I might think about my own life plans, my hopes and dreams, and take this verse as a straightforward promise that God is going to bring my plans to fruition—plans for getting into the college I'm hoping to attend, plans for landing a new job, or plans for finding that special someone.

As Scot McKnight points out, though, this way of reading the Bible chops it up into tiny morsels (verses) of truth, promises and blessings that are divorced from any sense of the larger story of the Bible.[5] When we read the Bible this way, our view of God gets skewed, and he becomes like a genie or Santa Claus. Or God becomes a helicopter parent, hovering over our life to prevent anything bad or difficult from occurring. The view put forth here is of a god who revolves around us and whose primary concern is to make our wishes come true and our life turn out the way we think it should. We pull verses like Jeremiah 29:11 out of context and fashion them to fit our notions of what God should do and what our lives should look like, including promises of our best sex life now. But is this what God intends when he makes promises and speaks of blessing in Scripture?

If we pay attention to the surrounding context of Jeremiah 29:11, we see there is more going on than God rubber-stamping our desired outcomes for our lives. There is a promise and a blessing here, but by reading it through our Disney lens of all our dreams coming true, we miss the depth and richness of this blessing. Let's unpack the context of Jeremiah 29:11 a bit more in order to better understand God's blessings and promises.

In this part of the book of Jeremiah, God is sending his people into exile in Babylon as judgment for their lack of covenant faithfulness. In Jeremiah 27, Jeremiah warns God's people that God is giving the kingdom of Judah over to Babylon and their king, Nebuchadnezzar, and that the people of Judah ought to submit to Babylon's rule rather than rebel against it. This, however, was not the message the king or the people wanted to hear.

In contrast, the false prophet Hananiah was prophesying a message of victory for God's people and defeat for Babylon, saying that God was going to restore all the items from the temple that Nebuchadnezzar had taken within two years and that Babylonian rule would also end during that timeframe (Jer. 28:3).

In response, God declares through Jeremiah that Hananiah will die, which he does (Jer. 28:16–17). Jeremiah's letter in chapter 29, then, is to the leaders of Israel who had been taken to Babylon. They lost their homeland, their livelihood, and their place of worship. In short, they were not in a good spot.

I imagine most of them would rather hear the message of Hananiah that this bad dream would be over soon and that they could go back to some semblance of normal life. Jeremiah, however, tells them to settle down in Babylon, build houses, plant gardens, and raise children and grandchildren in this foreign land (29:5–6). He underscores that they will be in Babylon for 70 years (29:10), which means that any adult hearing this message should expect to die in exile. Those people would not be going back to the land of Israel/Judah.

It's at this point that we get to the famous verse 11. Observe, however, the point of emphasis in the first part of the verse: "'*I* know the plans *I* have for you,' declares the Lord" (emphases mine). The hope, promise, and blessing of this verse are rooted in God's plan for his people, which includes a time of suffering and exile they would likely never choose for themselves. God is not working out their plan or their version of blessing, but his.

My point here is not that God is a killjoy or unconcerned with the suffering of his people in exile. Rather, it is to see that there is truly joy, hope, and blessing in what God promises but that his blessings may not align with our expectations or definitions. In fact, his richer, better version of hope and blessing often happens in and through times, circumstances, and experiences that are not what we would choose (or even define as a blessing). But the type of deep blessing promised in Jeremiah 29:11 brings true comfort because it goes beyond our surface-level understandings of blessing and helps us see the God who is with us even when our surrounding circumstances may not be what we would like.

The story of the sexual prosperity gospel distorts not only how we think about God but also how we view sin and redemption. It gives a distorted answer to the questions "What's the problem?" and "What's the solution?" For the prosperity gospel, the primary problem involves external factors and circumstances: I lack health and/or wealth, and the solution is to make the right moves, thereby leveraging God into providing me with my best life now. This mindset also characterizes the sexual prosperity gospel, which makes the common theological mistake of assuming that all suffering should be avoided.[6] As pastor and writer Ed Shaw puts it, the main operating assumption of many Christians is, "If something makes you really suffer, you stop doing it. If something will make you happy, you sign up for it."[7] This is blunt but accurate.

The "redemption" offered by the prosperity gospel—including the

THE MYTH OF SEXUAL PROSPERITY

sexual prosperity gospel—has no place for suffering, which is seen as the enemy of God and his people, a problem that God must solve rather than a place where God is present. Like the false prophet Hananiah, prosperity preachers see "salvation" or "redemption" as God's action to fix the circumstances we don't like and to give us what we want. Similarly, since our culture values romantic and sexual fulfillment so highly, the peddlers of purity culture are often false prophets insofar as they hold out simplistic promises and a formulaic approach to getting God to rain down an abundance of relational and sexual blessings.

The Bible never simply reduces "the problem" to our surrounding circumstances. Certainly, we must recognize that sin and the fall have had a profound effect on every dimension of our lives, including our physical and economic wellbeing. Many people live in poverty because of unjust economic structures. Many people suffer the ravenous effects of disease due to factors beyond their control. Likewise, sin affects our relationships and our sex lives, so that we sin against others, and they sin against us. This is not the way God intended things to be.

Yet the root problem put forth by the biblical narrative is an internal problem of my heart—unfaithfulness to God—rather than an external problem of my circumstances. My infidelity to God can't be blamed on circumstances; rather, it is the result of my own warped and disordered desire. Indeed, one of the main effects of sin is that I fail to see God where he is truly at work and instead try to see and understand God in terms of my own framework. The true gospel, though, turns what seems natural upside down in light of the cross.

EMBODYING SEXUAL PROSPERITY: PURITY CULTURE

I grew up in the 1980s, which was the heyday of televangelists like Jimmy Swaggart and Jim Bakker. I remember watching them on my grandparents' television (not because my grandparents bought into their theology, but because they were a spectacle), hearing their pleas for money and promises of financial windfalls and physical wellbeing. Their prosperity gospel promised health and wealth for all those who would invest in their ministries. In more recent decades, Joel Osteen has popularized a version of the prosperity gospel that still underscores material wealth but slightly softens the approach, including personal fulfillment along with the more tangible benefits of fiscal and physical wellbeing.

Scholar and historian Kate Bowler contends that the prosperity gospel revolves around four key themes: faith, wealth, health, and victory.[8] By faith, she means the spiritual power that brings about what is spoken or hoped for and turns that into reality. Health and wealth are the tangible demonstration of faith. As she puts it, the "material reality" is "the measure of the success of immaterial faith."[9] Finally, the focus on victory underscores that no forces or powers, spiritual or otherwise, can stop believers from experiencing full victory in the here and now. In the face of an ascetic, disciplined orthodoxy that may emphasize delayed gratification and self-mortification, the prosperity gospel promises "demonstrable results," a calculus that sees real faith and produces real, positive results in the present.[10]

As Bowler points out, many Christians are skeptical—even critical—of this prosperity gospel. It features elements of consumerism, even greed, and paints a simplistic picture of what God promises to his people. However, I think many Christians who would criticize the prosperity gospel of Jim Bakker and Joel Osteen have bought into a different version of the same flawed message when it comes to sex and the promises made by the purveyors of purity culture. Purity culture is not usually talked about in the same context as the prosperity gospel. But when we compare the two, we start to see similarities that should give us pause. Using Bowler's main descriptors as a grid, we can see that purity culture is actually a form of the prosperity gospel.

Before turning to Bowler's description, I want to briefly note the distinction between the purity culture that developed in the 1990s and a biblical sexual ethic more generally, because some conflate the two. Purity culture is not merely an emphasis on sexual abstinence outside of marriage (which the Bible teaches and is part of the historic Christian sexual ethic). Rather, it holds together three of the distorted stories I'm surveying in this book: legalism, sexual prosperity, and an anti-body theology. It often looks at the body as bad and the source of evil, thus emphasizing that anything physical, such as kissing, outside marriage is wrong.

Those who want to remain truly "pure" set up boundaries in addition to Scripture. This legalistic approach is often reinforced through a variety of symbols, from abstinence pledges to purity rings. And following this purity code leads to its reward: a great marriage and amazing sex! While these strands of legalism, sexual prosperity, and anti-body theology may be present in different times and places in church history, they coalesced in a particular way in the 1990s as a backlash to the sexual revolution.[11]

The textbook for purity culture was Joshua Harris's *I Kissed Dating Goodbye*, and curriculums like True Love Waits, along with their accompanying pledges, were key teaching tools. And these messages resonated with many people. For example, in 1994, a True Love Waits rally in Washington, DC, had over 25,000 participants, and the movement displayed over 210,000 commitment cards signed by teens throughout the US.[12] As we briefly survey the symbols and praxis of purity culture, then, we need to distinguish between the distortions of purity culture and the sexual ethic taught in Scripture. With that distinction in mind, how is purity culture a form of the prosperity gospel?

First, purity culture often underscores the need for faith that goes against the grain of what's normal in the broader culture. That is, it doesn't seem easy, right, or natural to follow the Bible's teaching on sexual ethics, including an emphasis on abstinence apart from marriage, and especially on the further legalistic steps demanded by purity culture, such as saying no to dating or kissing before marriage. As Pastor Mike Todd puts it, "Dating—the word—is not in the Bible, but the concept of what we call dating is honestly practicing divorce."[13] This is a contemporary remix of Joshua Harris's point in *I Kissed Dating Goodbye*: "Try looking up 'dating' in your Bible's concordance. You won't get very far."[14] So purity culture first asks for faith on the part of its followers to reject something considered normal and acceptable even by most Christians.

Second, purity culture promises a tangible blessing for that faith. That is, there is a cause and effect to purity promises. Whereas prosperity preachers often promise health and wealth if you do the right thing, the purveyors of purity culture often promise a good marriage and a great sex life if you follow the rules. As Joshua Harris put it in *I Kissed Dating Goodbye*, "Intimacy is the reward of commitment."[15] I greatly appreciate that Harris is trying to avoid casual hookups and slow things down, but I can't help but think that seeing sex as a "reward" for following the rules sets us up for a simplistic view of marriage and sex.

Similarly, others promise that sex within marriage "is able to reach its fullest and most exciting potential within those limits. There is no fear of rejection, no need to pretend, no need to sneak around, no guilt, no fear of a baby ruining your life."[16] Again, these statements need more nuance and clarity. I'd love to ask pastors and counselors whether they've had good Christian married couples struggle with rejection, faking it, less-than-transparent behavior, not to mention an extra kid or two "accidentally" coming on the scene. I can agree that there are definite benefits to following the Bible's teaching and detriments to not doing so. But I know that life is a lot more complicated than these teachers convey. I imagine that many people reading those lines (including me) feel a bit like Job reading the book of Proverbs, which provides general rules of moral cause and effect and not specific promises that speak to every circumstance in our world. "Yes, but . . ." Not only is this view misleading, but its main premise of blessings following automatically from keeping the rules ends up distorting a truly biblical view of sex and marriage in several ways.

By holding up marriage and sex as the "blessing" for following the rules, the sexual prosperity gospel reinforces the unbiblical notion that marriage and sex are superior to singleness and celibacy. In other words, purity culture says, "Save yourself *for* marriage." Singleness could not possibly be the goal or even an equally valid action. If you take the right action, you'll get the reward: sex and marriage.

Grace Thornton speaks powerfully to this mistaken posture in her blog post "I Don't Wait Anymore."[17] Grace did all the right things. She got a purity ring when she was 16. She kept a card from her youth leader that reminded her that if she hadn't found someone yet, it was because she wasn't "fully satisfied in God." She resonated with the motto "true love waits." But eventually she started asking: For what? This framework, she points out, ends up making Jesus a means to an end: sexual fulfillment and marital bliss. It turns out the Jesus who rewards abstinence with marriage is an idol. By God's grace, Grace didn't walk away from her faith or from God's call to chastity and celibacy. But she did walk away from the sexual prosperity gospel that sees God as divine dispenser of marriage and sex to those who have their act together. She rightly points out that by telling the story of sex and bodies within the story of the sexual prosperity gospel, we devalue singleness and miss the ultimate point of *all* bodies, married or single: The body is for the Lord (1 Cor. 6:13).

Third, the sexual prosperity gospel often implies an automatic connection between faith and obedience in your single life and great sex and a great marriage in your married life. For example, the classic 1980s abstinence book *Why Wait?* lists numerous reasons to save sex for marriage. The book outlines some of the negative physical, emotional, relational, and spiritual consequences of having sex before marriage, such as sexually transmitted diseases, the psychological and emotional damage that comes from breaking up with someone with whom you've had sex, the relational damage to a future marriage that comes from comparing sexual partners or from a posture that affirms sex outside marriage, and the spiritual burden of guilt and the missed blessing of purity. This way of setting it up, however, risks following the logic of the prosperity gospel: If you truly have faith and behave the way you are supposed to, a good marriage and great sex will be the tangible blessings that result. In other words, if you wait to have sex until marriage, then your marriage and sex life will attain physical, emotional, relational, and spiritual fulfillment. But what if they don't?

That was the case for Ryan Navero.[18] Raised in a Southern Baptist church (the denomination that produced the True Love Waits curriculum), he and his wife struggled with sex. Having been raised with the calculus that waiting for marriage produces great sex, Navero says, "When I did get married, we encountered our sexual dysfunction and we didn't know how to talk about it. . . . The advice we got was simply to read these books or pray about it more." These supposed solutions didn't help, and things did not get better. Because of the promises of purity culture, Navero felt "divinely broken," and after fifteen years of marriage without sex, Navero and his wife ended up getting a divorce.

The story of the sexual prosperity gospel sets people up to romanticize and idealize both sex and marriage. In doing so, many Christians assume that a fantastic marriage and great sex will just magically happen because they followed the rules of abstinence. As a result, they are often underprepared for the communication and work it will take to make marriage and sex better.

Fourth, like the prosperity gospel, purity culture holds out the promise that, for those who truly have faith and follow this path, there is a promise of sure "victory." Purity culture is not prudish. The movement was not anti-sex or shy about talking about sex. Indeed, many proponents of purity culture openly talked about how great sex is and recommended that married folks seek out resources that would enable them to maximize the techniques they employed in bed. Like the prosperity gospel, purity culture held out the promise that God really and truly wants what is best for you here and now—your best sex life *now.* So promoters of the sexual prosperity gospel exclaim, "Save sex for marriage. If you do, it will be amazing, beyond your wildest dreams! God has so many blessings in store for you!"

By fixating on a supposedly amazing sex life as the reward for abstinence, the story of the sexual prosperity gospel fails to incorporate sex into the larger biblical view of marriage, which is more about self-giving love than it is about getting amazing sex as part of the victorious, blessed life.

Finally, this story applies a simplistic "behave and be blessed" logic to sex and marriage. If you have a good marriage or a good sex life in marriage, it must be because you did the right thing and God is blessing you. If not, you must have fallen short in some way—your faith or your behavior wasn't quite good enough. This story can make us puffed up and prideful when we think about our own life and behavior. For example, part of the message of purity culture is that you should save yourself for marriage and that you deserve another virgin for a spouse. There's a kind of merit or value in living up to this expectation. So if someone is *not* a virgin, then God couldn't bless me through them because my high moral standing clearly deserves someone who is "better" than that. If I'm blessed, it's because I *deserve* to be blessed. Just like the story of legalism, this behavior-based approach to sex and bodies is rooted in a deep distortion of God and the gospel.

CHAPTER 10

THE STORY OF
GOD'S HOUSEHOLD

"Jesus Is the Suffering Servant"

The stories of sexual prosperity and romance offer hope that we'll find fulfillment, completion, and blessing through a significant other. But the gospel offers different answers to the questions "Who is God?" and "Who are we?" In doing so, it casts a substantially different vision for how we think and act in relation to sex, bodies, singleness, and marriage, and how our life in all those areas embodies the gospel. The gospel is not just the story of God's covenant faithfulness, but also the story of God uniting us together in a family. As Romans 12:5 puts it, "In Christ we, though many, form one body, and each member belongs to all the others." Our first family is not the biological family but the household of God, the family of God. This belonging thus shapes how we view singleness and marriage and how we live those out as the household of God. How do we embody the gospel? By living as the family of God as both married and single people.

WHO IS GOD? THE SUFFERING SERVANT

In light of the gospel, the view of God put forth by the story of the sexual prosperity gospel doesn't hold up. Why? Consider the body of Jesus, which hangs at the heart of the gospel, the story of God's covenant faithfulness and love. When we look at the body of Jesus, we do not see someone who is the epitome of health and wealth but, in fact, quite the opposite: He made himself poor for our sake, his body was bruised and broken so that we might have life, and his entire life was characterized more by suffering than by what we would generally call blessing. If we are going to understand how marriage and singleness are called to embody the gospel, we must grasp the way the gospel overturns our expectations about suffering and blessing.

The great reformer Martin Luther helps us see this by drawing a sharp contrast between what he called a theology of glory and a theology of the cross. In the Heidelberg Disputation, Luther draws out this contrast first by asserting that a "person does not deserve to be called a theologian who looks upon the invisible things of God as though they were clearly perceptible in those things which have actually happened."[1] When Luther talks about a "theologian" here, he is talking about anyone who engages questions of the nature and character of God: What is God like? How does he reveal himself? Where do we see him at work?

Luther contends that a "theology of glory" constructs our view of God and his character based on our own assumptions and expectations.[2] Although the term *glory* is usually a biblical and positive one, Luther uses it here to highlight what is glorious according to human standards, not God's standards. Thus, a theology of glory constructs God and God's work in the world on the basis of our ways of thinking. This, says Luther, is not a biblical or legitimate way to do theology.

This theology of glory sounds suspiciously like the sexual prosperity gospel of purity culture. An American culture that values romantic relationships and sex ends up preaching a god who pours out the blessings of a good marriage and great sex on those who are virtuous and pure. This view of life, God, relationships, and sex works from *our* definitions of what counts as a "blessing," framing sex and marriage in self-serving terms.[3] It is a theology of glory that builds from our assumptions and expectations to a view of God's character and action that is rooted in our projections of God, not how God has revealed himself to be.

In contrast to this way of interpreting God and the gospel, Luther states, "He deserves to be called a theologian, however, who comprehends the visible and manifest things of God seen through suffering and the cross."[4] In other words, we only see God truly when we see him hanging on the cross. This is scandalous. Jesus's own disciples could not wrap their minds around it, repeatedly failing to understand that the Messiah would suffer and die.

This doesn't fit with our idea of God or God's presence. How can a suffering servant be the embodiment of the kingdom come? Luther here points to Paul's words on the scandal and wisdom of the cross: "We preach Christ crucified: a stumbling block to Jews and foolishness to Gentiles, but to those whom God has called, both Jews and Greeks, Christ the power of God and the wisdom of God. For the foolishness of God is wiser than human wisdom, and the weakness of God is stronger than human strength" (1 Cor. 1:23–25).

As Luther comments on this passage, he emphatically asserts that it does us "no good to recognize God in his glory and majesty" unless we also recognize him "in the humility and shame of the cross."[5] Luther relentlessly hammers home the point that we must be centered on the cross, for it is only there, in the depths of suffering, that God is truly known and fully revealed. The offense of the cross is not simply the cross itself or Christ's suffering but that, in the cross, the very nature of God is revealed.[6]

Of course, the story of the gospel doesn't end with the cross. Christ is risen! The hope of the resurrection is what empowers us to take up our cross and follow Jesus with joy. Still, the path of cross and resurrection is not the cause and effect of the prosperity gospel. This is not a "have faith, obey, and you'll be blessed" formula. The cross is not just a hurdle to get to the real blessing. The cross is not an incidental and accidental stepping-stone to something else. The cross is where the self-giving God gives himself completely to us. It is the manifestation and embodiment of God's abundant love. This is why when John sees a vision of the resurrected and ascended Jesus taking his rightful place in heaven, he sees a Lamb "looking as if it had been slain" (Rev. 5:6). In the fullness of his glory, Jesus remains the Crucified One.

We must not distort the cross and resurrection by making them part of a calculus to get the "blessing" held out for us by a theology of glory or the prosperity gospel. The cross and resurrection simply do not fit within that paradigm. Rather, they are the cornerstone of a completely different paradigm that flows from the nature and character of the One who did not see equality with God as something to be held on to but who became a servant. The height of God's covenant faithfulness and love is revealed not in a glorious display of power, might, and blessing, but in the broken body of Jesus. The story of God's faithful covenant love reaches its climax with the cross and resurrection.

But this raises a vital question: If the cross-centered lens of the gospel sheds new light on all reality, how do marriage and singleness embody this story? What would it mean for us to abandon a sexual prosperity gospel in favor of a view of marriage and singleness that centers on the cross and resurrection?

EMBODYING THE GOSPEL: SUFFERING AND SINGLENESS

The sexual prosperity gospel's message about singleness is clear. Singleness is suffering. It is a time of waiting, a time of deprivation, a time of testing, a wilderness where God is evaluating whether you are good enough for or worthy of a lifetime soulmate. Singleness is, in some sense, less than truly and fully human. In other words, the sexual prosperity view of singleness is a christological heresy.

Christians worship a single Savior. We confess that our single Savior, Jesus, is fully divine and fully human. Many people in the modern world reject the divinity of Jesus, but many people in the New Testament world struggled to accept his full humanity. The fact that he had a physical human body was a difficult concept for Jew and Greek alike. Yet the New Testament repeatedly emphasizes the full humanity of Jesus in numerous ways. Even in his resurrected state, he was fully human; he could be touched, and he could eat with his disciples. This is significant because the salvation of humans depends on Jesus being fully human, yet without sin. The full humanity of Jesus is an essential doctrine of our faith. But Jesus's humanity is also significant because it reminds us that a life of singleness is not in any way deficient or lacking.

We subtly deny the full humanity of Jesus when we operate with the mindset that only people who are married or in a relationship are fully and truly human. If being single is somehow lacking an essential component of full and complete humanity, then Jesus was lacking in this way. If having sex and being in a relationship or married are essential components of full, complete humanity, then Jesus wasn't fully human. To be clear, I don't think most Christians would say this explicitly. But when we pressure single people (young and old alike) toward romantic relationships and talk about singleness as a state of inherent incompleteness, deprivation, and suffering, we subtly perpetuate this christological heresy.

What is more, this is also an ecclesiological heresy. This view of singleness as suffering and marriage as blessing not only conveys a wrong idea about Jesus but also conveys a wrong idea about the church, the people of God, in Scripture. Our assumptions and attitudes about singleness reveal that we either do not understand or do not really live out our call to be the family of God. We see our biological family or romantic relationships as our true family rather than embracing the gospel message that Jesus has created a new family through his Spirit and that our commitment and allegiance to that family are supposed to be our first priority.

How can we begin to recapture a biblical picture of the church as family of God? Rather than talking about people as "single," we should use a more biblical term for all Christians (single or married): family members. When we hear the word *single*, many of us have been trained to hear "solitary," "alone," or "disconnected." And if "it is not good for man to be alone," then the solution must be a romantic relationship or marriage. In contrast, the New Testament describes us as members of Christ's body who belong to one another and as members of the family of God. Whereas "single" implies lack of family, the New Testament opens our eyes to the way Jesus and the Spirit are forming us into a new family. This was central to the witness of the early church. As John Nugent summarizes,

> The early church clearly viewed one another as family. They referred to one another as brothers and sisters. They used adoption language to describe what it meant to join God's family. They shared possessions and took care of one another's financial needs. They encouraged one another to share their blessings and curses, their losses and their victories.[7]

Don't miss the practical implications of this view. Because early Christians saw themselves as members of the family of God, they lacked urgency around marriage. This is why Paul encouraged unmarried members of the Corinthian church to remain unmarried (1 Cor. 7:8).

We often fail to understand how radical Paul's advice is.[8] Whereas our culture tends to see marriage as necessary for emotional and personal fulfillment, in the Greco-Roman culture of Corinth, marriage was necessary for survival. Marriage and family were the social and economic security of the day. Marriage and children were usually necessary for economic survival. Your family was obligated to take care of you. Paul could encourage "singleness" because to be a Christian means you already have a family. You already have people looking out for you in practical, everyday ways.

Far from being a state of inherent suffering and deprivation, as the sexual prosperity gospel implies, singleness can be a place of blessing, connection, and real relationship when we are part of the family of Jesus. If we have bought into the lie that singleness is suffering, we need to take a hard look in the mirror and ask whether that is because we as the church have stopped being the family of God. If the church functions less like a family and more like a once-a-week program, then it's no wonder that many Christians assume you must be married to be in a real relationship and real community. Only when we recover a biblical view of the church as family will we be able to recover a biblical view of singleness, which is not solitude but membership in the household of God.

Of course, a biblical view of the church and singleness does not rule out real suffering. But what kind of suffering should characterize the single members of the family of God? Jesus endured intense suffering, including abandonment by many of his friends in his darkest hour. Nevertheless, for most of his life and ministry, Jesus was surrounded by his disciples and friends. They were his family. We should not overlook that Jesus's transformation of his disciples into an alternative family was, as N. T. Wright points out, "outrageous" and "scandalous" to Jesus's contemporaries.[9]

It sounds equally strange to us in our day. As one Twitter user wittily put it, "Nobody talks about Jesus' miracle of having 12 close friends in his 30s."[10] In other words, the suffering of the single Jesus was not generally a suffering of aloneness. Rather, it was fundamentally a suffering *with*, a suffering that came from his familial connection to and solidarity with disciples, friends, and the sinners he came to save, including you and me.

The cross is the obvious example, but we see this suffering

throughout Jesus's life. I'll explore more examples below, but his commitment to connect with others is one example showing how he faced derision and ultimately persecution from religious leaders because of the new family he was forming around himself. This is the suffering Paul speaks about when he says of married and unmarried Christians alike that "if one part suffers, every part suffers with it; if one part is honored, every part rejoices with it" (1 Cor. 12:26). In short, this suffering comes from connection, relationship, and love—not isolation and loneliness.

As with Jesus, Paul didn't view the suffering of unmarried Christians as arising from a lack of fellowship and relationship, but rather as stemming from solidarity and connection with Jesus and the family of God. Paul looks at his own life as an example. Driven by his love for Jesus and for the family the Holy Spirit was forming throughout the world, Paul suffered imprisonment, beatings, stoning, shipwreck, and hostility from various groups of people, as well as nakedness, hunger, and cold, not to mention the pressure and concern of planting and nurturing numerous churches throughout the Roman Empire (2 Cor. 11). Paul knew perhaps better than anyone what a self-giving, cross-shaped single life looked like. (That's right—like Jesus, Paul was single.) But again, this suffering was not the suffering of abandonment or loneliness.

Throughout all his hardship, Paul knew the joy and challenges of relationships with numerous coworkers in the gospel, as well as churches with whom he shared his life and ministry. Certainly, these relationships were messy. Read Acts or Paul's letters, and you will see that Paul and these churches were far from perfect. But my point is this: Paul's suffering was a suffering *with*, a suffering that came from connection and devotion to Jesus and the family Jesus was forming by his Spirit. The shape of our single Savior's life was one of suffering and solidarity, not isolation and loneliness, and the single apostle's life took on that same shape.

The gospel tells a story about singleness and suffering that is different from the sexual prosperity gospel. The sexual prosperity gospel sees singleness as loneliness and deprivation, whereas a Jesus-centered view sees singleness through the lens of the family of God. As members of Christ's body and the family of God, we suffer with one another and bear each other's burdens. When we clarify how singleness embodies the gospel through the suffering of solidarity, we can begin to see how our view of marriage needs to shift as well. Just as embodying the gospel in singleness involves a suffering that comes from solidarity, so embodying the gospel in marriage involves an embrace of suffering.

EMBODYING THE GOSPEL: SUFFERING AND MARRIAGE

In the sexual prosperity gospel, if singleness is a place of suffering, then marriage is a place of blessing. If singleness is a time of waiting, deprivation, and wilderness, then marriage is a place of fulfillment and abundance. According to the sexual prosperity gospel, marriage and sex are the promised land you earn when you are spiritually strong enough to survive the drought of sexual abstinence and power through. In other words, the sexual prosperity view of marriage is a satanic temptation.

The sexual prosperity gospel mirrors the way Satan sought to tempt Jesus away from the cross and suffering. When he approached Jesus in the wilderness, Satan offered Jesus a path to kingship that didn't involve suffering. He tempted Jesus to turn stones into bread rather than have his own body broken as the bread of life. Satan knew Jesus could be king by providing economic security. We see a picture of this possibility in John 6:1–15. After Jesus fed the 5,000, they wanted to force him to be king. Satan also tempted Jesus to throw himself down from the temple to force God to miraculously save him. Finally, Satan promised Jesus political power if he would worship Satan.

In all these temptations, Satan promised a way to be king that avoided suffering and the cross. In other words, Satan is the first prosperity gospel preacher. That's why, when Peter attempted to rebuke Jesus for saying the Son of Man must suffer and die, Jesus reacted so strongly: "Get behind me, Satan!" (Mark 8:33). Jesus had heard this temptation before. "You don't have to suffer." "Your path of kingship can't *really* involve suffering and death, can it?" Jesus recognized that the true path of the gospel led to the cross.

My friends Laurie and Matt Krieg help me better understand how to answer this question because their marriage doesn't make sense. In fact, it seems downright impossible.[11] Their story helps us see how perverted the sexual prosperity gospel is, and it speaks to our need to let a theology of the cross shape our view of marriage. You see, Laurie is attracted to women, and Matt has battled porn addiction. Their story exposes the fundamental lie at the heart of the sexual prosperity gospel: that following the rules inevitably leads to the so-called blessed life and that the end goal in this life is to escape suffering. Laurie's attraction to women didn't just go away once they got married. Matt's struggles with pornography didn't just disappear because he was a married man. Thanks to their vulnerability in sharing their story, we see that marriage involves suffering. Why on earth would they stay together? Why would they keep working at something that seems so unnatural and painful, something that seems so impossible?

Their answer is simple: the gospel. That might seem like a Sunday school answer, but if you read Laurie and Matt's story, you'll realize they are more about exploding simple Sunday school answers than perpetuating them. Their story is possible only because of the gospel of Jesus. When faced with their own sin and brokenness, Matt and Laurie could have walked away from their marriage. But they didn't. They are clear that their road has not been easy. They are open about the way God's work in their lives has involved incredible suffering but has also been life-giving and transformational.

Laurie willingly shares how she was on the verge of divorce, ready to walk away from her marriage to Matt and toward life with another woman. Further, she recounts how her experience of sexual abuse as a child was a roadblock to physical intimacy with Matt. Matt willingly talks about how his sexual brokenness manifested itself in a porn addiction, an outlet through which he sought security and acceptance. But he also recounts his more acceptable and respectable idolatries: losing himself in sports and his career in a way that was damaging to his relationship with God and his marriage.

When I listen to their story, I trust Laurie and Matt because their own vulnerability about their suffering, their struggles, and God's faithfulness shows they practice what they preach. And what they preach is the gospel of Jesus Christ. The only way their marriage makes any sense is if it is meant to manifest "Jesus' embodied, self-sacrificial love for us."[12] This is why we have to renounce the sexual prosperity view of marriage just as vigorously as Jesus renounces Peter's echo of Satan that there's a way to avoid the cross (Mark 8:33–34).

If the gospel includes the suffering of the cross, and if marriage is meant to embody the gospel, then all marriages are impossible in human terms. Given how my Christian subculture has often demonized same-sex attraction, I'm tempted to say that Laurie and Matt's marriage is impossible because Laurie is generally attracted to women, not men. But sexual orientation isn't the ultimate issue. Laurie and Matt remind us that we straight people have an orientation problem too: we are naturally oriented toward sinful selfishness, not self-sacrificial faithful covenant love.[13]

This notion of an "impossible marriage" hits exactly the right biblical chord. When Jesus explains marriage to his disciples, he goes back to God's creational intentions and says that faithful covenant love means that divorce is not permissible except in cases of sexual immorality. His disciples are shocked at this standard of faithful covenant love! Their response is telling: "If this is the situation between a husband and wife, it is better not to marry" (Matt. 19:10). In other words, that is impossible! My question to you is this: When Christians describe marriage, do people say, as the disciples did, "Wow, that sounds hard. Sign me up for singleness!"?

We usually pitch marriage as a romantic relationship where you'll be fulfilled in every way. Jesus did just the opposite. Dietrich Bonhoeffer said, "When Christ calls a man, he bids him come and die."[14] Based on what we've learned above, we can put a twist on that famous quote: "When Jesus calls people to marriage, he bids them come and die." The apostle Paul doesn't shy away from this reality either. He puts it bluntly: "Those who marry will face many troubles in this life" (1 Cor. 7:28). (As a professor, I offer extra credit to any engaged students who would put this verse on the front of their wedding program. For some reason, I can't get anyone to take me up on this.) Although marriage certainly brings numerous blessings, the Bible is clear that this path of love is also a path of suffering. To embody the gospel, then, our marriages will need to learn the path of forgiveness, the path of loving our enemies. In other words, loving our spouses.

It might seem strange to think of a spouse as an enemy. But in one sense, they are. Think about it. Who will hurt you more over the course of your life, in big and small ways, than your spouse? Whose mere presence will constantly call you out beyond yourself and your selfishness? Who will say and do things that are not morally wrong but that you find irritating beyond belief? Who knows just what to say to really stick the knife in and turn it just so? Who will sin against you more in your life than your spouse?

Although he is not talking about marriage, Russian novelist Fyodor Dostoyevsky captures well what happens when our high ideals about love come crashing into the reality of living in close quarters with someone:

> The more I love humanity in general the less I love man in particular. In my dreams . . . I often make plans for the service of humanity, and perhaps I might actually face crucifixion if it were suddenly necessary. Yet I am incapable of living in the same room with anyone for two days together. I know from experience. As soon as anyone is near me, his personality disturbs me and restricts my freedom. In twenty-four

hours I begin to hate the best of men: one because he's too long over his dinner, another because he has a cold and keeps on blowing his nose. I become hostile to people the moment they come close to me. But it has always happened that the more I hate men individually the more I love humanity.[15]

Most of us tend to idealize and proclaim our love for humanity in general while struggling to love those particular humans closest to us. Love sounds good until you have to put it into practice. Because of this, walking the path of forgiveness and faithfulness is perhaps the most central way your marriage can embody the gospel. So how do we forgive?

A first step is simply naming sin for what it is. In other words, forgiveness doesn't mean I gloss over sin or act like it's no big deal. I want to be clear here: We must not justify abuse of any kind. All too often, the language of suffering and forgiveness is used as a theological justification for abuse within a marriage. That is biblically and theologically unacceptable. If someone engages in ongoing abusive behavior, it needs to be named, acknowledged, and made known to those who need to know to ensure the safety and care of all parties, including bringing in pastors, therapists, and/or civil authorities where relevant. Forgiveness doesn't mean suppressing or avoiding the truth that my spouse can, does, and will sin against me, as I do against them. The more we buy into the notion that marriage is a place of ease, connection, and romance, the less likely we will be to acknowledge that we are both sinners and that the road of any marriage will be one of inevitable suffering.

In order to forgive, we also have to fix our eyes on Jesus and truly embrace our own need for the gospel. When my spouse sins against me, I have to recognize that my first impulse is to focus on the injustice she has done and start working out the moral calculus of what she needs to do to make things right. I am tempted to take it upon myself to punish my spouse for what she has done wrong and withhold my love and care until she makes it right. And let's be honest, many of the day-to-day "injustices" we spouses worry about are not big things, but the little mundane grievances that repeat over time.

I find myself having to embrace my own need for the gospel when it comes to the small, everyday matters. Who's gotten up with the early-rising kids more? Yes, it's true that she breastfed all six kids with all the nighttime feedings that requires, but I get up first with them Sundays through Fridays, and that still happens even now that they are all weaned. So why am I stuck with this ongoing task in our household pattern?

But this self-righteous, performance-based approach to marriage needs to come to the foot of the cross. I need to stop and ask what I am angry about. Well, in part, I'm angry that the prosperity gospel doesn't seem to be working out. *I* did what *I* am supposed to as a good husband, but *I* am not getting what *I* deserve! It's at this point that I need to stop and fix my eyes on Jesus. And I don't mean that just figuratively. I literally stop what I'm doing, picture Jesus on the cross, and meditate on Philippians 2:5–11, which talks about how Jesus completely humbled himself and died for me. When I do that, it's very apparent that *he* did not get what *he* deserves. Rather, he has taken my suffering on himself. When we see him and his great love for us, his Spirit enables us to embody that same love toward our spouses.

Jesus's self-giving, suffering love was not a one-time event but the central posture of his life. So we should ask, "How do I embody the love of Jesus *every day*? After all, the cross was a one-time event; loving my spouse is not!" This is a fair question. Wendell Berry points out that we tend to gravitate to the stories of characters (including biblical characters) who perform one-time acts of heroism rather than those who perform everyday acts of faithfulness. In contrast, Berry contends that a courageous, faithful life is not so much about singular heroic acts but about perseverance. As he puts it, "It may, in some ways, be easier to be Samson than to be a good husband or wife day after day for fifty years."[16]

Jesus's suffering, self-giving love was not a one-time act but the shape of his whole life. The cross of Christ was not an anomaly but the

147

natural consequence of Jesus's entire ministry, which was shaped by self-giving love. For example, when Jesus proclaims the arrival of God's kingdom—the good news it means for Gentiles as well as the bad news for some of the house of Israel—the people of his hometown try to kill him (Luke 4:14–30). When Jesus enacts the kingdom of God, welcoming sinners and tax collectors to eat with him, he suffers the anger of the religious leaders of the day. In his life and ministry, Jesus suffered with no regular home and place of comfort to call his own (Luke 9:58). When faced with Lazarus's death and Mary and Martha's grief, Jesus suffered deep grief (John 11:33–35). When he pondered the path of the cross, Jesus's soul was troubled (John 12:27), and as he prayed, his suffering was such that he sweat drops of blood (Luke 22:44). Suffering love was not a one-time act in Jesus's life.

As we follow Jesus, we are called to die daily, to live a consistent pattern of self-giving love. Sometimes I act as though I can ignore the daily demands of love in my marriage but try for sporadic, heroic acts of suffering and service to try to rectify things. But as I fix my eyes on Jesus, I see that the cross is the culmination and continuation of a daily life of consistency that is poured out for his bride, the church.

In contrast to the story of sexual prosperity, the gospel focuses on the suffering Savior and what it means to follow him as single and married members of God's household. Like the story of sexual prosperity, the story of romance focuses our attention on our significant other as the source of fulfillment. In contrast, the gospel holds out the promise of fulfillment in God alone. Yet that fulfillment does not exclude human community. Rather, those who find rest in God are called into the household of faith, the family of God.

PART 4

CHAPTER 11

THE MYTH OF NATURALISM

"Your Body Is Matter in Motion"

The stories of individualism and romance emphasize that I need to create and express myself and find a soulmate who acknowledges and affirms that authentic self. But those two stories are interwoven and interdependent with a third: the story of naturalism. It says that matter has no meaning, that there is no inherent meaning in nature/creation or in our physical bodies. The material world is simply matter in motion. This meaningless world of matter is the flip side of individualism, where the "real me" is an invisible, nonmaterial reality that is expressed through the body but has no inherent connection to the body.

WHAT'S THE STORY OF NATURALISM?

The TV show *Ted Lasso* was an instant hit because the titular Ted is so optimistic, encouraging, and inspirational. Beyond that, though, Coach Lasso sees people *as people*, not simply objects to be used on his own path to success. His attentiveness to people and his ability to connect with them in a deep way are key aspects of his success as a coach. The one deviation from this depth comes when Ted has a one-night stand with his boss Rebecca's friend Sassy. Feeling guilty about the situation, Ted consults his friends, one of whom asks why Ted is beating himself up over this, noting that Ted hasn't done anything wrong. And his assistant coach, Beard, narrows the focus to one question: Was it fun? Ted acknowledges that it was, and that seems to be that. Unlike Ted's behavior in virtually all other episodes of the first season, the sense that something deeper is going on is lacking. And while that may be inconsistent for the character Ted Lasso, it was certainly consistent with the show *Ted Lasso,* which often features unrelenting sexual references and encounters in a very casual manner. In this way, the show certainly embodies and purveys key elements of our secular age, including a focus on individual authenticity and romance combined with a view of bodies and sex as primarily physical and recreational.

Who or what are we as humans? According to naturalism, we are nothing but matter in motion, animals who are born, breed, and die. We have certain physical needs and urges, and sex is central among them. But there is no bigger picture and no deeper, spiritual dimension to material reality or the human body.

This view of sex and the body is summarized by philosopher Caroline Simon, who calls it the "plain sex" view. Drawing on the thought of Alan Goldman, Simon notes that, for this view, "sexuality is now best seen as simply an acute physical desire for an intensely pleasurable physical activity that naturally leads to engaging in bodily exploration and intensely pleasurable activity."[1] In other words, this view asserts that connecting sex with love and commitment is an unnecessary cultural construct. Perhaps some cultures have made these links, but there is nothing about physical sexual activity that inherently entails some kind of ethical commitment or involvement. Thus, rather than loading more ethical weight onto sex than it should bear, we can perhaps see that it is nothing more than a physical, animal urge that needs to be properly channeled.

This view of sex and bodies, though, stems from an entire story about how to understand the world and our place in it as humans. Christians need to understand the story of naturalism for two key reasons. First, we may unknowingly adopt and adapt practices arising from the story of naturalism into the biblical story and our lives. Second, we need to understand the appeal of naturalism so we can see how the gospel tells an even better story that meets our deepest needs and longings. With that in mind, let's look at key components of the story of naturalism and see how it affects our thinking and practice in our secular age.

Where are we? How do we name reality? We use the term *nature* all the time to talk about the natural world and our place within it, but Norman Wirzba draws attention to the fact that this naming is not neutral.[2] In fact, Wirzba points out that there is a fundamental difference between seeing the world as creation and seeing the world as nature.[3] When we adopt the biblical view of the world as God's creation, we see it as an icon through which the love of God is poured out and seen. Unlike atheism or the watchmaker God of deism who winds up the world and then steps back, the biblical view of God is that he is constantly present to and with his creation and is continuously interacting with the world.

In contrast, the modern view of the world as nature sees it as "a self-standing or autonomous realm, a material mechanism or random biological process that has no life or purpose in God."[4] As scientist Edward O. Wilson summarizes, "All tangible phenomena, from the birth of stars to the workings of social institutions, are based on material processes that are ultimately reducible . . . to the laws of physics."[5] In other words, all reality is matter in motion. This way of telling the story, this way of seeing the world, has profound effects on how we diagnose what's wrong with reality and what should be done about it.

What's wrong with reality? And what should we do about it? According to the story of naturalism, the first step is to increase our knowledge of nature. This is why our culture values science so much. If we can understand nature, we can understand why it sometimes produces suffering. And if we can alter nature so that human suffering is diminished and human flourishing is increased, we will have made life better than it was before us. Note carefully the villain in this story: nature itself. As ethicist Allen Verhey puts it, "Nature is the enemy. Nature may be—and must be—mastered. It may be—and must be—altered."[6] Humanity is thus pitted in a constant battle with nature, where "nature threatens to rule and ruin humanity."[7]

Of course, this is not merely a battle with elements outside of us but a battle that runs through us. We are part of nature, physical beings who are constantly under attack from disease without and decay within, so "the nature we are is the nature we suffer from."[8] That is, nature is fundamentally ambiguous, something that allows us some level of understanding and control of the world, but also something that often rules over us more than we control it.

It's worth letting this point sink in: The story of naturalism sees bodies as the enemy. This might seem counterintuitive because the story is often told that Christianity looks down on bodies and, in contrast, naturalism embraces the fact that we are material creatures. There may be an element of truth in this, but our modern society also sees bodies as the enemy because they are ultimately part of nature. Bodies limit us. They, in some ways, define us and tell us who we are. The body is thus something to be managed and perhaps even overcome and transcended through science, medicine, and technology.

If Christianity has sometimes valued the soul over the body, then modern naturalism has done something similar in valuing the mind over the body. The mind allows us to manage nature, to manage our bodies and bring them into subjection to our will and desires. In that way, far from valuing our bodies as they are, the story of naturalism charts a path with the goal of complete dominion over the body by the (immaterial?) mind.[9]

So what is the solution to the problem of nature's unpredictable rule over us? For the story of naturalism, the solution is found in technology. Science allows us to better understand the world, and technology enables us to gain greater mastery over things that were previously out of our control. Our advances in technology produce numerous benefits, and we profit from them every day. For example, in the field of medicine, we can cure diseases and provide treatments for a myriad of ailments and illnesses. Matters that were once mysterious have become common knowledge. I am very thankful that scientists, doctors, and pharmacists have collaborated in ways that allow people to live remarkably better lives, at least physically, than in previous eras of history.

For example, scientists have been able to alter DNA for decades, but recent advances have led to the development of CRISPR (Clustered Regularly Interspaced Short Palindromic Repeats) technology. These are essentially "molecular scissors" that allow scientists to easily add, alter, or delete portions of any organism's DNA.[10] This technology can be used to alter mosquito DNA[11] in an effort to limit and ultimately eradicate malaria, a mosquito-borne disease that infected 241 million and killed 627,000 people worldwide in 2020 (over 480,000 of those deaths were children under 5 in Africa).[12] Science—the hero—conquers the villain of nature—annoying and deadly mosquitoes.

The applications of medical technology are deeply personal in many cases. In my family, my grandfather and two brothers have hemophilia, a genetic condition where the blood does not clot properly. For most of my grandpa's life, there was no real treatment for this. My brothers benefited from infusion treatments developed in the '80s and '90s, but the science has continued to advance at a light-speed pace, with clinical trials in gene therapy now reducing and in some cases apparently "curing" hemophilia.[13] Though the development of a cure is still in the early stages, I can hardly wrap my mind around the fact that a disease that had no treatment and wracked and crippled my grandpa's body could be essentially cured in my lifetime.

Yet the story of naturalism doesn't merely embrace science but often tends toward scient*ism*, which hails science and technology as our ultimate savior. Within this story, scientific knowledge is seen as the "paradigm of truth and rationality."[14] And our culture has largely embraced this scientism as a new form of religion, with scientific voices often operating with a kind of unquestioned authority that mirrors that of the Roman Catholic Church in medieval times.

But this story has some cracks in it. For starters, the story of naturalism generally assumes that human wellbeing inevitably follows from greater mastery over nature.[15] But is that *always* the case? As the character Ian Malcolm in *Jurassic Park* puts it, "Your scientists were so preoccupied with whether they could, they didn't stop to think if they should."[16] Malcolm's skepticism gets at the heart of the story of naturalism, which features a kind of technological determinism. That is, the essential assumption of this story is that any and every step of further technological mastery should be taken because it will inevitably be good. And it may seem that way for a while—at least until the velociraptors break loose and start killing people.[17] If we are honest, we will recognize that sometimes scientific and technological advancements produce unintended conditions and effects that lead to destruction and devastation rather than the flourishing of humanity or nature.

That was certainly the case for one of science's biggest mistakes: margarine. Or to be clearer: promoting margarine over butter. Margarine might seem innocent, especially when compared with fictional velociraptors, but Dr. Paul Offitt points out that it led to literally millions of deaths from heart disease.[18] In the twentieth century, scientists began uncovering the link between diet and heart disease, and some studies seemed to show a link to saturated fats, a category that includes butter. So what was the proposed solution? Switch to alternatives like margarine or other hydrogenated vegetable oils, which are unsaturated fats. In the mid-twentieth century, these products were far and away the most used products for baking and frying. Later studies revealed, however, that these products were deadly, the source of a quarter of a million heart attacks and related deaths per year. Over the course of decades, that's millions of people slowly killed by their food habits based on the best scientific research. It's true that science ultimately came to the right answer. But it's also true that the science, at least for a few decades, had the *wrong* answer. If science isn't infallible (a truth good scientists recognize), then we have to acknowledge that one day we might look at our best science today as nothing more than a big tub of margarine. My point is not to discount science, but to recognize the proper limits and scope of science so we don't veer into a kind of messianic scientism and naturalism, inflating what those things can actually provide.

Another effect of the story of naturalism is a sense of isolation and separation from each other. We see the mechanistic world as an object that we, as subjects, learn to control and engineer. But this means we no longer see ourselves as part of a larger, meaningful whole (creation) or as creatures of God, but rather as isolated selves seeking to master and manage the mechanistic processes of nature to bend them to our vision of what should be.[19] To be fair, this is the rationalistic strand of naturalism and doesn't necessarily reflect all of naturalism.

Another strand of naturalism is found in Romanticism, which looks at the whole as interconnected and interrelated (found today in a wide variety of "spiritual but not religious" people). The more rationalistic stream of naturalism can end up alienating us from nature, from other people, and even from our own bodies. Rather than seeing an interconnected and meaningful whole, we see particles, atoms, matter in motion that must be given meaning through our control and mastery. That's true not only of natural resources that we use and use up, but also of other people, other bodies. That is, our naturalism leads us to a place of utilitarianism, where something is good insofar as it is useful for making our (or just my) life better. So how does the story of naturalism show up in the way we use our bodies and in our everyday praxis?

157

EMBODYING NATURALISM:
GENDER IDENTITY AND MEDICAL TECHNOLOGY

The story of naturalism informs numerous practices around sex and bodies in our culture. Because sex and bodies, in this story, are simply matter in motion, pornography and hookup culture are widely accepted. Because sexual union is not a covenant-making act but is purely physical, objections to sex outside of marriage, cohabitation, and adultery are easily set aside. Another way (and one rapidly on the rise) that we embody the story of naturalism is through the use of hormones or surgery to alter one's sex or gender.

"I just wanted you to know that I'm transgender." This was a message from one of my favorite students. He (I use *he* because that's how he identified at the time) loved church history and led a book club that read Eusebius's *History of the Church* for fun—for fun! Plus, he loved Harry Potter, so we clicked immediately. I had several conversations with this student about issues surrounding gender identity, and he asked thoughtful questions. I knew he was wrestling with these questions, so I wasn't surprised when he messaged me and officially came out as transgender. I thanked him for his courage and willingness to share this with me. Our relationship didn't change much—we continued to have good conversations about church history and Harry Potter. After graduating, he officially changed his name to a feminine name, began cross-sex hormone therapy (CHT), and transitioned to presenting socially as a woman.

In recent decades, it has become common for transgender people who desire to transition socially and physically to embrace CHT. Some go further and undertake sex reassignment surgery (SRS). To be clear, *transgender* is "an umbrella term for the many ways in which people might experience and/or present and express (or live out) their gender identities differently from people whose sense of gender identity is congruent with their biological sex."[20] Because this is an umbrella term, people can mean a wide variety of things when they identify as *transgender*. And there are various approaches to medical interventions like CHT and SRS.

So how should we think about these kinds of medical interventions? This is a highly complex topic, so I can't pretend to address all of the conceptual, personal, and pastoral concerns here.[21] Before digging into this specific use of medical technology, it's worth taking a step back and asking a much broader question: Is it morally legitimate to change or enhance the human body in any way we want?

This question might sound like science fiction, but it's a pertinent question today. Can we custom design babies so they have the hair color or body shape we desire? If you could, would you take a pill that unleashed the full potential of the human mind? If you could harness science and technology to alter your body so you could transcend normal human boundaries, would you? (Both failed and successful attempts to do so usually produce the origin stories of villains and superheroes alike in the mythology of many comic-book universes.) Asking these questions helps us see that there are two ways to use science, medicine, and technology with respect to our bodies: to remedy something that has gone wrong (remedial) or to enhance something that is working just fine (enhancement).

For example, if I break my arm, my doctor will set it and take measures to ensure that what has gone wrong will be made right and that full healing will take place. In contrast, if my doctor were to suggest that my basketball skills would be greatly enhanced if he could add a third arm to my body, that would be enhancement. This example is absurd, of course, but we often undertake procedures that are purely for the sake of enhancement and have nothing to do with remedying a malfunctioning body. It is a huge industry. People get various forms of plastic surgery because a body part or their body type does not fit their desired ideal. There is no medical reason for these procedures—nothing has gone wrong in the body—rather, the body has failed to align with the ideal in someone's mind.

Sometimes the same exact procedure can be remedial or enhancing, depending on the case. If someone gets into a car accident that causes damage, and they need reconstructive nose surgery, elements of that procedure can and should be done by a plastic surgeon who specializes in cosmetic surgery. That is an example of remedial treatment. The same doctor could do a nose job on someone else, however, who simply wants a nose of a different size or shape, and it would be a surgery that is not necessary in any medical sense. It's not fixing something that is wrong but changing the body to fit our image of what we want the body to be and do.

The naturalistic notion that we can change our body in any way we desire has flowered into the movement known as transhumanism. Transhumanism views humanity as merely one cluster of characteristics on an evolutionary scale. To be clear, the problem here is the philosophical assumption that being "human" is the result of a completely natural process with no purpose or goal. In other words, there is no reason (theologically or philosophically) why we are the way we are, and there is no reason to stay the way we are. Remember, for naturalism, the problem is the way nature, including our own bodies, does not conform to the reality we desire. Thus, advocates of transhumanism argue for "morphological freedom," the use of technology to change the body in any way we might desire. Researcher and futurist Anders Sandberg summarizes this concept: "If my pursuit of happiness requires a bodily change—be it dying [sic] my hair or changing my sex—then my right to freedom requires a right to morphological freedom."[22] In this concept, we see a key marker of naturalism, in that the body itself does not have inherent meaning but is raw matter to be fashioned in whatever way the mind or will desires.

This priority of mind over matter seems to be the dominant idea behind cross-sex hormone therapy and sex reassignment surgery. Preston Sprinkle crystallizes the main philosophical, bioethical, and theological question this way: "If someone experiences incongruence between their biological sex and their internal sense of self, which one determines who they are—and why?"[23] The story of naturalism, combined with the individualism we explored earlier, predisposes our culture to answer this question with "internal sense of self."

For individualism, it's an affront for someone else to try to define who I really am. Only I have the right to do that. For naturalism, my body is just matter in motion, potentially an obstacle to me being the "real me" just as much as any external person. I didn't choose my body, so in a way, I might have to "overcome" my sexed body so the "real me" can be properly expressed and realized.

The bioethical issue here, though, is that medical technology is not being used in a remedial way but rather for enhancement, altering something essential about who we are as embodied creatures. That is, CHT and SRS are not treatments to fix an unhealthy body; they radically alter a healthy body. And unlike a nose job (which might commit the sin of vanity), these procedures are meant to alter the distinctive male and female features of the human body. From a biblical standpoint, upholding this embodied biological distinction, which is core to our identity as the image of God, is not incidental but essential to who we are.

EMBODYING NATURALISM: BIRTH CONTROL

I remember the first time my wife (then fiancée) and I went to Planned Parenthood. I never imagined darkening their door, given their advocacy for abortion, but the nurse at our Christian college had recommended that we go there to get free birth control. We were going to be married in the near future and were planning to move to Toronto, where I would pursue my master's degree and my wife would work to support us (I couldn't work with my student visa). Given those circumstances, we figured it made sense to wait to have kids.

My wife had taken a bioethics class that had made us aware that some forms of birth control might be abortifacient, but the consensus from that class and professor was that birth-control pills were not. In the course of thinking about family planning, we researched a number of different options. Growing up as good Christian kids, however, we knew that sex within marriage was okay and that abortion was wrong. Other than that, the question of family planning was simply a matter of personal preference. The idea that using contraceptives (including sterilization) within the context of marriage and family planning might have theological or ethical implications never crossed our minds.

There's a good reason for this: Churches all across the theological spectrum—from mainline churches like the Episcopal Church, United Methodist Church, and Evangelical Lutheran Church in America to evangelical churches like the Southern Baptist Convention and Pentecostal Assemblies of God—all see birth control as a matter of individual liberty and conscience. This theological stance is borne out in practice as well: Among women who do not want to get pregnant, 90 percent of mainline Protestants and 89 percent of evangelicals are using a contraceptive method. Even among Roman Catholics, whose church teaches that contraception within marriage *is* morally wrong, the numbers are the same: 89 percent use some form of contraception.[24]

Until 1930, all churches, not just the Roman Catholic Church, taught that contraception was wrong, even within (*especially* within) marriage. How did contraception become almost universally acceptable? As theologian Dennis Hollinger points out, "What is most significant about this change is not that it happened, but that there was so little theological reflection in the process."[25] According to Hollinger, in most Protestant circles (mainline and evangelical), this shift happened without careful biblical and theological argumentation; the broader culture shifted, and the church simply shifted as well. This fact makes me pause. If every body tells a story, then what story does birth control tell about sex, bodies, and marriage?

To understand how birth control is linked to the story of naturalism, we need to consider how naturalism views bodies generally and sex in particular. I use the term *birth control* here to refer to any means of disconnecting sexual union from conception and birth as the natural result of sexual union. My guess is that even approaching this topic might raise strong feelings and concerns among some readers from a variety of angles. What about couples who are infertile? What about women who need to take the pill for health reasons? Are you saying women are just baby-making machines? Are you saying couples can't choose to delay having children if God is calling them to something else, perhaps adoption? What about the world's population and the strain on the environment? Are you telling me what I can and can't do with my body? These are all relevant questions, and I promise we will work through each one in chapter 12. My goal is to see how every body tells a story and to understand how we embody the story of naturalism. The practice of birth control is worth examining because it is a prime example of how we can adopt a practice that profoundly affects our bodies without necessarily thinking through the deeper story woven into that practice.

The first thing to keep in mind here is that, for naturalism, the body itself is not significant or meaningful. That is, our body is matter in motion and merely serves as the housing for and source of our mind or self. But our body does not in and of itself *mean* anything. Our bodies are not the image, the physical icon, of God. For naturalism, we are not the result of a teleological process—that is, a process with a purpose or goal. Rather, we are a complex piece of biological machinery. Sex, then, is simply a biological act without a deeper meaning. It is what it is.

For the story of naturalism, the fact that sexual union produces children does not tell us anything about the morality of sex or what should be the case. It's just a scientific fact about the nature of things. So what happens if the children who might result from sex are not wanted? Can we intervene to prevent procreation as a result of sex? The story of naturalism says yes. But why? Here's where we need to return to the previously discussed concepts of medicine as remedial versus medicine as enhancement.

With those concepts in mind, a key question is this: What sickness or illness does birth control treat? Is it remedial or enhancement? In his book surveying the history of the birth-control pill, Bernard Asbell answers that question: "The Pill has led each of us, women and men alike and in a most personal sense, into a new era of potential mastery over our bodies and ourselves. As the first systemic contraceptive, it altered the routine functioning of the healthy human body. It opened the gateway to what I shall call the Era of BioIntervention . . . it is taking us beyond medicine into an eventual ability to modify—genetically—other body functions as well as our physical form itself."[26]

Asbell clearly charts the connection between the pill and the story of naturalism. This use of medical technology is not remedial but enhancing. It is not about fixing what goes wrong with our bodies, but about altering bodies that are perfectly healthy. Far from affirming or embracing our bodies and the natural limits of the healthy human body, naturalism seeks to completely subjugate the body to the will and the mind. For many people, including many Christians, the practice of birth control does not seem to be morally problematic because it flows from our cultural autopilot of naturalism, which sees nature and the body as merely matter in motion to be controlled and mastered. If there is a consequence we want to avoid (in this case, children), we should do what needs to be done to prevent that unwanted result. In other words, we embody the story of naturalism.

CHAPTER 12

THE STORY OF GOD'S MISSION

"Your Body Is God's Home"

Let's go back to one of our driving questions: What are bodies for? What is the foundational story that we are called to embody? In 1 Corinthians, the apostle Paul works hard to set right the Corinthians' confused way of thinking about a number of matters, including bodies. As new Christians, the Corinthians lacked clarity about what following Jesus meant for their lives, including their sex lives. One man was sleeping with his stepmother (1 Cor. 5:1), and apparently a number of men were having sex with prostitutes, a practice that was considered standard male behavior in their time and place (1 Cor. 6:15). On the opposite end of the spectrum, some Corinthians were teaching that having sex at all was evil and wrong—even for husband and wife! In the midst of this discussion, Paul says something that should transform our thinking about bodies and serve as a powerful antidote to the myth of naturalism and the notion that our bodies are nothing more than matter in motion.

Paul first tells us what bodies are *not* for: "The body . . . is not meant for sexual immorality" (1 Cor. 6:13). I have to admit, when I hear Paul say this, I start to anticipate what I think he's going to say next. In my mind, it sounds like a lot of youth-group sex talks. Don't have sex outside of marriage. Flee sexual immorality. And on the flip side, "The body is meant for sexual morality." Be good. Be moral. Have sex but keep it within marriage. Do what you are supposed to do. Or maybe, "The body is meant for your spouse, not a prostitute."

But Paul doesn't say that. He ups the ante and jumps right past instructions about sexual morality or spouses. He gets to the heart of the question: What are bodies for? The body is "for the Lord, and the Lord for the body." In other words, the end goal of your body—of you—is that you become a member of Christ himself, so much so that "your bodies are temples of the Holy Spirit." (1 Cor. 6:13, 19). Let's stop for a minute and let this sink in. What does it mean that our bodies are temples of the Holy Spirit?[1]

WHO ARE WE? OUR BODIES, GOD'S HOME

Throughout Scripture, we see that God's desire and intention is to live with, to abide with, to dwell with his people. When God calls out the people of Israel from Egypt, his goal is to dwell with them (Ex. 29:44–46; Lev. 26:11–12). In the Old Testament, the central dwelling place of God with his people is the tabernacle and then the temple. They were God's home on earth, the center of God's presence and power.

Because of God's glory and power, though, the tabernacle and temple were not to be taken lightly. God is good, but not safe, to paraphrase C. S. Lewis's famous saying about Aslan. There is a weight, a majesty, a gravity that comes with the glory of God's presence. It is a reminder of the calling to respond faithfully to God's action. As the Israelites live faithfully as God's people, the surrounding peoples and nations will see who God is and be drawn to God (Isa. 2:2–3). At the dedication of the temple, Solomon reminds the Israelites of this purpose: God has blessed them and called them to follow him with all their hearts "so that all the peoples of the earth may know that the LORD is God and that there is no other" (1 Kings 8:60).

Think about what it means to say our bodies are now God's temple. Our bodies are the dwelling place of the God of the universe. Our bodies are God's home on earth. Our bodies are the place where God's mission is launched and where his presence is made known to a watching world.

Too often, we reduce Christianity to some kind of benefit that comes from God's presence with us or his work on our behalf. In other words, we want God for the benefits he brings rather than for his own sake. But first we have to grasp that God wants to dwell with us and that our bodies—our physical, fleshy, material, mundane bodies—are God's temple today. Far from being disposable, meaningless, or a problem to be fixed, Scripture wants us to see that our bodies are the place where the presence and the story of the invisible God are made manifest. Just as the crucified and resurrected body of Jesus accomplishes and reveals God's faithfulness on our behalf, so our bodies today continue that story and point to the work of Christ for us.

EMBODYING THE GOSPEL: RELEASING CONTROL AND EMBRACING CHILDREN

The gospel says that our bodies are God's home, which sounds great but also a bit abstract. In chapter 14 below, we'll dig into how this shapes marriage and singleness, but I want to focus on one question here that stems from our discussion in the previous chapter: What does the gospel have to do with using birth control, especially in the context of family planning? We often approach ethical questions like these through a somewhat legalistic framework, where we focus on a specific act and ask whether it's right or wrong. Biblically, we zero in on a few specific verses and debate whether there is a specific command or prohibition about this topic. Or, especially with a complex topic like this, we throw our hands up and just encourage people to be wise and make the best choice they can.

In what follows, I want to think bigger and broader. I want to reflect on how the gospel informs our view of the body, using the framework we have established thus far to inform the way we think about our attempts to control our fertility and infertility. I want to ask how embracing the limits of our bodies, and thus the reality of children, embodies the gospel before a watching world.

Now you might be thinking, *Wait a second, didn't you say earlier that you and your wife used free contraceptives (the pill, in our case) from Planned Parenthood when you were first married?* Yes. Part of our own journey as a couple has been a shift from using contraception to embracing the path of theologically and scientifically informed natural family planning taught in books like *The Art of Family Planning* and support groups like the Couple to Couple League.[2] This wasn't merely an intellectual journey, though. It was a deeply personal and painful one that included the loss of our son.

When we decided we were ready to have kids, my wife, Sarah, got pregnant almost right away. However, our first pregnancy ended in a miscarriage at around 12 weeks. A few months later, we were expecting again. We made it past the 12-week threshold and were elated to find out that we were expecting a son at our 20-week ultrasound. A few days later, however, our joy turned to dread. Sarah's water broke, and she was hospitalized. The doctors tried to slow the labor that had been initiated, but things were in motion that couldn't be stopped.

Our son Stephen was born right around 22 weeks. The day he was born, the doctors talked to us about our options. Their neonatal equipment was made for small babies, but not that small. Either they could take him away as soon as he was born and try to work to save him, even though their equipment wouldn't fit his small body, or we could spend a short time with him. We were devastated. What were we supposed to do? In that moment, it was clear that God was saying, "There's nothing more than can be done beyond letting go." We asked our pastor, "Is God okay with this?" He wrapped his arms around us and said, "God is right here with you. He loves you. It's okay to let go." We got to spend precious moments with our son Stephen. Then we let go. And God was in the letting go.

I had experienced loss and pain before, but losing Stephen reinforced how utterly not in control I really was. I like control. I've worked hard in my life to control a lot of things, including my education and career. I went to school, got my PhD, and got hired as a tenure-track professor at 27. But losing Stephen made me feel utterly out of control. It was not a good thing insofar as it involved death and loss, but insofar as it made me realize my place in the world—a creature, not the Creator—I can see that God was teaching me a lot about my posture in the world. It also made me realize that I took a basic posture of control toward having children. Like most good, modern people, I assumed that having children was one more life choice I could and should dictate and control through the use of medical technology. What if I'd been treating my own body, my wife's body, and the bodies of our children no different from the myth of naturalism, as matter in motion to be manipulated and controlled according to my expert (or so I thought) planning?

Not long after Stephen died, my wife, Sarah, challenged me to think more theologically about sex, bodies, and contraception. She was given a book by a friend titled *Theology of the Body for Beginners* by Christopher West, which outlined a theological vision of singleness, marriage, and sex that was winsome and compelling.[3] Being a good Protestant, I was admittedly suspicious of West's Roman Catholic background and his focus on the theological writings of Pope John Paul II. Not only did this book launch my interest in a theology of the body, but it also made us think practically about how big-picture theology connects with everyday practices of sex, including contraception. What follows in this chapter comes from both who I am as a theologian, someone who wrestles with big concepts, and also who I am as a husband and father, someone who is trying to be faithful to God's call in my everyday practice of sex. As we think about big theological concepts and everyday practical realities, we need to again root ourselves in the gospel.

When we reflect on the gospel and how it relates to sex and bodies, three things stand out. First, bodies matter. Matter matters. God has created us in his image with bodies that are good. The eternal Son of God has taken our humanity onto himself, including a body. Second, bodies are linked to God's covenant faithfulness. God makes and keeps covenant promises to us through the body of Jesus. In the cross and resurrection, Jesus gives himself fully to and for us. Similarly, sexual union between a man and woman is a covenant-making act. Marriage is a covenant, and sex is the sign and seal of that covenant. Third, God's covenant is made through the suffering body of Jesus. That is, the reality of God's faithful covenant love includes the dimension of suffering, as Jesus gives himself fully so that we might live. When we are drawn into that story, we see that we too are called to a life that is both self-giving and life-giving to others. Let's unpack in more detail how this story affects our view and practice of birth control and what we are saying with our bodies.

ONE FLESH

When it comes to marriage and sex, bodies matter. In sexual union, a man and woman enter into a covenant with one another. In other words, sex is a kind of body language that communicates a real, objective message. Sex is not something that is meaningless or just means whatever we make it mean. As we've seen, Genesis 4:1 speaks to the covenant-making nature of sexual union when it talks about Adam and Eve "knowing" one another in and through sexual union. But the story of Genesis 1–2 helps us see that this covenant occupies a central purpose and function in God's creation: producing and nurturing new life. In Genesis 1, we get a picture of the creativity, goodness, and life-giving love of God, who brings all things into being and gives all life what it needs to flourish. In the context of creating humanity as male and female, God declares words of blessing and calls them to "be fruitful and multiply" (Gen. 1:28 NLT). This is at least one key dimension of what it means to bear God's image.

The Trinitarian God is an eternal communion of life and love. This complete and perfect love, however, is not self-enclosed or self-contained; rather, God's abundant and perfect love overflows and gives life to all creation, to you and me. God's love is the source of all life. And God has powerfully woven this dimension of who he is into our very biology and being. As husband and wife know each other in the covenant act of sexual union, the result is new life. That is not just an accidental feature of biology, but a profound spiritual truth. The biology of our bodies tells the story of the Trinitarian God.

The fact that sexual union is a covenant-making act profoundly affects our theology of children. Children are not merely a bundle of biology but are persons made in the image of God. But there's another dimension to how we should think about children: They are the embodied, "one flesh" sign and seal of the marriage covenant of their parents. In Genesis 2:24, marriage is seen as a one-flesh union, where two people are joined in this new covenantal relationship. There are layers to the phrase "one flesh," including a focus on creating a new family or kinship group and the one-flesh act of sexual union. But "one flesh" also reflects the reality that children embody in themselves the one-flesh union of their parents. They are the one flesh in which two have become one. Their very existence is rooted in the covenant of their parents.

We can see how children embody the marriage covenant from a different angle when we think about the way divorce affects children. As Andrew Root points out, divorce is painful for children not merely on a psychological or even spiritual level, but on an ontological level.[4] That is, divorce strikes at the core of the being of the child. If my very being stems from my parents' marriage, their covenant, then the dissolution of that covenant is, in a sense, the undoing of the root of my existence.

In the movie *Back to the Future*, Marty McFly goes back to the 1950s, when his parents were just meeting and starting to date. Part of his existential crisis in that movie is that if his parents don't get together, then his very existence will be undone. As it begins to look like his parents won't, in fact, connect, he looks at a physical picture of himself and his siblings from the 1980s and they begin to fade. Their being is rooted in their parents' covenant.

In the same way, divorce undermines a child's source of existence. The pain of divorce reinforces the power of marriage: It is the source of life itself. As someone whose parents are divorced, I can't help but feel that this sounds rather bleak for those of us who walk that road. But Root's intent isn't to leave us in despair but to point out the true nature of the pain experienced by children of divorce. Who we are, our very being, is mirrored in our foundational relationships, including the parent-child relationship. When that mirror is cracked, it's even more important that the church, through its praise, proclamation, and education, show young people who they are as children of God and where they belong: in the church family.[5]

THE NEW ADAM AND THE NEW EVE

We need to see how Jesus gives himself to us, the church, in order to see why the question of fruitfulness, or having children, is linked to the gospel.[6] Jesus also gives himself to us freely. In other words, Jesus wasn't forced to love us by anything outside of himself. He chose to enter our world, to seek and serve us, freely of his own accord, because that is his character.

Jesus gives himself to us totally. He holds nothing back from us. Body and soul, he pours out his life for us, even to the point of death, so we might have life. This is a completely self-giving love.

Jesus also gives himself to us faithfully. His love is unfailing. It doesn't waver, quit, walk out, or back down. His love is not conditional or a one-time deal. He has loved us from all eternity. That love is revealed fully on the cross, and even death could not hold back or overcome his great love for us! His love is faithful.

Finally, Jesus gives himself to us in a fruitful way. That is, when Jesus gives himself to us, the result is new life. He comes in order to bring us life and bring it more abundantly. By his Spirit, we are born again, born from above. He is the new Adam, and we as the church are the new Eve. Just as the first Adam entered a deep sleep and Eve was formed from his side, so Jesus's side was pierced on the cross, producing blood and water (birth imagery), and he was put to the sleep of death so we might be brought to new life, born from above by the Spirit. Jesus's free, total, faithful love does not return void but bears fruit and produces new life.

The covenant love of Christ for the church is embodied in the covenant of marriage, according to Ephesians 5:21–33. There, Paul notes that marriage, the covenantal and sexual oneness of husband and wife, is meant to embody the story of Christ and the church. In other words, to properly reflect the love of Christ and the church, sexual union should exhibit the characteristics of free, total, faithful, and fruitful love. Let's unpack these a bit more and think about how they relate to the question of children and birth control.

First, the fact that sexual union should be freely entered into is largely obvious to our culture, which rightly values consent. Any kind of forced sexual relationship violates the character not only of proper human love, but of Christ's love as well, which is freely given. If sex is forced, that force violates the fundamental, objective meaning of sex and the way it is meant to point to Christ's love for the church.

Second, the notion that sexual union is a total giving of the self explains why reducing sex to just a physical act misses the point. Because we as humans are whole and holistic creatures—body and soul—what we do with our bodies affects and involves our whole selves, our whole persons.

Third, sexual union makes the promise of faithfulness, that this relationship is not just a one-time interaction but part of a covenant that makes and keeps promises. To have sex is to promise to be around for your spouse, not only the next day, but also the next year and the rest of your life.

Fourth, freely giving your whole self to your spouse in sexual union involves an openness to the possibility of new life. This biological reality is simultaneously a spiritual reality about the whole purpose of sex and marriage. When spouses give themselves to each other in this free, total, and faithful act, new life (fruitfulness) becomes a real possibility.

BIRTH CONTROL AND FRUITFULNESS

If matter matters, if sex actually says and does something (makes or renews a covenant), then what are we saying with our bodies when we alter them in order to still have sex but avoid the possibility of new life as a result? If sex is meant to be free, total, faithful, and fruitful, are we fully embodying the gospel when we choose to alter our body's fruitfulness? I know this is not the typical question Christians ask when considering whether or when to have kids or whether or when to use birth control or undergo sterilization procedures. But just as the free, total, faithful love of Jesus is aimed at fruitfulness, at giving new life to you and me, so also the free, total, faithful love of spouses in marriage is aimed (at least in part) at fruitfulness, at bringing forth new life from love.

We need to recognize that, on a cultural level and an individual level, when we remove the fruitful, life-giving dimension of sex, the other three dimensions almost inevitably get removed as well. In other words, once we say that sex has nothing to do with children and new life, we generally end up saying that sex is not really faithful, free, or total (I'll address the obvious question about how this relates to infertility below).

Why does the story of naturalism emphasize absolute control over the fruitfulness of our bodies? Let me state the obvious: Kids complicate things. Less obvious is this: Kids force the story of naturalism to acknowledge the free, total, and faithful dimensions of sex. In other words, children explode naturalism's story that sex doesn't mean anything, that sex is just about matter in motion, that sex is nothing more than a physical urge to be satisfied by a purely physical act. The fact that children result from sex inscribes us into the much bigger story of the gospel, the story of self-giving and life-giving love. The fruitful result of sex reinforces that sex is meant to be faithful, total, and free.

When a child is in the picture, we acknowledge that some level of faithfulness and commitment is inherent in sex. Even if it's just financial support, we recognize that this person is the result of sex and that the promise to care for them is built into that act. This faithfulness to our children grows out of the faithfulness we promise to the one with whom we have sex. Though our culture acts as though sex does not obligate us or connect us in a fundamental way to another person, children disprove that. It's no wonder, then, that a culture that downplays faithfulness would attempt to engineer sex so we can eliminate any possibility of obligation stemming from sex.

Further, a child serves as a reminder that sex involves more than just bodies; it involves total persons. The child is not just a bundle of biology; the child is a person. Their connection to their parents is not merely biological but deeply personal. The story of naturalism attempts to deny this in its affirmation of abortion. If sex is nothing but matter in motion, then the result of sex, a child, is just matter in motion as well, to be disposed of when inconvenient or unwanted. The reality of a child as a person, however, disrupts and dispels the notion that sexual union is mere matter in motion.

Finally, the reality of the child is a reminder that sex is meant to be entered into freely. Freedom and responsibility go together. We do not hold people responsible for things they do involuntarily. If sex were nothing more than the result of a necessary, involuntary physical urge, then we could not and would not hold parents responsible for caring for their children. But we do. Even when there is a divorce or a parent is not part of the same household as their child, the common practice of child support recognizes that there is not only freedom but also responsibility in this relationship. The fact that we see parents as obligated to care for and provide for their children reminds us of the promise and covenant built into the act of sexual union. The one-flesh covenant act of sexual union forms the one flesh of the child, the embodied reality that, in sex, two become one (Gen. 2:24).

PRACTICAL QUESTIONS ABOUT FERTILITY

Our culture as a whole, including Christians, does not often connect children with the meaning of sex. Understandably, my contention that they are connected raises a number of practical questions. Working through these questions should clarify further the links between the meaning of sex, marriage, children, and bodies, as well as give pastoral guidance on how to think and live with respect to these matters. These kinds of detailed, practical questions might seem obscure. We might be tempted to say, "Who cares? Just love Jesus." But here again we need to recognize that our bodies matter. If every body tells a story, these kinds of questions have to be considered in light of the big story we want to tell with our bodies.

On the other hand, we might be tempted to go along with our culture and see these as questions of personal preference and concern. But if our goal is to embody the gospel, we need to think carefully and biblically about significant questions that affect everyday life. I don't pretend to be able to answer every question or speak to the complexity of every person's situation here. But these are some of the most common general questions that I often hear on this topic.

WHAT ABOUT COUPLES WHO ARE INFERTILE?

This is a huge question. Does this approach imply that infertile couples are somehow lesser than those who can have children? Am I saying that somehow their marriage isn't complete or legit because they physically cannot have children? No. In fact, when we see the biblical link between marriage and children, it helps us understand and affirm the deep pain that often stems from infertility. It may be helpful to think through how this approach stands in contrast to the story of naturalism on the question of infertility. If our bodies are just matter in motion, then infertility is simply a biological fact. If I desire a child, that's simply a subjective, personal preference. If I cannot have children due to infertility, the logical response of naturalism is to try my best to change my desires. I just need to get over it because there's no inherent connection between marriage, sex, and children. Or another option is to embrace assisted reproductive technologies, which many people use without fully understanding the theological and ethical implications of this technology.

In contrast, recognizing the link between marriage, sex, and children enables us to truly weep with those who weep. The desire for children isn't just an individual preference but something that is built into the structure of sex and marriage. The love of husband and wife for one another is meant to be life-giving. When it is not, there is grief, and the approach outlined here allows us to affirm that such grief is deeply rooted in the way God intended the world to be. This approach, far from diminishing the marriage of infertile couples, actually allows a proper pastoral response to the struggle and grief of infertility.

At the same time, we also need to emphasize that God's mission for marriage is far more than just having children. If a couple's mission of making disciples does not include their own biological children, they need to ask how God is calling them to exercise hospitality and connect with those who need to know the good news of Jesus. The "how" and "what" of this mission may look a bit different from a marriage with children, but the fundamental "why" is the same.

MAY A MARRIED COUPLE CHOOSE NOT TO HAVE BIOLOGICAL CHILDREN AT ALL?

Based on the biblical links between the meaning of marriage, sex, and bodies, I believe married couples are called to be open to biological children and that saying "absolutely not" to children runs counter to the way sex and marriage are meant to embody the gospel. Openness to new life is part of the meaning of sex and marriage and the way that sex and marriage point to the reality of Christ and the church. I recognize that some couples choose not to have children for good reasons. Perhaps they feel especially called to adopt children who need parents. Perhaps they feel especially called to use their time and resources in focused ways that serve the kingdom of God. I understand the reasoning behind those kinds of choices. But if the self-giving, life-giving gospel is woven into the meaning of our bodies and the meaning of marriage, married people are called to be open to the possibility of children in order to embody the self-giving, life-giving gospel.

BUT CAN'T MARRIED COUPLES FOCUS ON SPIRITUAL FRUITFULNESS INSTEAD?

One common response to this line of thinking is something like, "Yes, God calls us to be fruitful and multiply, but can't married couples 'be fruitful' in a variety of ways, including bearing spiritual fruit and spiritual children, even if they don't have biological children themselves?" This is a good and fair question.

It's certainly true that God bears a variety of spiritual fruit through the lives and marriages of married people. The central question is whether children are simply an add-on to the meaning of marriage or an essential part of it. All Christians are called to be spiritually fruitful. But those who are married are called to be fruitful and multiply in a way that embodies the life-giving gospel. To completely spiritualize the fruitfulness of marriage risks setting aside a foundational biblical point about marriage. To see the full biblical picture, we must include both biological and spiritual fruitfulness, not emphasize one at the expense of the other.

The spiritual fruitfulness of marriage includes and builds on the foundational reality of physical fruitfulness. After all, any relationship between two people can bear spiritual fruit, but that is not to say that any relationship bearing spiritual fruit is a "marriage." Marriage is a specific kind of relationship, existing in part for the sake of bringing forth children. If that purpose is totally spiritualized, we are missing a key dimension of how the Bible explains marriage.

WHAT ABOUT TAKING THE PILL FOR OTHER MEDICAL CONDITIONS?

This question pushes us back to the distinction we made earlier between medical technology that is remedial versus enhancing. The difference here is treating something going wrong with the body (endometriosis, for example) versus altering a normally functioning part of a healthy body. This may seem like a minor distinction, but it's not. In the first, doctors and patients treat an illness through medication, which may have side effects, even unwanted ones such as infertility. That is different from taking a medication intentionally for nonmedical purposes.

This is precisely why most medications are highly regulated. Abusing a substance means using it for a treatment that is not medically necessary. Taking painkillers after a surgery is different from taking opioids for the high. To use a different analogy, a firefighter who dies trying to rescue someone else is not committing suicide even though their own intentional actions led to their death. That death is a side effect of trying to achieve something good. Someone who takes the pill to address a genuine medical need is not intentionally trying to avoid children, even if infertility is a side effect of that medication.

In a similar way, surgeries or other treatments that unintentionally render people sterile are not morally wrong. For example, if a man or woman has to have essential parts of their reproductive system removed because they are cancerous, we wouldn't say they could not get married or should not have sex because they are infertile. Those medically necessary treatments render them infertile, but infertility is not the aim of those procedures.

SO ARE YOU SAYING THAT GETTING AN ELECTIVE VASECTOMY OR GETTING YOUR TUBES TIED IS WRONG?

This is a complicated question. For most people, these procedures don't even register as needing biblical, theological, or moral consideration. Again, that is part of how deep the story of naturalism goes. We assume that choosing to fundamentally alter our body's reproductive system for nonmedical reasons (finances, quality of life, not wanting more kids, etc.) is not a moral issue. Our cultural autopilot sees these as questions of personal preference and life planning. So most people, including most Christians, who elect sterilization do so without much thought. Although I would not say that these procedures are morally wrong in every instance, I hope Christians will ask, What story am I embodying when I embrace this procedure? What does it mean to let the story of the gospel shape the life-giving capabilities of my body? What kinds of questions do I need to ask myself (and have other Christians ask of me) to ensure I'm not just operating on cultural autopilot here but embodying the life-giving love of God?

CHAPTER 13

THE MYTH OF EVIL BODIES

"You Are Not Your Body"

The story of naturalism says we are nothing but matter in motion, but it's not the only story that has a low view of the body. Unfortunately, many Christians have put forth a distorted version of the biblical story as well, one in which the body is not simply morally neutral or incidental but the enemy. This story offers not just a distorted view of sex and bodies, but a distorted view of the gospel and Jesus, the eternal Son of God who took on our full humanity, including a body, so we might have the hope of the resurrection of the body and an embodied life everlasting.

WHAT'S THE STORY OF EVIL BODIES?

Every story has a plot. And every plot has a villain, a bad guy, or a conflict that needs to be overcome, defeated, or resolved. Many Christians mistakenly tell the biblical story as "the story of evil bodies." According to this story, the body is the root of evil, including sexual sin. In this way of telling the story, our bodies are not an essential part of who we are. We are not our bodies. Rather, our bodies are an unhelpful and sinful container for what we *really* are: a soul. The solution is, as the old hymn puts it, to "fly away" from the prison house of the body to the heavenly home where there will be no sin and suffering because there will be no bodies.

If we want to understand the story of bad bodies, it may be helpful to begin at the end. Why? Because the resolution of any story reveals the chief conflict or problem of the story. And in the story of evil bodies, the happy ending occurs only when we are free from the physical body, which weighs us down literally and morally.

But here we need to stop and ask, How does this story of evil bodies accord with the actual story of Scripture? How does the biblical story end? Most of us learn the answer to this question not by sitting down in a formal class on eschatology (the doctrine of last things) but through a mix of church experiences, sermons, and songs. When I was young, I got one explanation in a Sunday school song, which declared (I kid you not) that "somewhere in outer space / God has prepared a place for those who trust him and obey!" At the end of this song, we would literally count down from ten to one and then shout, "Blast off!" (taking our lives into our hands by jumping off those classic metal folding chairs). I don't know if this song was written with a view toward relevance in the space-age heyday of the 1960s, but I look back on those lyrics with a mixture of horror and incredulity. "Somewhere in outer space?" In retrospect, that's not very sound theology. But it provided a clear answer to the question of how the story ends. This song's story ends by leaving earth and our bodies behind and going to heaven forever.

Here's another classic line from my evangelical childhood: "Do you know where you will go if you die tonight?" As a kid, I remember hearing repeated altar calls to follow Christ, to get saved, so we would know where we'd go if we did die. In retrospect, I appreciate the relentless emphasis that what we do in this life will echo for all eternity. Taking that long view is crucial. However, the eschatology of these frequent altar calls is questionable. The story told here says, "The end goal is to die, leave the body behind, and make sure your soul is secure for eternity." Whatever role the body has to play is minimal. In other words, Christianity is an exit strategy because salvation is something for our souls, not our bodies. At best, our bodies are incidental and, at worst, a real hindrance to the goal of this story.

THE END OF THE STORY

The story I was taught through songs and altar calls had an implicit view of the body. But does it hold up with Scripture's view of where this story is going? When I talk about eschatology here, our view of last things, I'm not talking specifically about answering questions on the millennium or the rapture. Instead, I'm thinking through the differences between what theologians refer to as the "final" and "immediate" states of human beings. Confusing these two states is one telltale sign of the story of evil bodies.

The intermediate state refers to what happens when we die. Scripture teaches that when we die as Christians, to be absent from the body is to be present with the Lord.[1] Our bodies are dead, but our souls are with God. The Bible doesn't give much detail about this time or state of being because it's not the focus of the biblical story. We know it's not an embodied existence but a time of waiting for the resurrection of our bodies. Other than that, we don't get a lot of detail. Suffice it to say that God holds us and takes care of us in this time between our death and the final resurrection.

In contrast to the intermediate state, our condition in the final state is clearer. At the end of the story, we will be given resurrected, glorified bodies. As 1 Corinthians 15 makes abundantly clear, just as Christ died and was resurrected, so we will share in his resurrection. We will have bodies that are transformed, glorious, and imperishable, just like Christ's resurrected body. In other words, our eternal existence is an embodied one, which is why we profess in the Apostles' Creed that we believe "in the resurrection of the body and the life everlasting." According to

Scripture, the final state and our current state are similar in that we enjoy an embodied existence in both.

The problem comes when we equate our intermediate state with the final state. Why? Because in our intermediate state, we lack bodies. When we make it seem like disembodied existence is part of our final goal or ultimate destination, we are telling the story as though bodies are a key part of what's wrong with the way things currently are. If the goal is to escape my body, then the implicit message is that there must be something wrong with my body. If every *body* tells a story, then a story that ends without bodies is a story where bodies are (wrongly) identified as part of the problem.

Another place we find this mistaken view is in our funerals and our practical theology of death. When people die, I've heard pastors state that what's left is just "the shell" of who they really are. The "real you," the soul, has gone to heaven to be with Jesus. In other words, "You are not your body." Now, in the face of modern materialism, which says that we are nothing more than matter, I think it's right and fitting that Christians emphasize that we are more than matter. But erasing and denigrating the body is not a tactic that rings true with the Bible, which makes it clear that our bodies—the matter that makes us—are essential to who we are.

To use the theological language above, the intermediate state is not normal. To have the soul and body ripped asunder in death is not good, as though death frees the "real" thing that had been confined to the prison of the body. No! That sounds much more like the Greek philosophy of Plato or the Gnostic heresies the church wrestled with in its early years. In this confused version of the biblical story, the enemy that Jesus came to defeat—death—ends up getting portrayed as the right and normal state of humanity. It's not.

Not only is our final state one of embodied existence; it's also an existence that takes place on a glorified earth. I was in college the first time I realized this, and I have to admit, I was shocked and startled. I had read Revelation 21–22 before, but I had overlooked this important aspect until one of my professors stopped and pointed out that this vision of the life to come was not one of human souls being whisked away to a spotless and ethereal heaven, but of the New Jerusalem, the dwelling place of God, who comes to dwell with humanity in a renewed and cleansed planet earth.

This was jarring because for so long I'd heard that the whole point of my faith was to get saved so I could go to heaven when I die. But what about after we're not dead anymore? What about the resurrection or "life after life after death," as N. T. Wright puts it?[2] Suddenly, it sank in that the stream of Christianity I grew up in had a low or nonexistent theology of the body and of the resurrection. Certainly, we celebrated Easter. And we were intent on affirming the resurrection in the face of modern scientific skepticism. It's just that the goodness of bodies and the reality of the resurrection didn't fit into the everyday language and practice of our faith—including our teaching on bodies and sex.

THE GOD OF EVIL BODIES

Who is God? A dangerous theological error lies at the heart of the story of evil bodies. The notion that sexual sin is natural, inherent in our bodies, places the blame for sin ultimately on God. This is just another riff on the blame-shifting tactics we see with Adam and Eve: "The woman *you* put here with me—she gave me some fruit . . ." (Gen. 3:12, emphasis mine). "The maleness *you* gave me—it caused me to lust . . ." If sexual sin is the built-in, normal trajectory of maleness, then it is ultimately not my fault as a man. Rather, the fault lies with the One who made me this way, the One who created humanity male and female. God made me naturally lustful and unable to control my thoughts, feelings, and actions when I see a woman. Plus, God made her body in such a way that I have this so-called natural reaction. In other words, God is at the root of the problem of sin and evil.

Not only is this biblically inaccurate and theologically dangerous, but it's also a practical, pastoral problem. It hamstrings us in our daily battle against sin because it misdiagnoses our real problem. The root cause of my struggle with sexual sin is not the natural tendencies of my maleness or femaleness but my own battle with sin in general and the fallen structures of a society selling me false hope. That is, I am looking for love in all the wrong places. I am looking for acceptance, security, and hope (all of which are good things), and our fallen society offers these things to me via pornography, sex, and romance. My heart is then enticed by the false hope and false fulfillment offered by the culture around me. My unnatural, sinful tendency assumes that loving something more than God will bring me true fulfillment.

EMBODYING EVIL BODIES: SHAME AND BLAME

Every body tells a story. But what if the story you tell is that the body and sex are villains, problems to be overcome? If we are not our bodies, if the goal is to get rid of the body to go to heaven forever, if death is seen as a good release rather than an enemy to be defeated, then how does this affect our view of the body and sex? How does it skew our answers to the questions, What are bodies for? What is sex for?

Several years ago, a young married couple came to talk with me in my office, and I could sense right away that there was deep struggle and hurt. Admittedly, as a professor, I often operate on an intellectual level, so I wasn't surprised when the conversation opened with a heady discussion about sex. I was surprised, however, when one of the spouses started putting forth their views that all sex was ultimately sinful, contaminated by lust. As the conversation continued, the couple slowly revealed that they had not actually consummated their marriage, though they had been married over a year.

The body language of both spouses was telling: fear, sadness, defeat. Clearly, a lot more was going on than just bad theology. Yet bad theology *was* in play here: If our bodies are bad and sex is inherently sinful, then sex—even sex *within* marriage—was a sinful act. Bad theology had bad consequences. This couple struggled and eventually ended up divorced, victims, in part, of an unbiblical view of the body.

We can see the tendency to blame our bodies and feel shame about them at the very beginning of humanity's rebellion against God. In the beginning, Genesis tells us, Adam and Eve were naked and felt no shame (Gen. 2:25). God created them to be in relationship with him and with each other, and these harmonious relationships characterized humanity's interactions with God, one another, and all creation. Their nakedness shows their complete trust in God and openness to each other, just as a small child's nakedness in their home shows a complete trust in their parents and family.

However, when Adam and Eve sin and disobey God, they have an interesting reaction: They attempt to cover their bodies, to hide their nakedness. Why? Is nakedness morally wrong? That doesn't seem to be what the Bible is trying to convey. After all, the biblical text is clear that Adam and Eve's original state of being naked and unashamed was good. So why did they cover themselves with fig leaves? Had they done something wrong with their genitals? Not according to Genesis. Even the physical act of eating forbidden fruit was not the real sin. Rather, the root sins here are pride, lack of trust, and disobedience. Yet because they felt shame about their physical nakedness, they covered their bodies in an attempt to cover their spiritual failure and shame. This misplaced shame still haunts our experience of our bodies today. How do we distort what the Bible teaches about bodies? We'll discover two ways below.

SHAMING THE BODY: SPEAKING OF GENITALS

One way many people have been trained to experience shame around their bodies is in the words they use and don't use. That is, we rarely refer to our genitals in a clear and straightforward way. As a parent of young children, I've experienced this challenge. Many parents are more comfortable teaching their children euphemisms for their genitals, instead of simply saying "penis" and "vagina." Why are we—why am I—hesitant to just call a boy's penis a penis and a girl's vagina a vagina? (Are you feeling a level of discomfort just reading these words?) Perhaps some parents feel that these words sound too clinical or complex for a potty-training toddler to learn. Or perhaps we know that our toddlers will be sure to use these new words at the most inopportune time, such as during the silent prayer of confession on Sunday morning or when they meet the new neighbor for the first time.

But my sense is that many Christian parents struggle to use those words because they have been taught and trained by their Christian upbringing (and the broader culture in general) that those words are inappropriate. In essence, our euphemisms for genitalia function like linguistic fig leaves, covering the misplaced shame we feel about our ~~bodies~~ (see, I almost used a euphemism there) vaginas and penises.

Misplaced shame about our bodies in general and our genitals in particular can have devastating implications around sexual abuse. For example, psychologists Maureen Kenny and Sandy Wurtele point out in their research that most preschoolers know the correct terms for their nongenital body parts, but few know the correct terms for their genitals.[3] These scholars note that this is a problem because children who cannot properly name their genitals are more susceptible to sexual abuse. As Kenny and Wurtele highlight, the more a child relies on euphemisms, the more likely they will be misunderstood when trying to tell someone about an abusive encounter. In contrast, children who use anatomically specific terms are more likely to be understood if or when they describe a sexually abusive encounter. In fact, these scholars note that some sex offenders report avoiding children who knew the correct terminology for genitals.

Not only is it important to speak directly about our bodies and genitals for practical reasons, but it is also theologically significant. When we treat our genitals as that-which-must-not-be-named, we convey to ourselves and to others, including our children, that our sexual organs are a mysterious and nefarious source of evil that should not be talked about. We grant linguistic and symbolic power to the story of evil bodies. But that only compounds the problem. Conversations and questions about sex and bodies do entail some level of difficulty, awkwardness, and maybe even conflict, but when we refuse to speak in a clear and straightforward way, we only reinforce the sense that our sexed bodies are somehow bad and shameful in and of themselves. Avoidance is a bad long-term strategy, and it reveals a deeply flawed theology. In that way, it misidentifies what the gospel says is our true problem (sin) and sets us up for a gospel that tries to deliver us from our bodies rather than our sin.

BLAMING THE BODY: MODESTY

A second way we attach blame to our bodies is a framework for modesty that wrongly identifies bodies—particularly women's bodies—as the source of lust and evil. To be sure, the Bible affirms modesty. I'm not here to bash modesty, properly understood. Too often, though, it has not been properly understood, and *someone else's* body has been identified as the root source of *my* lust.

In her book *Pure*, Linda Kay Klein interviews a variety of women who grew up in the purity culture of 1990s evangelicalism.[4] Story after story relay the ways in which women and women's bodies are identified as the source of evil, including cases where girls are sexually abused and assaulted, yet are still blamed for their assailant's attack. The faulty thinking about modesty goes along these lines: Women need to cover their bodies and be as discreet as possible because there is an inevitable and unstoppable link between a woman's body and a man's sexual desire or lust for her body. As Jo, one of the interviewees in Klein's book, notes, "Women are taught that their bodies are evil; men are taught their minds are."[5] Therefore, a woman is responsible to make sure men are not drawn into sinful, lustful thoughts about her due to the way she dresses. But again, is this a biblically accurate understanding of how we should view our bodies? Let's unpack what's wrong with this line of thought.

The key here is to discern what is normal and abnormal when it comes to human life and behavior. Dutch theologian Abraham Kuyper argues that there are basically two ways to look at the world and human nature as we know them in our experience. From a Christian perspective, there is something fundamentally "abnormal" about the way the world is now.[6] Sin has perverted our experience, our history, and our minds such that what is in our experience, history, and minds is not the way the world should be. In other words, we must understand how God created and redeemed us to be versus how we often operate in our sinful, fallen state. In contrast, though, we sometimes end up interpreting the abnormal perversion of sin as the normal state of things. When politicians are corrupt, police are unjust, spouses are unfaithful, and corporations exploit their workers, we shrug and say, "That's just the way it is." But that's not the way it should be.

Admittedly, it can sometimes be hard to distinguish between what is a normal, creational part of how God intended life to be and what is a perverted, sinful intrusion into God's intentions for his world. This is difficult because our experience of the world is rooted in our own sin and fallenness. Thus, we tend to assume that what's normal for us sinners is just normal. But that is why Scripture is so vital: It shows us a different way, a way that involves untangling the good, creational gifts of God from the abuse and misuse we've made of those gifts.

So how did God create us? How are we meant to be? As we see in Genesis 1 and 2, there is nothing morally wrong with naked bodies. Adam and Eve are naked and unashamed. Moreover, God quite clearly has no issue with this. In their state of innocence and goodness, he doesn't try to cover up the nakedness of either of them, as though their nakedness would somehow skew their behavior so they're constantly preoccupied with sex or objectifying the other's naked body. It's only after sin enters the picture that they cover themselves and God provides a covering for them. This indicates that the issue is not a naked body but a sinful heart.

Why do we cover bodies, then? Bodies need to be covered not because they are inherently bad or provoke evil, but because perverted *hearts* warp how we see other humans. Rather than seeing others as God's image bearers to be treated with respect, dignity, and love, we see people as objects to be used and consumed. That's why Jesus says to gouge out your eye (Matt. 5:29) if you have a lust problem, not "tell that person to cover their body better." Their body isn't the problem; your heart (and how it shapes your vision) is. According to the Bible, that objectifying way of seeing people is not normal, so we shouldn't normalize it.

Unfortunately, that's just what some popular Christian approaches to lust and sexuality do. In their popular book *Every Man's Battle*, Stephen Arterburn and Fred Stoeker discuss some of the reasons men struggle with sexual temptation. Although I'm sure their book has been helpful for many men, their theological framework is skewed in some places, particularly in a chapter titled "Just by Being Male." In this chapter, the authors raise the question, How did we get to a place where sexual sin is so prevalent among men? According to Arterburn and Stoeker, the answer is simple: "We got there naturally—simply by being male."[7] They reiterate, "Our very maleness" is a key reason for "the pervasiveness of sexual impurity among men." Our very maleness! So sexual impurity is something that flows from the essence of being a man?

This is a strong—and theologically wrong—statement. As the authors continue, they argue that men are rebellious by nature, that men find the "straight life" (the responsibility of working and caring for a wife and family) boring, that men have a strong regular sex drive, and that men receive sexual gratification through visual stimulation. All of these statements are oversimplified, but in particular, I want to note a deep-rooted theological problem here.

This approach to lust and sexuality naturalizes and normalizes sin. Why do I as a man struggle with sexual impurity? "Well, it's just who I am as a male. It's normal! C'mon, every man thinks and operates that way, right? After all, boys will be boys." Certainly I'm not denying that all men struggle with sexual sin in some way, shape, or form. However, if we keep in mind the normal/abnormal terminology of Kuyper introduced above, we can see that the problem lies not in maleness but in fallenness.

If we follow the biblical narrative, the fact that all people (including men) struggle with sexual sin is not because they are male, female, or human. That would be looking at a sinful, fallen world and concluding that, well, this is just the way things are. No! Such a view conflates our human nature or even our sexual nature with our sinful nature. Sin is not natural. Sexual sin is not natural. If sexual sin is every man's battle, it's not because they are men but because *sin* is every person's battle, including sexual sin. But sexual sin is not woven into the essence of what it means to be human, what it means to be male or female, or what it means to be sexed beings. It's a distortion of our good, creational essence.

To sum up, Christians have often told a story that sees the body as something to be discarded. The body is not the real you, and the goal is to be free from it. This anti-body theology shows up in how we blame and shame the body. We refuse to talk about our genitals in a straightforward way, and following the lead of Adam and Eve, we try to cover our bodies in order to hide our spiritual shame. Our language around modesty also tends to see women's bodies as an inherent source of temptation and men's "maleness" as sexually sinful by nature. This anti-body theology has had negative effects on how Christians view bodies and sex. But there's an even deeper issue here. Not only does the biblical gospel identify a different villain (sin, including my own struggle and the fallen structures of society around me, not bodies), but the gospel actually places an almost unimaginably high value on the body. In fact, the gospel proclaims that we are saved through a body—the body of Jesus.

CHAPTER 14

THE STORY OF GOD'S MISSION

"The Word Became Flesh"

The story of naturalism and the story of evil bodies both have a fundamentally flawed view of material reality, including our physical bodies. The story of naturalism sees us as nothing more than matter in motion, with bodies as our enemies to be mastered by science and technology so they will conform more perfectly to our will. The story of evil bodies sees our bodies as the source of sin, the problem to be solved by death. In the face of both stories, we need to retell the gospel.

The good news is that we belong, body and soul, to our faithful Savior, Jesus Christ. But we belong to him because he was first made like us: fully human, including a fully human body. And just as Jesus came with a mission, so too we are given a mission: to be his witnesses. This gives us a new perspective on our bodies as God's temple, the dwelling place of God, and helps us see that our bodies are meant to be the place where God's name and nature are revealed to a watching world. This is the mission of our bodies and our whole lives.

WHO IS GOD? THE WORD MADE FLESH

The Bible is a story about bodies. The biblical story is about how we are redeemed by a God who actually has a body in the person of Jesus, whose goal is to make our bodies his dwelling place. Our bodies are the place where he reveals his love, grace, and faithfulness to a questioning world. And at the heart of the biblical story, the gospel, is the body of Jesus. As such, when we learn to tell the gospel story correctly, we will see that it provides a helpful antidote to the body blaming and shaming that have often plagued Christian visions of sex and the body. When we get the gospel story right, we get the story of bodies right. When we get the gospel story right, we get the story of sex right.

BEGIN AT THE BEGINNING

Let's start with beginnings. As a kid, I remember visiting the Gateway Arch in St. Louis, Missouri. Given that I wasn't exactly enamored with heights or small spaces, the lurching ride to the top in an egg-shaped elevator pod was not fun, although the view from the top was indeed stunning. As part of our visit, we stopped in the gift shop, toured the museum and exhibits there, and watched a brief documentary, "Monument to the Dream," about the construction of the Gateway Arch. It was fascinating in large part because my mind definitely does not work like an engineer's. One fact that stuck out to me was how crucial it was to lay the foundations correctly. The two sides had to be set up perfectly to meet as a single arch. The documentary noted that any errors when laying the foundations would be catastrophic. A miscalculation of less than an inch would result in the two sides of the arch missing each other by yards in the air. As somebody who struggles with the basic engineering feat of making sure pictures are hung straight on the wall, this fact stuck with me. Clearly, just as endings reveal something crucial about the stories we tell, so also beginnings are crucial.

To get the gospel right, we have to start at the beginning—the "in the beginning" of Genesis 1. The story of the gospel doesn't just start with Jesus. He stands at the center of the story, but if we don't know the whole story, there's a good chance we'll get Jesus wrong, get the gospel wrong, and get bodies and sex wrong. At the very least, we will have a much thinner slice of the Jesus story, a diminished understanding of who Jesus is and of his mission in the world. To try to get the gospel by starting with the New Testament would be like trying to understand the story of Harry Potter by starting with *The Deathly Hallows* or *The Lord of the Rings* with *The Return of the King*. If we tried that reading strategy, we might have some sense of what was going on in the story, but we would lack the background, context, and fullness that give the story its power and complete meaning. So we need to start at the beginning.

In the beginning, God affirms the goodness of bodies and sex. You might have read over this many times without realizing it, but the first command in the Bible is to have sex. Maybe we're so used to how the story starts that we've overlooked what is staring us in the face. Maybe we've been so deeply trained by an anti-body Christianity that we can't fathom that God's first blessing and command in Scripture has to do with sex and bodies. But it does.

God creates a material world that is bursting with life, and at the apex of creation, God creates humanity, male and female. These humans bear the image of God, and to be the "image of God" is a physical, material reality. There is no such thing as an invisible image. Rather, human beings are the visible, physical image of the invisible God. In other words, the bodies—the sexually differentiated male and female bodies—of humanity are an essential and essentially good dimension of what it means to be God's image bearers. In the beginning, the Bible affirms that bodies are good. Far from being evil, embodied humans are God's icons, the primary place where God is revealed to the world.

Then God calls humanity to use those bodies to do something else good: have sex. God's first words after creating humanity, male and female, are a blessing and calling that he has woven into their bodies, the blessing and calling of participating in the power of life-giving, creative love: "Be fruitful and multiply." Just as God is the triune, relational God who brings forth life out of his love, so God calls the husband and wife to enter into a covenant relationship and bring forth life out of a love that is embodied and expressed in and through our bodies and sex. Bodies, and multiplying bodies, are essential to God's mission in the world. God's goal in forming and shaping his creation is for it to be a dwelling place not just for humans but also for himself, so he can dwell with the people he created. And he makes himself present to his creation in and through his icons, his image bearers, to fill the earth with his glory.

GOD HAS A BODY

The theology of the body in Genesis 1 lays the crucial foundation for getting the gospel right. In the gospel, bodies are not the source of evil; they are fully good. Bodies are not nonessential parts of our humanity to be discarded when we die; they are essential to the gospel, which makes the startling claim that God has a body. Even Christians can find this claim startling if you phrase it the right way.

Years ago, an adjunct professor caused a stir at Kuyper College by starting a theology course on Christology with this phrase: "Jesus has a penis." I wasn't there, but as the story goes, that definitely got the students' attention. Supposedly, one person fell out of their chair, and another spit the coffee they'd just sipped. Even if those are semi-mythical tales, they accurately capture the sense of shock that pervaded the class. "Jesus has a penis." Does that sound strange? How about "God has a body"? How about "The Word became flesh"? That way of thinking about God certainly did sound strange to many in the first century who heard the gospel message about Jesus. For many in Jesus's world and in ours, the physical, material, earthy reality of fleshy bodies was contaminated by evil—or maybe even the source of evil. But if you start to pay attention, you see the New Testament writers repeatedly emphasize that Jesus was not only fully divine but also fully human. He had a human body.

The Gospel of John starts with startlingly high claims about Jesus: He is the eternal Word, the Son of God, who was with God in the beginning and who is himself God. It's hard to get more divine than that. But then John goes on to make some shockingly low or mundane claims about this Word: "The Word became flesh and made his dwelling among us" (John 1:14). The God revealed in Jesus is not a God who stands afar or aloof from humanity, but descends to become fully human. For many in John's day and in ours, this just doesn't fit with our idea of who God should be. God should be omnipotent, immutable, and free from entanglement with human affairs. God doesn't need to get his hands dirty. (He is spirit, after all; he doesn't even have hands!) But a God who stands apart from us and our humanity is a figment of our imagination, the ultimate product of our anti-body theology. This is a god created by us, as our polar opposite, lacking a body because of our deep sense that our bodies are the real problem. This god is an idol, not the God revealed in Scripture.

The epistle of 1 John, like the Gospel of John, begins with a focus on the humanity and body of Jesus that is central to the gospel: "That which was from the beginning, which we have heard, which we have seen with our eyes, which we have looked at and our hands have touched—this we proclaim concerning the Word of life" (1 John 1:1). Later in this letter, John affirms how central Jesus's body is to the gospel: "This is how you can recognize the Spirit of God: Every spirit that acknowledges that Jesus Christ has come in the flesh is from God" (1 John 4:2).

John goes on to say that those who deny Jesus's bodily reality and divinity—that he has come in the flesh and come from God—have the spirit of antichrist. That's a strong statement! It makes me wonder whether many Christians who would affirm the gospel and affirm Jesus's humanity have subtly allowed this spirit of antichrist to take root through our body shaming and blaming. It's not exactly what John is talking about here, yet it's a real and powerful denial of the gospel—a spirit of antichrist—insofar as it misdiagnoses the body as the source of evil and thus warps our view of Jesus's own body.

But the Bible doesn't just affirm that Jesus had a body; it also says that our salvation in Christ *depends* on the body of Jesus. The body of Jesus tells a story—accomplishes a story—about who we are in relation to God and who God is for us. This is crucial. How does God accomplish his work of salvation and redemption? It isn't just a mental or spiritual transaction that depends primarily on mental assent and belief or God's spiritual posture of forgiveness. Our salvation is accomplished physically through the body of Jesus. But don't take my word for it. Listen to the New Testament. In these passages, notice how our redemption depends on the body of Jesus (emphasis added):

- "Once you were alienated from God and were enemies in your minds because of your evil behavior. But now he has reconciled you *by Christ's physical body* through death to present you holy in his sight, without blemish and free from accusation. . . . This is the gospel" (Col. 1:21–23).
- "So, my brothers and sisters, you also died to the law *through the body of Christ*, that you might belong to another, to him who was raised from the dead, in order that we might bear fruit for God" (Rom. 7:4).
- "'He himself bore our sins' *in his body* on the cross, so that we might die to sins and live for righteousness; 'by his wounds you have been healed'" (1 Peter 2:24).
- "We have been made holy through the sacrifice *of the body of Jesus Christ* once for all" (Heb. 10:10).
- "Therefore, brothers and sisters, since we have confidence to enter the Most Holy Place by *the blood of Jesus*, by a new and living way opened for us through the curtain, that is, *his body*, and since we

have a great priest over the house of God, let us draw near to God with a sincere heart and with the full assurance that faith brings, having our hearts sprinkled to cleanse us from a guilty conscience and having our bodies washed with pure water" (Heb. 10:19–22).

- "For he himself is our peace, who has made the two groups one and has destroyed the barrier, the dividing wall of hostility, by setting aside *in his flesh* the law with its commands and regulations. His purpose was to create in himself one new humanity out of the two, thus making peace, and *in one body* to reconcile both of them to God through the cross, by which he put to death their hostility" (Eph. 2:14–16).

These biblical texts reinforce what we may know but maybe don't always say explicitly: Redemption happens through the body of Jesus. Without his fully human, fully good body, you and I would be dead in our sin, unable to walk in newness of life. We would be alienated and separated from God, content to go our own way, which leads to death. We would be separated from the family of God, the church that nourishes and sustains us. In his body, Jesus fully obeyed the Father and lived the life of love that we were all called to live. In his body, Jesus bore the full penalty of our sin and rebellion against God. But the story of Jesus's body—and our bodies—doesn't stop with Jesus's death. The gospel is that Jesus died, was buried, and rose again on the third day. The full gospel, the whole story of Jesus's body and the redemption accomplished through it, affirms not just that Jesus had a body but also that Jesus *has* a body.

The resurrected body of Jesus tells the story that the new creation has begun. The good news of the gospel is not just that Jesus died but also that he rose again and has ascended to the right hand of the Father. In theological terms, there is no dis-incarnation. The Word is still flesh. In the story of the resurrection, we see over and over an emphasis on the resurrected body of Jesus.

In Luke 24, Jesus appears to his disciples and shows them his hands and feet. Not only is he likely showing them his healed wounds as an identity marker, but by showing them his feet, he is also proving he is not merely a ghost or spirit. In their culture's view of ghosts and spirits, those beings didn't walk from place to place—they hovered. They didn't quite touch the ground. So when Jesus shows them his feet, it's a way of saying, "I'm not a ghost."

To take his case a step further, Jesus asks for a piece of fish and eats it (Luke 24:42–43). Does a ghost or spirit need to eat? No! I love the way this story is illustrated in *The Jesus Storybook Bible.*[1] The resurrected Jesus has discarded fish bones on his plate while wiping the back of his hand across his mouth, with a twinkle in his eye. The image perfectly conveys the full humanity, the bodily reality of the resurrected Savior who eats, juices dripping down his chin. Jesus is alive, and he's no ghost!

Singer/songwriter Andrew Peterson captures well the materiality of Jesus's body in his resurrection anthem "His Heart Beats," which focuses on the materiality of Jesus's resurrection body.[2] Peterson's song is full of biblical imagery, but he makes crystal clear that our redemption depends on the bodily resurrection of Jesus. This is a theological truth, yes. But Peterson won't let us forget that this theological truth is tied to the earthy, fleshy materiality of the body of Jesus. His heart beats. His lungs expand. His resurrected body tells the story of God's faithful love—his Father would not leave him in the grave, but would burst the chains of sin and death so not only Jesus could live but we can too. The resurrected body of Jesus tells the story of God's faithfulness and victory over death.

Jesus's victory over death applies to our bodies as well. In 1 Corinthians 15:20, Paul talks about the glorified and resurrected body of Jesus as the "firstfruits" of the resurrection. In other words, Jesus was raised first, but when he returns, his people will be raised to life as well with bodies that are glorified, free from sin and death. The good news of the gospel is that our bodies will also be like Jesus's body in telling the story of God's faithfulness and love. For Christians, though, the resurrection life doesn't just take place in some far, distant future. It begins now. Through the body of Jesus, our bodies are incorporated into the gospel story of God's faithfulness and redemption.

EMBODYING THE GOSPEL: SEXUAL HOLINESS

The gospel is the story of God's faithful covenant love in the suffering body of Jesus. This understanding of the gospel helps us understand why Christians are called to sexual holiness. Why are Christians called to a life of sexual discipleship and discipline in following Jesus? Jesus as the Word made flesh and the temple theology of 1 Corinthians 6 that we explored earlier help us see the big picture here:

> The body . . . is not meant for sexual immorality but for the Lord, and the Lord for the body. . . . Do you not know that your bodies are members of Christ himself? . . . Do you not know that your bodies are temples of the Holy Spirit, who is in you, whom you have received from God? You are not your own; you were bought at a price. Therefore honor God with your bodies. (1 Cor. 6:13, 15, 19–20)

Too often Christians have reduced sexual purity to a matter of self-focused legalism. In other words, I try to stay morally pure for my own sake and the sake of being in right relationship with God. But the language of temple here helps us see the other-focused dimension of witness through our sex lives. Remember, the whole point of the temple was to be a place where God was worshiped and made known. God's people are called to lives of holiness and faithfulness so "all the peoples of the earth may know that the LORD is God" (1 Kings 8:60). This helps us see why Scripture takes sexual discipleship so seriously. It's a matter of putting the character of God on display.

When I treat someone as an object to be lusted after, when I treat someone as something to be used for my own ends and then tossed aside, when I seek pleasure over fidelity, or when I set myself above others in my sexual habits, I am a dysfunctional temple. And if you know anything about Jesus's relationship with the temple in his own time, you can expect he's ready to turn the tables of our hearts, driving out sexual immorality in a forceful way. When Paul sees dysfunctional temples at the church at Corinth, he calls them out. Having sex with your stepmother makes you a dysfunctional temple (1 Cor. 5), having sex with prostitutes makes you a dysfunctional temple (1 Cor. 6), and not having sex with your spouse makes you a dysfunctional temple (1 Cor. 7). The goal here, though, isn't just to shame people. Rather, it's to get them reengaged and on mission.

Allow me a sports analogy. If a basketball player doesn't have their head in the game and is not performing in a way that contributes to the good of the team, they need to get their act together. Their coach might bench them to talk to them or just to send them a message. They know what to do, but they are not executing. The point is not to shame them or punish them. It is to get them back on track so they are a properly functioning member of the team.

We see the same kind of motivation at work in the biblical idea of discipleship and discipline. In 1 Corinthians 5, Paul says, essentially, you need to call out people who are refusing to embrace their calling to be God's temple, the place where God's love and faithfulness shine through, even in their sex lives. When he writes again to the church, he clarifies further that the goal is restoration for any Christian who repents: "You ought to forgive and comfort him, so that he will not be overwhelmed by excessive sorrow" (2 Cor. 2:7).

When someone has their head in the game and is ready to get back on the court and contribute to the team, let them play. The goal is not simply to punish Christians who commit sin or to shame those who are sexually immoral. The goal is a well-functioning temple that is putting God's love, holiness, and faithfulness on display to a watching world.

It's to restore those who stumble and remind them of their high calling: The body is for the Lord. This focus shapes how we see both singleness and marriage.

THE HIGH CALLING OF SINGLENESS

First, this view of the body as God's temple underscores that singleness is a worthy and high calling. If the ultimate purpose of bodies were to get married, have sex, and have kids, then single people would occupy a second-class status in the Christian community. But Scripture here puts forth something different. Our bodies are not ultimately for sex or marriage or our spouse. They are for God's Spirit to dwell with us in order to make himself known to us and to a watching world. In fact, the Bible says that those who are single have a level of "undivided devotion to the Lord" that should make singleness the default option (1 Cor. 7:35).

Most churches convey a much different posture. Having spent 13 years as a professor at a Christian college, I see the way many college students are constantly pressured by their families and churches to be in a romantic relationship. "Why isn't it enough?" I remember one student asking, sitting in my office after a class where we talked about singleness. "Why isn't it enough for people that I'm growing in my faith? Why don't they ask what I'm learning through my Bible classes and the friendships I'm building?" Instead, he lamented, he was constantly peppered with questions about his romantic status when he went back to his home church.

Too often, our Christian families and churches convey the idea that real spiritual maturity and real acceptance in the Christian community come through marriage. In contrast, Scripture underscores that those who are single can be "devoted to the Lord in both *body* and spirit" (1 Cor. 7:34, emphasis mine). The bodies of single people are meant to be clear signs and symbols that point to the kingdom of God. Since this is true, the main question our churches should be asking teens and twentysomethings is not "Are you in a relationship with a significant other?"

but "Given that you are already in a relationship with Jesus, how are you bearing witness to him in your life right now?"

My friend Rochelle is an amazing example of this. On Wednesday nights, I can sometimes hear her leading singing before we're even in the church building. She has third through sixth graders belting out songs to Jesus at top volume. She bought an ambulance and converted it to an ice cream truck, which, as you might imagine, is a big hit with kids (and let's face it, adults too). She runs camp programs in the summer and is constantly looking for ways to disciple young people from all over our state into mature followers of Jesus. My kids have benefited immensely from the way she pours her life into serving others and encourages them to do the same. She is searching for ways to grow in her own faith and serve Jesus, and she clearly absolutely loves being around other people. I love that my girls who are 13 and 11 can see Rochelle as a model of what it means to love and serve Jesus. Rochelle makes it easier for me to remember to say things like "*if* you get married" rather than "*when* you get married" in conversations with them. Rochelle embodies what it means to be the temple of God.

FAITHFULNESS IN MARRIAGE

This temple theology of bodies also underscores why sexual faithfulness in marriage is so crucial. In other words, Paul's language in 1 Corinthians 6 helps us see why sleeping with prostitutes—or any kind of sexual unfaithfulness—is not simply a moral mistake but a fundamentally mistaken account of the gospel story. If the gospel story recounts a faithful Savior seeking us out and serving us in a life-giving way, then husbands in Corinth had to understand their actions through this lens.

In contrast to this understanding, though, they were not being faithful to their wives. They were not focused on serving their wives. They were not focused on sex as a life-giving power (in a literal or a figurative way). The story they were embodying in their sex lives was not the gospel of Jesus Christ. By buying into their culture's notion of sex as nothing more than a physical need to be gratified, and by buying into a social system that saw prostitution as a lowly and vulgar but necessary part of life, they were failing to bear witness to the gospel.

This same danger lurks in our own culture, just in a different form. Prostitution may be considered out of bounds morally, even for most non-Christians, but internet pornography has taken its place as a culturally normal sexual outlet. Even though this easily accessible pornography is having a massive effect on our society,[3] from the perspective of our individualistic, consent-focused culture, pornography is not a moral issue. If consenting adults agree to participate in porn production and others consent to consume porn, who is being harmed?[4]

Jesus's words in the Sermon on the Mount point to a different measure of morality: "You have heard that it was said, 'You shall not commit adultery.' But I tell you that anyone who looks at a woman lustfully has already committed adultery with her in his heart" (Matt. 5:27–28). Again, the issue here is not merely one of legalistically trying to be morally perfect. Rather, a spouse—man or woman—who looks at someone else with a lustful gaze is displaying something other than a gospel orientation. Jesus is our faithful Savior, and a lack of fidelity to my spouse casts doubt on Jesus's faithfulness. But as I develop a Spirit-filled heart of faithfulness to my spouse, the world will see something of Jesus's faithfulness in me. In other words, when I refuse to engage in the culturally acceptable sexual outlet of porn, I'm offering a different way of looking at bodies, at people, and at reality—a way that points back to the reality of the gospel.

CONCLUSION

Every body tells a story. Our secular age embodies the stories of individualism, romance, and naturalism, living out the reality that there is no higher calling than achieving self-fulfillment and meaning on my own terms. In response, many Christians have countered with the stories of legalism, sexual prosperity, and evil bodies—stories that fail to embody the gospel before a watching world. In contrast, Christians are called to embody the gospel, the good news of God's covenant faithfulness that produces households of faith witnessing to the gospel in every facet of life, including sex, marriage, and singleness. In the midst of all these stories, it might be tempting to refuse to give credence to any story. Who can say which one is right? Who can say which is the true story of the world—or if such a thing even exists?

Blaise Pascal, the French philosopher, pondered many deep matters of philosophy and theology, including the question of God's existence. He recognized that many people, Christian and non-Christian alike, struggled with whether you could rationally prove the existence of God. In his day, many people were defaulting to agnosticism, the view that we can't really know if there is a God or not. In their view, we can't definitively say that there is a God. In a similar way, many people today might default to a kind of agnosticism about our bodies, sex, marriage, and singleness. Can we really establish one of these stories as true? What if we are not in a place where we want to commit to any of these stories, whether it's the gospel or the stories of our secular age? We may not be able to say for sure that any of them is, without a doubt, the way to go.

Pascal's response is helpful, in his day and in ours: You may not be able to rationally prove God, but your life is the concrete answer to the question of whether there is a God.[1] That is, no matter what you think, you are embarked on the journey of life every single day, and the way you live your life *embodies* the answer to the question of what you think about God. There's no such thing as a functional agnostic. Every life embodies an answer to the question of whether there is a God and who that God is. You may feel conflicted about these competing stories about what bodies and sex are for. You may want to retreat and not give a definitive answer about what you think. Nevertheless, you have to live your life every day. And because you are embarked on the journey of life, the way you live *embodies* what you think is the true story of the whole world. What story will your body tell?

GREAT LAKES CATECHISM ON MARRIAGE AND SEXUALITY[1]

1 Q: Is human sexuality a good thing or not?

A: It is good! We see in Scripture that God created us male and female as part of the creation order, that our sexuality is an inherent part of being human, and that our sexuality is part of what God calls "very good" in the beginning.[2]

Moreover, God created man and woman as full partners, together bearing God's image[3] and together receiving God's blessing and call to "Be fruitful and increase in number; fill the earth, and subdue it. Rule over the fish in the sea and the birds in the sky and over every living creature that moves on the ground."[4]

2 Q: But isn't the body or the "flesh" the root cause of our sin and temptation?

A: Certainly not! Our sin problem is not ultimately a body or sex problem; it is a heart problem—we do not desire God as we should and so we desire other things in a way we should not.[5]

---

1. This catechism is titled "Great Lakes Catechism" because it was developed at the request of the Executive Committee of the Synod of the Great Lakes (RCA), 2017.

2. Gen. 1:31.

3. Gen. 1:27.

4. Gen. 1:28.

5. Jer. 17:9; James 1:14–15.

3 Q: May we then look to our bodies and sexual desires to learn what is right?

A: No. Our expressions of sexuality are distorted and twisted by sin. Sin warps us in many ways, including our desires, thoughts, and actions pertaining to our sexuality. Because our sexuality is affected by the fall, we should not act on our desires, inclinations, or thoughts without first testing them by what Scripture teaches is honorable, right, pure, and lovely.[6]

4 Q: So Scripture is the source from which we learn what it means to be a disciple of Jesus in our sexual lives?

A: Yes. Scripture is the infallible rule for our lives.[7] This means that we look to it to understand who God is and who we are called to be as God's people.

In this world, we are called to test all teaching about marriage and sexuality by Scripture, and we must not put human writings, custom or tradition, the majority opinion, the thinking of our own time and place, or even past decisions of the church, above the truth of God, for God's truth is above everything.[8]

5 Q: Who should we consider our family?

A: Though many may consider their biological family their first family, Jesus teaches us that those who are his disciples, who are united by one Lord and one baptism into God's covenant people, should be considered our primary family.

6 Q: Does this mean our earthly families are unimportant?

A: No. In fact, Scripture teaches us that we are to honor our parents,[9] and that we should faithfully love our spouses and children.[10]

---

6. Phil. 4:8.
7. Belgic Confession, art. 7.
8. Belgic Confession, art. 7.
9. Ex. 20:12; Eph. 6:1.
10. Eph. 5:21–6:4.

Nevertheless, we are called to seek first the kingdom of God.[11] God's mission and vocation must shape all my relationships. Though earthly families are good and a blessing, they may become an idol if we make them our ultimate priority or loyalty. All earthly loyalties and obligations, including those of family, must be subject to the lordship of Jesus.

7 Q: Since marriage and family are good, is it necessary to be married?

A: No. During his earthly ministry, Jesus showed us that true human fulfillment does not need to include marriage or sex. Yet the life of Jesus most certainly included close, intimate relationships with those he called family.

8 Q: But why do many people in my church expect young adults to get married and raise a family?

A: The goal for all Christians is not marriage but, whether married or single, to live decent and chaste lives.[12]

In the beginning, God blessed marriage and he calls many Christians to live out their discipleship in the context of marriage. Nevertheless, Christians sometimes idolize marriage and family and promote the unbiblical teaching that a person can only find fulfillment and happiness in the context of a marriage and family.

However, this expectation is contrary to Scripture, which teaches that many Christians will be unmarried,[13] whether through choice or circumstance, and that they live a true, fully human life, as our Savior did.

9 Q: How then should we view the single, celibate life?

A: Singleness can serve as a sign and reminder to married people that our most basic calling is to seek first the kingdom of God,[14] not

---

11. Matt. 6:33; 12:46–50.
12. Heidelberg Catechism, Q&A 108.
13. 1 Cor. 7:29–40.
14. 1 Cor. 7:33–35; Matt. 6:33.

our earthly families. In addition, the single person's life points us ahead to the life to come, when we will neither marry nor be given in marriage.[15]

10 Q: Why did God institute marriage between man and woman?

A: Though many see marriage simply as a path to personal fulfillment, happiness, or self-realization, or a relationship that may be dissolved if they are dissatisfied, Scripture teaches that God instituted marriage between a man and woman as a sign of Christ and the church,[16] as a state of mutual help for life's journey,[17] as a relationship in which married Christians are sanctified,[18] and in order to provide for the continuation of the human race[19] and the raising of children into a life of faith in Jesus Christ.[20]

11 Q: Should we view the duties and obligations of marriage and family as a hindrance to the truly spiritual life?

A: No. When properly understood, we see that faithful devotion to one's spouse and faithful care of one's children are not merely "earthly" or "natural" matters but are in fact key elements of a faithful walk with Christ.[21]

Furthermore, the married person is a sign and reminder to single people that, just as a husband or wife has obligations to their spouse and family, so we all have obligations to the family of God.

12 Q: What is the meaning of sexual union?

A: God created man and woman to be able to unite not only our

---

15. Matt. 22:30.
16. Eph. 5:31–32.
17. Gen. 2:18.
18. John 13:34; Gal. 5:13; Phil. 2:3; Eph. 5:21; 1 Peter 5:5; 1 Cor. 7:4–5; Gal. 6:2; 1 Thess. 5:11.
19. Gen. 1:28; Ps. 127:3.
20. Deut. 6:4–9.
21. Eph. 5:21–6:4.

bodies, but our very lives and selves as husband and wife. In marriage, husbands and wives give themselves completely to one another, and the one-flesh sexual union embodies the fact that these two persons are no longer two, but one flesh.[22]

13 Q: But isn't sexual union just a physical act?

A: No. It is certainly more than that. In fact, when we reduce sex to a merely physical or biological act, we end up reducing other image bearers of God to mere objects to be used.

We see this abuse and hatred of our neighbor all around us,[23] in pornography, prostitution, rape, promiscuity, cohabitation apart from marriage, and sexual union outside of the covenant of marriage.

14 Q: How, then, should we understand sexual union?

A: Sexual union is a part of the total giving of oneself—body and soul, indeed one's whole self—to one's spouse, just as God in Christ gave himself completely to his bride, the Church.[24]

And just as God is a faithful God who gives himself to us in covenant,[25] so sexual union is a covenantal act that commits one to faithful, lifelong love to one's spouse.[26]

Sexual union is also meant to be a free act, entered into without coercion, but freely and graciously, as God in Christ freely and graciously loves us.[27]

And finally, God created husband and wife so that they fruitfully participate in the miracle of new life.[28] Just as God's life and creativity brought us forth,[29] so children are not to be seen as a nuisance or

---

22. Gen. 2:24; Matt. 19:5; Mark 10:7–8; 1 Cor. 6:16; Eph. 5:31.
23. Heidelberg Catechism, Q&A 5.
24. Phil. 2:5–8.
25. Ex. 34:6–7.
26. Mal. 2:16.
27. Rom. 8:32.
28. Gen. 1:28; Ps. 139:13–14.
29. Gen. 2:4–7, 18–22; Job 10:8–9.

impediment to the marriage relationship but as gifts of God,[30] disciples to be raised in the training and instruction of the Lord.[31]

15 Q: Does Scripture limit marriage and sexual union to a husband and wife?

A: Scripture consistently teaches that the difference between a woman and man in marriage is essential to properly represent, symbolically, Christ and the church, to the one-flesh act of sexual union and one-flesh relationship of covenantal marriage, and for the bringing of children into the world.

In Scripture, bodies matter. We are saved by the body of Christ, broken for us, and his blood, shed for our sins. Without Christ's body, we cannot be saved.

Furthermore, in the sacraments, we see that the material elements matter. God does not merely give us grace through invisible means but gives us visible signs and seals, which are not empty and hollow signs but which have their truth in Jesus Christ, without whom they would be nothing.[32]

In a similar way, bodies matter in marriage, which is defined in part by the sexual difference of male and female, who together—body and soul—bear the image of God and symbolize Christ and the church. Thus, marriage is not defined merely by the will or desire of any individual but by the recognition that our Creator and Redeemer God has instituted marriage to take a certain form, with certain kinds of bodies: "A man leaves his father and mother and is united to his wife, and they become one flesh."[33]

16 Q: Does Scripture really condemn all same-sex sexual activity?

---

30. Ps. 127:3–5; Gen. 21:1; 30:22; 1 Sam. 1:19; Ps. 139:13–14.
31. Eph. 6:1–4; Deut. 6:4–9.
32. Belgic Confession, art. 33.
33. Gen. 2:24.

A: Yes. Scripture consistently and categorically condemns sexual activity between persons of the same sex as immoral. Genesis 1–2 presents the male-female relationship as God's design for marriage. The Torah given by God to Israel teaches that same-sex sexual activity is wrong.[34]

Jesus re-affirms the teaching of Genesis on marriage, that marriage is between a man and woman.[35] The early church condemns same-sex sexual activity when they condemn "sexual immorality," a term that points back to Leviticus 18 and encompasses all forms of sexual sin,[36] and the New Testament writers re-affirm the sexual ethics of Torah, including specific condemnations of incest, adultery, and same-sex sexual activity.[37]

17 Q: Does the Bible especially condemn same-sex sexual activity above other sins, sexual or otherwise?

A: No. Scripture never singles out same-sex sexual activity as a worse sin than others.

18 Q: What should characterize our attitudes and actions toward those who are same-sex attracted, whether inside or outside the church?

A: We must first remember that there is a difference between being same-sex attracted, and acting sexually on that attraction. Just as there is a difference between being attracted to people of the opposite sex, and acting sexually on that attraction.

Furthermore, though Scripture condemns sexual sin, it also condemns all forms of mockery, degrading words and thoughts, economic oppression, abuse, threats, and violence against anyone based on their sexual identity or activity.[38] Anyone involved in such behavior must repent and walk in obedience to Jesus's command to love.

---

34. Lev. 18:22.
35. Matt. 19:1–10.
36. Acts 15:19–20.
37. 1 Cor. 5:1–2; 6:9–20; 1 Tim. 1:10.
38. Belhar Confession, art. 4. Luke 6:31; Lev. 19:9–18; Prov. 6:16–19.

19 Q: What about those who fail to keep fully Scripture's teaching on marriage and sexuality? How should we view them?

A: We must first remember that "they" are us![39] We are all sinners saved by God's extravagant grace. We must therefore see all people with the eyes of Jesus, who looks on us with compassion.

We must also remember that we should not expect people who are not disciples of Jesus to act as though they are. Indeed, Scripture teaches us that we should expect to interact and associate with those who are idolaters and sexually immoral as part of our daily life in this world.[40]

But as disciples of Jesus, we are also called to teach, rebuke, correct, and even discipline one another,[41] for we know that without discipline, we dare not call ourselves the church of Jesus Christ.[42] And we do not love one another in this way merely for the sake of following the rules or keeping human traditions but because God's life-giving Spirit empowers and equips us for a life of faith and gratitude,[43] for which we were made and to which we are called.

---

39. Romans 2:1–4.
40. 1 Cor. 5:9–10.
41. Matt. 18:15–20; 1 Cor. 5:11–13; 2 Cor. 2:5–11.
42. Belgic Confession, art. 29.
43. Heidelberg Catechism, Lord's Day 32 & 33.

ACKNOWLEDGMENTS

I am thankful for the many students, colleagues, friends, and family who had a hand in shaping this book. Thanks to my students, who engaged with so many of these topics, shaping the material through their interaction and insight. Thanks to Josh Larsen at *ThinkChristian* for giving me the chance to do early explorations on several of the topics addressed in the book. I'm grateful to Ryan Pazdur for guidance and wisdom on crafting this project and to Kyle Rohane for feedback that greatly improved the final outcome. A special thanks to two early readers, Andrew Zwart and John Nugent. Andrew has been a constant sounding board and conversation partner on so many of these matters over many years. John's clarity and insight are a gift, and he always pushes me back to Scripture. A huge thanks to Jeff Fisher and Sarah Behm for being willing to step into what God has for us with The Foundry. I didn't expect to write this book while also jumping into this new thing God is doing, but it's been great to do it as a team! I'm grateful for Eric Schalk and Aaron Wetzel, who faithfully walk with God's people through these matters (and all the other ones) day in and day out. It's great to be in ministry with true friends. My kids, Eliana, Ruby, Christian, Ephraim, Marigold, and Amos, constantly remind me what's most important. Every day with you is a treasure. Above all, I'm grateful to my wife, Sarah. Your daily love is the surest sign of God's faithful love to me, and your boldness, grace, generosity, and love are a wonder to behold! "She is clothed with strength and dignity; she can laugh at the days to come" (Prov. 31:25). I'm grateful for the mission God has given us, and I'm blessed to walk this journey with you, now and always.

NOTES

INTRODUCTION: WHAT ARE BODIES FOR?

1. Mansoor Iqbal, "Tinder Revenue and Usage Statistics (2022)," *Business of Apps*, February 24, 2022, https://www.businessofapps.com/data/tinder -statistics/.
2. CNBC.com, "Things Are Looking Up in America's Porn Industry," January 20, 2015, https://www.nbcnews.com/business/business-news /things-are-looking-americas-porn-industry-n289431. The statistics from the sociological study *Relationships in America* are discussed in Mark Regnerus, *Cheap Sex: The Transformation of Men, Marriage, and Monogamy* (Oxford: Oxford University Press, 2017), 114.
3. Sheri Madigan, Anh Ly, Christina L. Rash, Joris Van Ouytsel, and Jeff R. Temple, "Prevalence of Multiple Forms of Sexting Behavior among Youth: A Systematic Review and Meta-Analysis" *JAMA Pediatrics* 172, no. 4 (April 2018): 327–35.
4. Jennifer S. Hirsch and Shamus Khan, *Sexual Citizens: A Landmark Study of Sex, Power, and Assault on Campus* (New York: W. W. Norton, 2020), 112.
5. One source of numerous helpful resources is the Center for Faith, Sexuality, and Gender. You can access many of those resources at https://www.centerforfaith.com/.
6. Daniel I. Block, *Covenant: The Framework of God's Grand Plan of Redemption* (Grand Rapids: Baker Academic, 2021), 1.
7. Timothy Keller, *Preaching: Communicating Faith in an Age of Skepticism* (New York: Penguin, 2015), 104.

CHAPTER 1: WE ALL HAVE STORIES

1. Allen Verhey, *Nature and Altering It* (Grand Rapids: Eerdmans, 2010), 13.

2. Timothy Wilson, *Strangers to Ourselves: Discovering the Adaptive Unconscious* (Cambridge, MA: Belknap Press of Harvard University Press), 6–7.

3. Julie Beck, "The Decline of the Driver's License," *The Atlantic*, January 22, 2016, https://www.theatlantic.com/technology/archive/2016/01/the-decline -of-the-drivers-license/425169/.

4. James K. A. Smith, *Desiring the Kingdom: Worship, Worldview, and Cultural Formation*, Cultural Liturgies 1 (Grand Rapids: Baker Academic, 2009).

5. Steve Wilkens and Mark Sanford, *Hidden Worldviews: Eight Cultural Stories That Shape Our Lives* (Downers Grove, IL: InterVarsity Press), 22.

6. Wilkens and Sanford, *Hidden Worldviews*, 21.

7. Smith, *Desiring the Kingdom*, 25.

8. Wilkens and Sanford, *Hidden Worldviews*, 12.

9. The connection between story, symbol, and praxis comes from N. T. Wright, *Jesus and the Victory of God* (Minneapolis: Fortress, 1996), 142.

10. Mary Midgley, *The Myths We Live By* (New York: Routledge, 2004), 1.

11. Midgley, *The Myths We Live By*, 1. See also Wright, *Jesus and the Victory of God*, 369–442.

12. See Wright, *Jesus and the Victory of God*, 406–28, for a fuller discussion of the temple and the controversy Jesus created in regard to this central symbol.

13. For Kaepernick's own words on his actions, see Nick Wagoner, "Transcript of Colin Kaepernick's Comments about Sitting during National Anthem," August 28, 2016, https://www.espn.com/blog/san-francisco-49ers/post/_/id /18957/transcript-of-colin-kaepernicks-comments-about-sitting-during -national-anthem.

14. U.S. Code, Title 4, Ch. 1, Section 8, https://www.law.cornell.edu/uscode /text/4/8.

15. Daniel Hill, *White Awake: An Honest Look at What It Means to Be White* (Downers Grove, IL: InterVarsity Press, 2017), 79.

CHAPTER 2: EMBODYING THE GOSPEL IN A SECULAR AGE

1. Charles Taylor, *A Secular Age* (Cambridge, MA: Belknap Press of Harvard University Press, 2007), 2.

2. Taylor, *Secular Age*, 3.

3. Taylor, *Secular Age*, 539–56.

4. Taylor, *Secular Age*, 37.

5. Taylor, *Secular Age*, 5.

6. Augustine, *Confessions*, trans. Henry Chadwick (Oxford: Oxford University Press, 1992), 1.1.1.

7. David Zahl does a great job exploring this in *Seculosity: How Career, Parenting, Technology, Food, Politics, and Romance Became Our New Religion and What to Do about It* (Minneapolis: Fortress, 2019).

8. Taylor, *Secular Age*, 10–11.

9. James K. A. Smith, *How (Not) to Be Secular: Reading Charles Taylor* (Grand Rapids: Eerdmans, 2014), 9.

10. Taylor, *Secular Age*, 11.

11. Taylor, *Secular Age*, 10–11.

12. William James, "The Will to Believe," in *Philosophy: The Quest for Truth*, 7th ed., ed. Louis P. Pojman and Lewis Vaughn, 7th ed. (New York: Oxford University Press, 2009), 139.

13. Justin Ariel Bailey, *Reimagining Apologetics: The Beauty of Faith in a Secular Age* (Downers Grove, IL: InterVarsity Press, 2020).

14. Bailey, *Reimagining Apologetics*, 4.

15. Jonathan Leeman, *How the Nations Rage: Rethinking Faith and Politics* (Nashville: Nelson, 2018), 165.

16. James Davison Hunter, *To Change the World: The Irony, Tragedy, and Possibility of Christianity in the Late Modern World* (Oxford: Oxford University Press, 2010).

17. Michael Frost, *Surprise the World: The Five Habits of Highly Missional People* (Colorado Springs: NavPress, 2015), 1–15.

18. Frost, *Surprise the World*, 6.

CHAPTER 3: THE MYTH OF INDIVIDUALISM

1. Russell Brand, "50 Shades - Has Porn Ruined My Chance Of A Happy Marriage? Russell Brand The Trews (E261)," video, hosted by YouTube, February 20, 2015, https://youtu.be/R6GdEnINhtQ.

2. Jonathan Haidt, *The Righteous Mind: Why Good People Are Divided by Politics and Religion* (New York: Vintage, 2012), 112–13.

3. Patrick Deneen, *Why Liberalism Failed* (New Haven and London: Yale University Press, 2018), 50.

4. For a thorough discussion of the political philosophy of liberalism, see David Koyzis, *Political Visions and Illusions: A Survey and Christian Critique of Contemporary Ideologies* (Downers Grove, IL: InterVarsity

Press, 2003), especially ch. 2, "Liberalism: The Sovereignty of the Individual."

5. Jean-Jacques Rousseau, *The Confessions* (New York: Penguin, 1953), 17.

6. Jean-Paul Sartre, "Existentialist Ethics," in *Philosophy: The Quest for Truth*, ed. Louis P. Pojman and Lewis Vaughn, 7th ed. (New York: Oxford University Press, 2009), 516.

7. Charles Taylor, *A Secular Age* (Cambridge, MA: Belknap Press of Harvard University Press, 2007), 475.

8. Ron Clements and John Musker, directors, *The Little Mermaid*, Walt Disney Pictures, 1989.

9. Hans Christian Andersen, *The Little Mermaid* (1836). Full text available at http://hca.gilead.org.il/li_merma.html.

10. Clements and Musker, *The Little Mermaid*, 1989.

11. Christopher West, *Our Bodies Tell God's Story: Discovering the Divine Plan for Love, Sex, and Gender* (Grand Rapids: Brazos, 2020), 5.

12. See the discussion of choice and freedom in Jana Marguerite Bennett, *Singleness and the Church: A New Theology of Single Life* (New York: Oxford University Press, 2017), especially ch. 2, "Choice: Never Married and Paul," 26–55.

13. As quoted in Jessica Bailey, "Twenty Years On, Carrie Bradshaw Is Still Teaching Us about Relationships," *Grazia*, https://graziamagazine.com/articles/carrie-bradshaw-relationship-quotes-2016/.

14. This definition comes from the website of California State University, Chico, "What Is Consent?" https://www.csuchico.edu/title-ix/consent.shtml. Most colleges and universities have similar definitions and are required to educate students regarding consent for the sake of Title IX compliance.

15. Rebecca Beitsch, "#MeToo Movement Has Lawmakers Talking about Consent," Pew Charitable Trusts, January 23, 2018, https://www.pewtrusts.org/en/research-and-analysis/blogs/stateline/2018/01/23/metoo-movement-has-lawmakers-talking-about-consent.

16. The following paragraphs are adapted from Branson Parler, "Aziz Ansari and the Limits of Consent," *ThinkChristian*, January 29, 2018, https://thinkchristian.net/aziz-ansari-and-the-limits-of-consent.

17. Katie Way, "I Went on a Date with Aziz Ansari. It Turned into the Worst Night of My Life," Babe, January 13, 2018, https://babe.net/2018/01/13/aziz-ansari-28355. Warning: The link contains explicit sexual content.

18. Bari Weiss, "Aziz Ansari Is Guilty. Of Not Being a Mind Reader," *New York Times*, January 15, 2018, https://www.nytimes.com/2018/01/15/opinion/aziz-ansari-babe-sexual-harassment.html.

19. Jenell Williams Paris, *The End of Sexual Identity: Why Sex Is Too Important to Define Who We Are* (Downers Grove, IL: InterVarsity Press, 2011), 41.

20. Paris, *End of Sexual Identity*, 69.

21. Paris, *End of Sexual Identity*, 51.

22. Gregory Coles, *Single, Gay, Christian: A Personal Journey of Faith and Sexual Identity* (Downers Grove, IL: InterVarsity Press, 2017).

CHAPTER 4: THE STORY OF GOD'S COVENANT FAITHFULNESS

1. Daniel I. Block, *Covenant: The Framework of God's Grand Plan of Redemption* (Grand Rapids: Baker Academic, 2021), 2.

2. Heidelberg Catechism, Q&A 1.

3. Justin Ariel Bailey, *Reimagining Apologetics: The Beauty of Faith in a Secular Age* (Downers Grove, IL: InterVarsity Press, 2020), 8.

4. See James H. Olthuis, "Be(com)ing: Humankind as Gift and Call," *Philosophia Reformata* 58 (1993): 153–72.

5. Augustine, *Confessions*, 10.8.15.

6. Wendell Berry, *Sex, Economy, Freedom, and Community* (New York: Pantheon, 1994), 168.

7. Berry, *Sex, Economy, Freedom, and Community*, 168.

8. David Cantor, Bonnie Fisher, Susan Chibnall, Reanna Townsend, et al., "Report on the AAU Campus Climate Survey on Sexual Assault and Sexual Misconduct," January 17, 2020, https://www.aau.edu/sites/default/files/AAU-Files/Key-Issues/Campus-Safety/Revised%20Aggregate%20report%20%20and%20appendices%201-7_(01-16-2020_FINAL).pdf.

9. David Matzko McCarthy, "Becoming One Flesh: Marriage, Remarriage, and Sex," in *The Blackwell Companion to Christian Ethics*, ed. Stanley Hauerwas and Samuel Wells (Oxford: Blackwell, 2004), 276.

10. Episcopal Church, *The Book of Common Prayer and Administration of the Sacraments and Other Rites and Ceremonies of the Church: Together with the Psalter or Psalms of David according to the Use of the Episcopal Church* (New York: Seabury Press, 1979). See "The Celebration and Blessing of a Marriage," 423–25.

11. McCarthy, "Becoming One Flesh," 282.

12. McCarthy, "Becoming One Flesh," 282.

CHAPTER 5: THE MYTH OF LEGALISM

1. Tim Keller, *Center Church* (Grand Rapids: Zondervan, 2012), 269.
2. Augustine, *Teaching Christianity* (Hyde Park, NY: New City Press, 1996), 1.22.20–21.
3. Sadly, after the first draft of this manuscript, one of my chickens was killed by a raccoon. Rest in peace, Nia. Our other chickens went to live with friends in the country, where they are currently enjoying life and laying eggs.
4. Augustine, *Confessions* (Oxford: Oxford University Press, 1992), 1.1.1.
5. Of course, not every command in Scripture given to the original audience of the biblical message is directly applicable to us today.

CHAPTER 6: THE STORY OF GOD'S COVENANT FAITHFULNESS

1. For an in-depth survey of the story of the Bible, see Craig Bartholomew and Michael Goheen, *The Drama of Scripture: Finding Our Place in the Biblical Story*, 2nd ed. (Grand Rapids: Baker Academic, 2014).
2. Gordon P. Hugenberger, *Marriage as a Covenant: Biblical Law and Ethics as Developed from Malachi* (Eugene, OR: Wipf & Stock, 2014), 215.
3. Hugenberger, *Marriage as a Covenant*, 215.
4. Hugenberger, *Marriage as a Covenant*, 193.
5. Hugenberger, *Marriage as a Covenant*, 211.
6. Hugenberger, *Marriage as a Covenant*, 205–11.
7. Thanks to John Nugent for the alliterative list here.
8. After all, if your target audience is reading at a sixth-grade level, a story about a man "knowing" a woman and then her getting pregnant could be very confusing for some younger readers who haven't yet had "the talk" with their parents.
9. Hugenberger, *Marriage as a Covenant*, 268.
10. Hugenberger, *Marriage as a Covenant*, 272.
11. Hugenberger, *Marriage as a Covenant*, 271.
12. Hugenberger, *Marriage as a Covenant*, 279.

CHAPTER 7: THE MYTH OF ROMANCE

1. Caroline J. Simon, *Bringing Sex into Focus: The Quest for Sexual Integrity* (Downers Grove, IL: InterVarsity Press, 2012), 32.

2. Simon, *Bringing Sex into Focus,* 33.

3. Carol Costello, "Ready for the Marriage Apocalypse?" CNN, April 7, 2015, https://www.cnn.com/2015/04/07/opinions/costello-marriage-millennials /index.html.

4. Anthony Giddens, *The Transformation of Intimacy* (Redwood City, CA: Stanford University Press, 1992), 58.

5. Giddens, *Transformation of Intimacy,* 45.

6. Giddens, *Transformation of Intimacy,* 45.

7. John Calvin, *Institutes of the Christian Religion* (Louisville: Westminster John Knox, 1960), 1.1.1.

8. Giddens, *Transformation of Intimacy,* 39.

9. Esther Perel, "The Secret to Desire in a Long-Term Relationship," *TED,* February 2013, https://www.ted.com/talks/esther_perel_the_secret_to _desire_in_a_long_term_relationship/transcript?language=en.

10. David Zahl, *Seculosity: How Career, Parenting, Technology, Food, Politics, and Romance Became Our New Religion and What to Do about It* (Minneapolis: Fortress, 2019), 30.

11. Ben Folds/Nick Hornby, "From Above," track 9 on *Lonely Avenue,* Nonesuch Records, 2010.

12. Kutter Callaway, *Breaking the Marriage Idol: Reconstructing Our Cultural and Spiritual Norms* (Downers Grove, IL: InterVarsity Press, 2018), 42–46.

13. Mark Regnerus and Jeremy Uecker, *Premarital Sex in America: How Young Americans Meet, Mate, and Think about Marrying* (New York: Oxford University Press, 2011), 192.

14. Obergefell v. Hodges, 576 U.S. 644 (2015), https://www.supremecourt.gov /opinions/14pdf/14–556_3204.pdf. See Syllabus, p. 3.

15. Obergefell v. Hodges, p. 3.

16. Obergefell v. Hodges, p. 13.

17. Obergefell v. Hodges, p. 17 (emphasis added).

18. Some elements of the following paragraphs are adapted from Branson Parler, "Cohabitation, 'Conscious Uncoupling,' and Christian Marriage," *ThinkChristian,* March 31, 2014, https://thinkchristian.net /cohabitation-conscious-uncoupling-and-christian-marriage.

19. Lauren Fox, "The Science of Cohabitation: A Step toward Marriage, Not Rebellion," *The Atlantic,* March 20, 2014, https://www.theatlantic .com/health/archive/2014/03/the-science-of-cohabitation-a-step-toward -marriage-not-a-rebellion/284512/.

20. I first heard this phrase used by Gwyneth Paltrow in John Koblin, "A Third Party Names Their Split," *New York Times*, March 28, 2014, https://www.nytimes.com/2014/03/30/fashion/gwyneth-paltrow-and-chris -martins-separation-gives-phrase-conscious-uncoupling-a-boost.html.

21. Barbara Defoe Whitehead, *Divorce Culture: Rethinking Our Commitments to Marriage and Family* (New York: Vintage, 1998).

22. Two key sources that helpfully explain polyamory are Elizabeth Sheff, *The Polyamorists Next Door: Inside Multiple-Partner Relationships and Families* (Lanham, MD: Rowman and Littlefield, 2013), and Deborah Anapol, *Polyamory in the 21st Century: Love and Intimacy with Multiple Partners* (Lanham, MD: Rowman and Littlefield, 2010).

23. Ann E. Tweedy, "Polyamory as a Sexual Orientation," *University of Cincinnati Law Review* 79 (2011): 1461–1515.

24. On the ethics of polyamory, see Dossie Easton and Janet W. Hardy, *The Ethical Slut: A Practical Guide to Polyamory, Open Relationships, and Other Adventures*, 2nd ed. (Berkeley: Celestial Arts, 2009). See also the chapters "The Ethics of Polyamory" and "The Challenge of Jealousy" in Anapol, *Polyamory in the 21st Century*.

CHAPTER 8: THE STORY OF GOD'S HOUSEHOLD

1. Augustine, *Teaching Christianity*, 1.3.3.

2. Augustine, *Confessions*, 1.1.1.

3. Augustine, *Confessions*, 2.1.1.

4. James K. A. Smith, *On the Road with Saint Augustine: A Real-World Spirituality for Restless Hearts* (Grand Rapids: Brazos, 2019), 13.

5. For more on co-housing, see Karen M. Bush, Louise S. Machinist, and Jean McQuillin, *My House Our House: Living Far Better for Far Less in a Cooperative Household* (Pittsburgh: St. Lynn's Press, 2013); and Julie Beck, "The Case for Buying a House with Friends," *The Atlantic*, December 13, 2019, https://www.theatlantic.com/family/archive/2019/12/how-buy-house -friends-without-going-crazy/603538/. Thanks to Kandi Zeller for pointing me to these sources.

6. Kristina LaCelle-Peterson, *Liberating Tradition: Women's Identity and Voca- tion in Christian Perspective* (Grand Rapids: Baker Academic, 2008), 119.

7. Wendell Berry, "Men and Women in Search of Common Ground," in *Art of the Commonplace: The Agrarian Essays of Wendell Berry*, ed. and intro. Norman Wirzba (Berkeley, CA: Counterpoint, 2003), 141.

8. Berry, "The Gift of Good Land," 298.

9. Berry, "The Body and the Earth," 133 (emphasis original).

CHAPTER 9: THE MYTH OF SEXUAL PROSPERITY

1. As far as I know, Katelyn Beaty was the first to coin this term. See Beaty, "Joshua Harris and the Sexual Prosperity Gospel," Religion News Service, https://religionnews.com/2019/07/26/joshua-harris-and-the-sexual -prosperity-gospel/.

2. Linda Kay Klein, *Pure: Inside the Evangelical Movement That Shames a Generation of Young Women and How I Broke Free* (New York: Touchstone, 2018), 134.

3. Klein, *Pure*, 135.

4. Klein, *Pure*, 143.

5. Scot McKnight, *The Blue Parakeet: Rethinking How You Read the Bible* (Grand Rapids: Zondervan, 2008), 42–48.

6. See Ed Shaw, *Same-Sex Attraction and the Church: The Surprising Plausibility of the Celibate Life* (Downers Grove, IL: InterVarsity Press, 2015), 115–28, for more reflection on this basic theological mistake.

7. Shaw, *Same-Sex Attraction*, 115.

8. Kate Bowler, *Blessed: A History of the American Prosperity Gospel* (Oxford: Oxford University Press, 2013), 7. What follows summarizes Bowler's main points about these terms.

9. Bowler, *Blessed*, 7.

10. Bowler, *Blessed*, 7.

11. A brief but helpful summary of the context and content of purity culture can be found in Joe Carter, "The FAQs: What You Should Know about Purity Culture," *The Gospel Coalition*, July 24, 2019, https://www .thegospelcoalition.org/article/faqs-know-purity-culture.

12. Carter, "The FAQs."

13. Dela (@Mzdelah), "The most interesting take I've heard on dating and marriage," Twitter, November 14, 2021, 3:25 a.m., https://twitter.com /Mzdelah/status/1459799741450104834?s=20.

14. Joshua Harris, *I Kissed Dating Goodbye: A New Attitude toward Romance and Relationships* (Colorado Springs: Multnomah, 1997), 23. Notably, Harris has since essentially renounced his earlier teachings and discontinued publication of his book. See https://joshharris.com/i -kissed-dating-goodbye/.

15. Harris, *I Kissed Dating Goodbye*, 47.

16. Josh McDowell and Dick Day, *Why Wait? What You Need to Know about the Teen Sexuality Crisis* (San Bernadino, CA: Here's Life, 1994), 225.

17. Grace Thornton, "I Don't Wait Anymore," *Grace for the Road* (blog), February 3, 2012, https://gracefortheroad.com/2012/02/03/idontwait/.

18. Ryan's story is found in Mark Wingfield, "They Grew Up in Purity Culture, Then Taught It and Now Want to Help Others Recover from It," *Baptist News Global*, June 3, 2021, https://baptistnews.com/article/they-grew-up-in-purity-culture-then-taught-it-and-now-want-to-help-others-recover-from-it/#.YdcIP_5OnIU.

CHAPTER 10: THE STORY OF GOD'S HOUSEHOLD

1. Martin Luther, "Heidelberg Disputation," in *Selected Writings of Martin Luther 1517–1520*, ed. Theodore G. Tappert (Philadelphia: Fortress, 1967), 78.

2. Carl Trueman, "Luther's Theology of the Cross," *New Horizons*, October 2005, https://opc.org/new_horizons/NH05/10b.html.

3. Kutter Callaway, *Breaking the Marriage Idol: Reconstructing Our Cultural and Spiritual Norms* (Downers Grove, IL: InterVarsity Press, 2018), 81.

4. Luther, "Heidelberg Disputation," 78.

5. Luther, "Heidelberg Disputation,"78–79.

6. Miroslav Volf, *Exclusion and Embrace: A Theological Exploration of Identity, Otherness, and Reconciliation* (Nashville: Abingdon, 1996), 127.

7. John Nugent, *Endangered Gospel: How Fixing the World Is Killing the Church* (Eugene, OR: Cascade, 2016), 153.

8. For some historical context on this matter, see Sarah Ruden, *Paul among the People: The Apostle Reinterpreted and Reimagined in His Own Time* (New York: Pantheon, 2010), 96–104.

9. N. T. Wright, *Jesus and the Victory of God* (Minneapolis: Fortress, 1996), 401.

10. LEGO Joseph Smith (@Mormonger), "Nobody talks about Jesus' miracle of having 12 close friends in his 30s," Twitter, March 18, 2018, 6:22 p.m., https://twitter.com/Mormonger/status/975497709548314624.

11. Laurie Krieg and Matt Krieg, *An Impossible Marriage: What Our Mixed-Orientation Marriage Has Taught Us about Love and the Gospel* (Downers Grove, IL: InterVarsity Press, 2020).

12. Krieg and Krieg, *An Impossible Marriage*, 4.

13. Krieg and Krieg, *An Impossible Marriage*, 2.

14. Dietrich Bonhoeffer, *The Cost of Discipleship* (London: SCM, 1948), 44.

15. Fyodor Dostoevsky, *The Brothers Karamazov* (New York: Signet Class, 1986), 65.

16. Wendell Berry, "The Gift of Good Land," in *The Art of the Common Place: The Agrarian Essays of Wendell Berry* (Berkeley: Counterpoint, 2002), 300.

CHAPTER 11: THE MYTH OF NATURALISM

1. Caroline J. Simon, *Bringing Sex into Focus: The Quest for Sexual Integrity* (Downers Grove, IL: InterVarsity Press, 2012), 35.

2. Norman Wirzba, *From Nature to Creation: A Christian Vision for Understanding and Loving Our World* (Grand Rapids: Baker Academic, 2015), 48.

3. Wirzba, *From Nature to Creation*, 40.

4. Wirzba, *From Nature to Creation*, 47.

5. Edward O. Wilson, *Consilience: The Unity of Knowledge* (New York: Vintage, 1999), 226.

6. Allen Verhey, *Nature and Altering It* (Grand Rapids: Eerdmans, 2010), 25.

7. Verhey, *Nature and Altering It*, 25.

8. Verhey, *Nature and Altering It*, 25 n. 27.

9. See Nancy R. Pearcey, *Love Thy Body: Answering Hard Questions about Life and Sexuality* (Grand Rapids: Baker, 2018), 50–51.

10. National Geographic Society, "Molecular Scissors," *National Geographic*, July 12, 2019, https://www.nationalgeographic.org/article/molecular-scissors/.

11. Megan Scudellari, "Self-Destructing Mosquitoes and Sterilized Rodents: The Promise of Gene Drives," *Nature*, July 9, 2019, https://www.nature.com/articles/d41586–019–02087–5.

12. "Malaria," World Health Organization, December 6, 2021, https://www.who.int/news-room/fact-sheets/detail/malaria.

13. "Gene Therapy for Hemophilia A," Boston Children's Hospital, https://www.childrenshospital.org/centers-and-services/programs/f-_-n/gene-therapy-program/conditions-we-treat/hemophilia.

14. J. P. Moreland, *Scientism and Secularism: Learning to Respond to a Dangerous Ideology* (Wheaton, IL: Crossway, 2018), 29.

15. Verhey, *Nature and Altering It*, 14.

16. Steven Spielberg, director, *Jurassic Park*, Universal Pictures, 1993.

17. You can see how the *Jurassic* franchise lives in the tension of the story of naturalism, though, as humans and raptors work alongside one another, albeit in a fragile state, in later *Jurassic World* movies. As the franchise explores, humans continue to try to harness the wildness of nature, and that enterprise is constantly teetering on the edge of chaos.

18. Paul Offit, *Pandora's Lab: Seven Stories of Science Gone Wrong* (Washington, DC: National Geographic, 2017), 41–60.

19. Wirzba, *From Nature to Creation*, 45.

20. Mark Yarhouse, *Understanding Gender Dysphoria: Navigating Transgender Issues in a Changing Culture* (Downers Grove, IL: IVP Academic, 2015), 20.

21. I would highly recommend Julia Sadusky and Mark Yarhouse, *Emerging Gender Identities: Understanding the Diverse Experience of Today's Youth* (Grand Rapids: Brazos, 2020) for a helpful introduction to all the dimensions of transgender issues, especially as faced by youth.

22. Anders Sandberg, "Morphological Freedom—Why We Not Just Want It, but Need It," in *The Transhumanist Reader: Classical and Contemporary Essays on the Science, Technology, and Philosophy of the Human Future* (Malden, MA: Wiley-Blackwell, 2013), 56. For a fuller engagement with Sandberg's concept, see Jacob Shatzer, *Transhumanism and the Image of God: Today's Technology and the Future of Christian Discipleship* (Downers Grove, IL: InterVarsity Press, 2019), 55–72.

23. Preston Sprinkle, *Embodied: Transgender Identities, the Church, and What the Bible Has to Say* (Colorado Springs: David C Cook, 2021), 24.

24. Rachel K. Jones and Joerg Dreweke, "Countering Conventional Wisdom: New Evidence on Religion and Contraceptive Use," Report of Guttmacher Institute, April 2011, https://www.guttmacher.org/report/countering -conventional-wisdom-new-evidence-religion-and-contraceptive-use.

25. Dennis Hollinger, "The Ethics of Contraception: A Theological Assessment," *Journal of Evangelical Theological Society* 56, no. 4 (2013): 683–96.

26. Bernard Asbell, *The Pill: A Biography of the Drug That Changed the World* (New York: Random House, 1995), 7.

CHAPTER 12: THE STORY OF GOD'S MISSION

1. For a thorough exploration of connection between the temple, the church, and mission throughout the entire Bible, see G. K. Beale, *The Temple and*

the Church's Mission: A Biblical Theology of the Dwelling Place of God (Downers Grove, IL: InterVarsity Press, 2004).

2. John and Sheila Kippley, *The Art of Natural Family Planning*, 4th ed. (Cincinnati: Couple to Couple League, 1996).

3. Christopher West, *Theology of the Body for Beginners: A Basic Introduction to Blessed John Paul II's Sexual Revolution* (West Chester, PA: Ascension, 2009). This has been revised and republished under the title *Our Bodies Tell God's Story: Discovering the Divine Plan for Love, Sex, and Gender* (Grand Rapids: Brazos, 2020).

4. Andrew Root, *The Children of Divorce: The Loss of Family as the Loss of Being* (Grand Rapids: Baker Academic, 2010), 54.

5. Root, *Children of Divorce*, 125.

6. The four characteristics of Christ's love and marriage (free, total, faithful, and fruitful) are explored in Christopher West, *Our Bodies Tell God's Story* (Grand Rapids: Brazos, 2020), 117. These four characteristics are outlined in *Humanae Vitae* by Pope Paul VI. They are also explored at length in Pope John Paull II, *Man and Woman He Created Them: A Theology of the Body* (Boston: Paulist, 1986).

CHAPTER 13: THE MYTH OF EVIL BODIES

1. There are a variety of interpretations of exactly what this means. My goal here is not to sort out the precise details of the intermediate state, but to note that being without a body is an intermediate condition, not our final state.

2. N. T. Wright, *Surprised by Hope* (New York: HarperOne, 2008), 148.

3. M. C. Kenny and S. K. Wurtele, "Toward Prevention of Childhood Sexual Abuse: Preschoolers' Knowledge of Genital Body Parts," in *Proceedings of the Seventh Annual College of Education Research Conference: Urban and International Education Section*, ed. M. S. Plakhotnik and S. M. Nielsen (Miami: Florida International University, 2008), 74–79, https://digital commons.fiu.edu/cgi/viewcontent.cgi?article=1121&context=sferc.

4. Linda Kay Klein, *Pure: Inside the Evangelical Movement That Shamed a Generation of Young Women and How I Broke Free* (New York: Touchstone, 2018).

5. Klein, *Pure*, 235.

6. Abraham Kuyper, *Lectures on Calvinism* (Grand Rapids: Eerdmans, 1931), 54.

7. Stephen Arterburn and Fred Stoeker with Mike Yorkey, *Every Man's Battle: Winning the War on Sexual Temptation One Victory at a Time* (Colorado Springs: WaterBrook, 2000), 61.

CHAPTER 14: THE STORY OF GOD'S MISSION

1. Sally Lloyd-Jones, *The Jesus Storybook Bible: Every Story Whispers His Name* (Grand Rapids: Zonderkidz, 2007), 320–21.

2. Andrew Peterson, "His Heart Beats," *Resurrection Letters, Volume 1*, Centricity Music, 2018.

3. For a thorough discussion of this point, see Mark Regnerus, *Cheap Sex: The Transformation of Men, Marriage, and Monogamy* (New York: Oxford University Press, 2017), especially ch. 4: "The Cheapest Sex: Trends in Pornography Use and Masturbation."

4. Nadia Bolz-Weber makes this point in *Shameless: A Sexual Reformation* (New York: Convergent, 2019), 144–46.

CONCLUSION

1. Blaise Pascal, "Yes, Faith Is a Logical Bet," in *Philosophy: The Quest for Truth*, ed. Louis P. Pojman and Lewis Vaughn, 7th ed. (Oxford: Oxford University Press, 2009), 129. Reprinted from Pascal, *Thoughts*, trans. W. F. Trotter (New York: Collier and Sons, 1910).